TO BRIAN PETERS

SOUND AND AUDIO ENGINEERING BY

LOVE YOU, PAL

Fifth Avenue Press is a locally focused and publicly owned publishing imprint of the Ann Arbor District Library. It is dedicated to supporting the local writing community by promoting the production of original fiction, non-fiction and poetry written for children, teens and adults.

Printed in the United States of America

First Printing, 2017

ISBN: 978-1-947989-03-0 (Paperback), 978-1-947989-04-7 (ebook)

Fifth Avenue Press
305 S Fifth Ave
Ann Arbor, MI 48104
fifthavenue.press

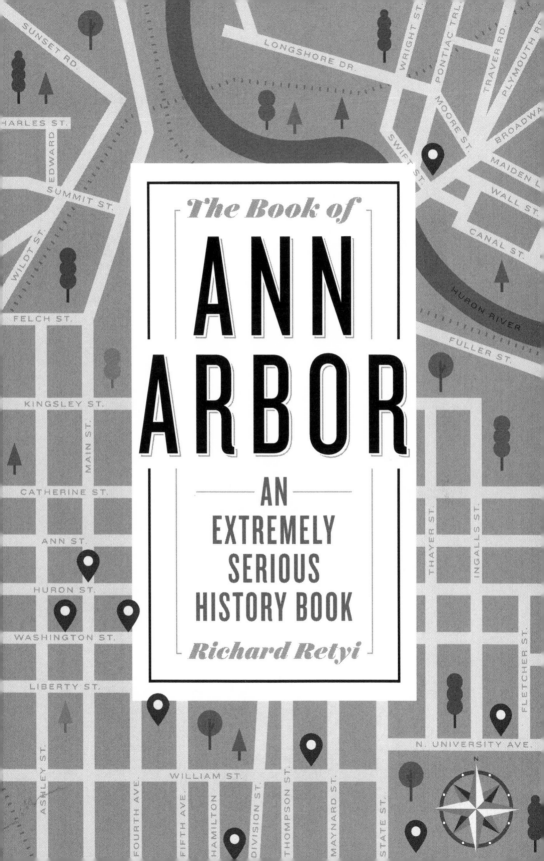

The Book of

ANN ARBOR

AN
EXTREMELY
SERIOUS
HISTORY BOOK

Richard Retyi

CONTENTS

CONTENTS

STREETS OF ANN ARBOR   1

DIRTY ROTTEN FOUNDERS   7

THE UFO INVASION OF 1966   15

THE NATIONAL MARBLES CHAMPIONSHIPS   21

THE MALLET MURDER   29

THE BIRTH OF IGGY POP   37

RIOT AT THE STAR THEATRE   45

HENRY FORD'S STRONG RIGHT FIST   53

THE LEGENDARY WEED CONTEST OF 1975   63

THE RED LIGHT DISTRICT   69

A COP KILLED IN COLD BLOOD   77

A BRIEF HISTORY OF POOP   81

MICHIGAN HOUSEWIFE FLIES AROUND THE WORLD   85

PRESIDENTS IN ANN ARBOR   93

THE NAKED MILE   105

THE SUICIDE SUBMARINE PARADE   111

THE TORCH MURDERS   117

THE GHOST OF FIRST METHODIST   125

THE HOTTEST GAY BAR IN ANN ARBOR   131

ANN ARBOR'S TOP 10 ASTRONAUTS   139

NAZIS VS. EVERYBODY   149

IT'S LOVELY TO DIE TOGETHER   157

THE BALLAD OF SHAKEY JAKE   161

THE GIRLS IN THE BAND   167

SANTA'S #1 HELPER   171

THE METEORITE HEIST   177

THE EMBASSY HOTEL   181

ANN ARBOR CAGES PUBLIC ANIMAL #1   187

THE DICTATOR COMES TO TOWN   197

THE INVENTION OF THE CUBICLE   207

GERALDINE SEEBACK AND THE MUSIC MOBILE   213

DAM ARBOR   219

THE CLAIRVOYANT PHYSICIAN   229

WE HAD A ZOO!   237

A VERY DIXBORO GHOST STORY   245

SKYSCRAPERS   251

100% TRUE: THE STORY OF WILLIAM DOUGLAS STREET   257

THE PIG BOWL   267

HOW THE HIPPIES ALMOST KILLED FOOTBALL .   271

TRAIN CRASHES   279

THE BLIND PIG   285

ACKNOWLEDGMENTS   291

STREETS OF ANN ARBOR

In 1824, they paid $1.25 an acre for 640 acres of prime Michigan land, dropping $800 on a desk in a tiny federal land office in Detroit. The purchasers were New Yorker John Allen and Elisha Rumsey of Connecticut, who scouted this location next to the Huron River and saw opportunity. On May 25, 1824, their town was formally named Annarbour.

Myths surround how the men came up with the name "Annarbour." One legend states that Allen's wife Ann and Rumsey's wife Mary Ann passed the days in a wild arbor built by their husbands, who wanted them to have a nice place to relax and converse in the shade. This sweet tale isn't true. Ann Allen didn't arrive in town until five months after Annarbour was formally named, and there wasn't a lot of time or space for lounging in those early days. It's more likely that the founders chose the name "Ann" to honor their wives, and added "Arbor" because there were a heck of a lot of trees in this new town.

Allen wrote the name Annarbour exactly how you see it, but Lewis

Cass, Second Territorial Governor of Michigan, transcribed it as two words. The Governor's choice set the standard and so Annarbour became Ann Arbour. At some point, it lost its "u" when residents decided to drop the dirty British spelling of "arbour."

Of the 640 acres purchased, Allen owned 480 and Rumsey the other 160.[1] They split the town into four sections, dividing it North/South at Huron, and East/West at Division. Rumsey chose to settle south of Huron, and named streets on his side of town Washington, Liberty, and William. Allen took the north side, naming his major streets Ann, Catherine, and North (which later became Kingsley).

For streets west of Division, they came to an easy consensus on a simple naming convention, calling these streets Fifth, Fourth, Third (later named Main), Second (later named Ashley), and First.

Ann Arbor had its first grid street plan.

Allen put down stakes at the corner of Huron and Main, while Rumsey settled a few blocks west at Huron and First. The men platted the land and placed ads in the Detroit Gazette offering lots for sale. A Mr. and Mrs. Smith and their infant daughter were the first to arrive, followed by a slow but steady flow of settlers. Many lived temporarily in Allen's home while they cut down trees and built homes of their own—the founders selling parcels of land for much more than $1.25 they paid per acre.

Log huts soon lined Washington and William as the town grew. Ann Arbor got its first sawmill and tannery. A shoemaker arrived to serve the community. The first schoolhouse was built. The first jailhouse was erected to keep horse thieves and bank robbers off the streets. The founders sold more and more plots and new arrivals spread in all directions.

Rumsey wasn't around long enough to enjoy his new town. Three years after settling Ann Arbor, Rumsey fell ill and died of fever. He was buried in Forest Hill Cemetery beneath a headstone bearing the inscription, "The first

---

1   640 acres is equal to one square mile. According to the Wikipedia in 2016, Ann Arbor is 27.83 square miles of land.

settler in Ann Arbor." His wife moved and remarried. But his co-founder John Allen lived on—one of 400 people who called Ann Arbor home at the time.

The town got a courthouse and its first bank. Hotels and music stores filled storefronts, while taverns flourished. Made mostly of wood, down to its brand new wood-plank sidewalks, Ann Arbor needed protection from fire. Volunteer fire companies with names like Eagle Fire Company, Defiance Hood & Ladder Company, and Mayflower Fire Engine Company protected the town from this very real threat.

After swapping Toledo for the Upper Peninsula in 1837, Michigan joined the union as the 26th state—territorial representatives signed the decree in the Ann Arbor courthouse. An ambitious little town in an up and coming state, Ann Arbor made a bid for the state capitol (losing out to Lansing) and another for the state's first prison (foiled again, this time to Jackson). But the third time was the charm. Six town boosters, offering 40 prime acres to the University of Michigan, lured the institution from Detroit. At just 13 years old, Ann Arbor had 2,000 citizens, four churches, and two mills—and now, a college.

Over the next four years, four faculty homes and a one-classroom dormitory were built on those 40 acres—mostly covered by grass and cows. A wooden fence ran the length of campus, keeping townie cows from mixing with college cows.

On the first day of classes in 1841, U-M had two professors and seven students, who each paid an annual $10 admission fee to attend.[2]

When the Michigan Central Railroad chose to lay track and run through Ann Arbor in 1839, the town really started booming.

In 1845, William Maynard platted the Old West Side, copying the town's existing number-naming system and creating unnecessary confusion. Rather than get creative, Maynard named his west-side streets Second, Third, Fourth, Fifth, Sixth, and Seventh. His solution to ongoing confusion about which street was which in a town with only a handful of them: designate the

---

2   The seven students were all men. Women wouldn't be admitted to the University of Michigan until 1870.

eest side's Fourth and Fifth streets as avenues instead. Problem solved.

Two years later, H.K. Stanley was elected the first marshal of the village of Ann Arbor—an office that was essentially police chief.[3]

Even with all this going on, John Allen grew bored. Ann Arbor's co-founder served as postmaster, village president, and even started a newspaper, but his personal life wasn't nearly as successful. He had an unhappy marriage and his southern wife was never fond of the midwest. The couple separated and Ann Allen returned to Virginia without her husband where she lived out the rest of her life. Ann Arbor's remaining founding father grew restless in the pseudo bachelor life. He left Ann Arbor and Michigan and moved back to New York to build on his fortune, but lost almost everything in a series of poor real estate deals. Undeterred, Allen struck out west to join the California Gold Rush, seeking fortune and fame. He never rebounded, dying somewhere in San Francisco in 1851.

Ann Arbor was declared a city that same year, electing its first mayor, George Sedgwick. The Civil War came and went. Brick replaced wood. A chemistry professor at U-M organized the first gas company. Another established the city's water and sewage systems.

Ann Arbor built proper roads connecting it to neighboring towns. Middle Ypsilanti Road (now Washtenaw) and Ypsilanti Street (which today would be North University and Geddes) connected Ann Arbor and Ypsilanti.

Ann Arbor's first public high school, Union High School, opened in 1856.[4] Ann Arbor's first streetcar track was laid in 1890 and just 35 years later, streetcars were already an outdated mode of transportation. A band played a funeral dirge marching in front of the final streetcar, which rolled down the tracks followed by 12 brand new buses. A banner hung on the streetcar reading, "Goodbye folks. The scrap heap for me."

---

3   As part of his compensation package, Stanley was paid by the arrest.

4   Union High School was one of the city's most prominent buildings. Erected on State Street between Huron and Washington, it burned to the ground 50 years later during a New Year's Eve inferno, and was replaced by Ann Arbor High School and eventually, U-M's North Quad.

At the turn of the century, the telephone arrived. The first automobile was sold. 14,500 people called Ann Arbor home. Workmen drank beer by the bucket and women earned pennies on the dollar. Buildings were constructed. Remodeled. Torn down. Built anew. Some caught on fire. One was hit by runaway train. Kerrytown grew. Lower town grew. The west side grew. The Masonic Block. The American Block. The Huron Block. The Union Block. Bloody Corners.

Arts and entertainment were easy to be had in the city packed with nickelodeons, vaudeville theaters, and an opera house. In 1906, state treasurer Frank Glazier built the tallest building the city had ever seen at the corner of Main and Huron—Ann Arbor's first skyscraper.

World War I came and went. The city grew faster than ever. Subdivisions sprung up—developers naming streets after their daughters and their daughter's classmates. Property values soared. World War II came and went. The town got its first parking structure. Art Fair was born. Ann Arbor elected its first black mayor. Sixteen years later, they elected their first female mayor. The first malls opened. The first mall closed. Saturdays in the fall became Michigan gameday.

The town that John Allen and Elisha Rumsey bought for $800 continues to grow and evolve. New businesses open. Old businesses fade. Ten-story residential high rises spring up, tech start-ups settle, a robot store offers to fix your metal friend, and a violin-playing monster prowls the streets.

All for $1.25 an acre.

DIRTY ROTTEN FOUNDERS

In 1824, a pair of men walked into a tiny federal land office in Detroit and bought 640 acres of prime Michigan land for $1.25 an acre—a speculatory purchase by two Yankees looking to make their fortune in the sparsely-settled Midwest.[5]

These pioneers were John Allen and Elisha Rumsey—founders of the town they thoughtfully named first after their wives and second after the leafy arbor they planted for their spouses where the women could relax and chat their days away. That story—like a good bit of the mythology surrounding Allen, Rumsey, and those early days in Ann Arbor—is bunk.

Allen's wife didn't arrive in Ann Arbor until well after the town had its

---

5   Michigan the territory, not Michigan the state. It wouldn't join the union until 1837, but *that* paperwork would be signed in Ann Arbor. Funny coincidence.

name, and in the wild beginnings of Ann Arbor, there wasn't a lot of time for lounging under arbors. There was a lot more working the land and hustling to sell plots on those 640 prime acres in the hopes of making heaps of cash money.

If you want the sanitized history of the men who found Ann Arbor, believe that malarky about the wives eating grapes under the arbor. If you want the real story, I present to you: Ann Arbor's dirty rotten founders.

Elisha Walker Rumsey

It's tough to tell someone's full story when even the year of their birth is unclear. Rumsey was born on or around 1785 in Sharon, Connecticut. At the age of 39 (give or take), he found himself in that land office in Detroit signing paperwork with a man 10 years his junior whom he'd only known for a month. He laid down his life savings on a government man's desk to purchase 160 acres of land next to a river named after the natives who settled the land and a creek that would be named after his business partner.

Rumsey was accompanied by his new wife, Mary Ann Sprague. They met in Bethany, New York four years earlier, when both Elisha and Mary Ann were married to other people. No details of their courtship exist, but two things happened that helped eventually deliver Rumsey to Ann Arbor. The first was Rumsey's first wife dying shortly after giving birth to their fifth child. The second was a company entrusting Rumsey with $3,000 cash to travel across the state and buy cattle on their behalf. He now had a dilemma: take the sacks of cash and capitalize on this chance to be the with good wife Sprague, or do the job and stay home with five motherless kids ranging from nine years to six weeks of age. In true dirty rotten founder fashion, Rumsey took the cash and the girl and bolted for Canada. The Great White North didn't really pan out, so the couple traveled south into Michigan where the law caught up with them.

Elisha and Mary Ann agreed to return to New York where Rumsey paid back the cow money and settled the charges against him. Sprague divorced her husband and properly married Rumsey back in his hometown in Connecticut, then returned to Bethany to begin anew. That probably went well, right? Returning home after stealing a small fortune, running away with another man's wife shortly after the death of his own, and letting relatives in town divvy up and raise his children.

Yeah, their fresh start in Bethany didn't last long. In the fall of 1823, Rumsey sold his 117-acre farm for $2,340, paying $900 to settle the mortgage and other debts around town. That left him with money enough to make a start somewhere else. Having spent time in Michigan, Rumsey thought the territory held a lot of promise, both personally and financially.

It was in Detroit that Rumsey met fellow founder John Allen. The pair had a common interest in finding promising tracts of land and making wagonloads of cash. Someone tried to get them to go in on land in Toledo, but Ohio, amirite? They chose to buy up the land that would become Ann Arbor instead.

The location they chose was better than most. Close to the growing city of Detroit but not too close in case the Canadians got feisty and decided to take the city again (see 1812, Battle of). Fertile soil, access to the Huron River and other waterways to provide sustenance and power. Trees. Lots and lots of trees. A functioning weather shield. This Ann Arbor of theirs had it all.

They built Rumsey's house first, a one-story log structure. Allen slept nearby in a tent. Rumsey and his wife were tasked with being the face of Ann Arbor for anyone considering settling down in the area, while Allen was the marketing man, placing ads in newspapers and trying to drum up interest in affordable plots of land.

The Rumseys shared their home/hotel with new arrivals—recent land buyers, new neighbors, or those just checking things out. They added a second, slightly larger building and called it the Washtenaw Coffee House. By all accounts, the Rumseys did a great job of feeding, boarding and showing these fine pioneer folk around.

Only two descriptions of Rumsey exist today. The first describes him as "a commonplace man both in ability and appearance." A little harsh. The second describes him as "a man of more than ordinary intelligence, and . . . he knew how to keep a hotel." Not a lot better, but we'll take what we can get.

The combination of Allen doing the selling and the Rumseys doing the hosting worked. By the Fourth of July of that first year, 50 people were living in the upper settlement of Ann Arbor. Log cabins popped up on Washington and William. The Coffee House bustled day and night. The town's first sawmill was built. They sold more and more land to new arrivals and Ann Arbor spread in all directions.

Then, three years after his arrival, Elisha Rumsey died of fever. He was in his 40s, which was about the normal life expectancy back then, even for a dirty rotten founder. Maybe especially for a dirty rotten founder. He was buried in Forest Hill Cemetery beneath a headstone with the inscription, "The first settler in Ann Arbor." Mary Ann moved away and remarried, leaving co-founders John and Ann Allen among the 400 people who now called Ann Arbor home.

As for Ann Arbor's other dirty rotten founder?

John Allen

Born in Augusta County, Virginia on May 17, 1796, John Allen came from a well-established family based in the Shenandoah Valley. Not quite as upper class as the Old South plantation owners, his family was said to have "possessed the same pride in family and good breeding as did the most aristocratic Virginians."

He grew up with all the advantages of a child of new money. Good schools. Good food. Good horses. Allen was described as "physically a very grand specimen of a man ... over six feet tall and well proportioned ... well educated, not a classical scholar, but a very good English scholar, and very apt in acquiring the elements of science."

He was charming and likeable, a decent businessman who took decent risks—not unlike his father. He parlayed this charm and his (almost) upper class bearing into a pretty sweet nuptial arrangement. At 19, he married the wealthy heiress Mary Crawford, whose well-established family owned hundreds of acres in Virginia and Kentucky. To celebrate the wedding, Allen's father gifted him 397 acres on which to begin his new life, along with additional land holdings worth a grand total of $12,000—15 times the amount he later paid for the land that became Ann Arbor.

This 19-year-old was set for life. However, six short years later, Mary Crawford was dead and Allen's father was in massive debt to the tune of $40,000. John sold and mortgaged everything he could to rescue his father, and used that Allen charm to wed a second time—once again, marrying up. This time, he wed a woman who not only came from wealth but had inherited her first husband's substantial fortune as well.

Mrs. Ann Isabella (Barry) McCue was descended from French nobility, attended finishing school, was deeply religious, and had zero sense of humor. Allen was rough around the edges, up for adventure, and looking for a fresh start because, oh yeah, his family's enormous debt.

In 1823, rather than use his new wife's considerable fortune to bail out his family, he transferred the debt back to his father (sorry, Dad) then left Virginia, never to return. The reasons for the move are murky. In the tax collection records for 1824, next to John Allen's name, the word "absconded" appears. Absconded from what? There's a story of him buying a considerable herd of cattle on credit with an agreement to drive them to Baltimore, sell them, and repay the loan plus interest. Allen took possession of the cattle, made it to Baltimore, and did in fact sell them, though he never quite got around to paying the men in Virginia back. Nor did he settle many of his own debts in the South.

With the proceeds of the cattle sale in hand, Allen went to Buffalo, then Canada, and ended up in Detroit in 1824 looking to buy up some land and start a-speculating. That's when he met Elisha and Mary Ann Rumsey.

Allen purchased the lion's share of the land that became Ann Arbor—480 acres to Rumsey's 160, spending $600 of his shady, "borrowed" cattle profits. They almost called the town Allensville, but settled on "Ann-Arbour" to honor their wives and the burr oaks that covered the land they'd purchased.

Allen was in heaven—pioneering in this new land in the winter months where he'd rebuild his family's fortune. He was content sleeping in a tent behind Elisha's log house because he was always on the move—doing his best to make this new settlement succeed. While the Rumseys played town host, Allen got to using that charm.

It took Allen five months to work some major magic, nudging Michigan Governor Lewis Cass to designate Ann Arbor the county seat, making it central to the running of the new Washtenaw County. That made Allen's sales job a lot easier, even if in return for being the hottest city in the county, Ann Arbor now had to provide an expensive courthouse, a "substantial" bridge over the Huron River, and plots of land for public use.

The ads Allen posted in the Detroit Gazette were amazing.

"The subscribers invite the attention of EMIGRANTS, particularly of Mechanics and Artisans, to the village of ANN-ARBOUR."[6]

They boasted of a growing town in the heart of a rich and rapidly populating country with lots for sale "on the most liberal terms, to persons desirous of permanently locating."

Conspicuously absent in all of this was Ann Allen. She loved life in the South and unlike her husband, didn't wish to leave. Allen finally sent for her in the summer of 1824, and, reluctantly, she traveled westward, leaving her own kids behind, knowing they would be ill-equipped for the journey and the destination. She traveled in a covered wagon with Allen's father and some of his children. They left Virginia in August and reached Ann Arbor on October 24, 1824.

Though they had cramped quarters that winter, Allen's speculation paid off. The population of Washtenaw County nearly doubled to more than 1,500 by 1825 and Ann Arbor's population rose appreciably. Allen sold plots hand over fist, using the proceeds to buy more and more government land.

It wasn't all burr oaks and arbors though. Allen's cofounder, Rumsey, died in 1827, and Allen's own father died the following year. He continued to add to his fortune, but as the town grew, Allen adopted more of a founder's role than he originally intended, sacrificing parcels of land for public use and the greater good.

---

6   ALL CAPS theirs.

A rich man now, he finally settled his affairs back in Virginia (better safe than sorry), and lived like a beloved prince in Ann Arbor, serving as postmaster, village president, and publisher of a local newspaper. He continued to take financial risks, using his personal wealth and borrowing from associates to invest heavily in further land speculation in Michigan. He set up a company right on Wall Street in New York City and was ready to become a true financial titan, only to lose it all in a financial crisis known as the Panic of 1837. Dejected and broke, he returned to Ann Arbor where they welcomed him with open arms, even if he owed a bunch of them a lot of money.

Allen licked his wounds and plotted his next move. He wasn't a young man anymore. He'd burned through not one, not two, but three fortunes. He talked about visiting Texas. Planned to explore the unexplored west. It was all too much for Ann, who'd endured Allen long enough out of sheer love and devotion. She returned to Virginia around 1843 where she lived another 30 years. In her will, she asked that a tombstone be erected not only to memorialize her, but also her husband, John Allen. Her family paid for one grave marker— for Ann.

With Michigan becoming well-settled, Allen looked to the west and the gold rush. He set out for California in the winter of 1850, writing three lengthy letters to family and friends back in Ann Arbor at various points in his journey.[7]

Allen arrived in the San Francisco territory on April 25, 1850, after a four-month journey that cost $200. He got right to work. After three months, he'd failed to make a strike. After six, he and his partners had barely paid for the expense of moving to California. They pivoted, buying 20 acres five miles outside the city and set up a farm with vegetables, chickens, and cows. In his final letter home, Allen closed with the ominous line, "My health has not been very good for some days, having a somewhat severe attack of the dysentry (sic) now prevailing here."

---

7   The *Ann Arbor News* published all three–people wanted to know how the founder was faring in the wild west!

His obituary, dated March 11, 1851, described the illness that ended his life as "painful and protracted." He was buried in the Yerba Buena Cemetery, then disinterred and re-buried in Golden Gate Cemetery when they built San Francisco's City Hall on the site.[8]

The town mourned their final fallen founder, but made no attempt to retrieve his remains on the other side of the continent.

The true story of John Allen and Elisha Rumsey goes to show you—out of pretty spectacular crap can spring something truly beautiful. They were dirty rotten founders, but they were ours.

---

8   They didn't move all the bodies, so there's a chance Allen is still on that spot. Construction of the City Hall building disrupted a number of graves that were missed, uncovering fragments of bone and whole skulls. The building didn't last long. City Hall was destroyed in the 1906 earthquake and fire, and eventually razed to build the San Francisco Public Library and later the Asian Art Museum. When renovations were being made to the museum in 2001, they once again found fragments of coffins and fully-preserved skeletons.

THE UFO INVASION OF 1966

In the wee hours of March 14, 1966, seven cops across two Michigan counties witnessed something unexpected, unexplained, and unidentified flying in the sky. Strange lights and weirdly-shaped craft zipped and hovered in the southeast Michigan skies. These sightings were reported by police officers, not run of the mill crackpots. Over the next few days, more than 100 witnesses reported similar sightings—dozens of accounts of football-shaped objects darting back and forth for hours in the sky—reports so numerous and so consistent that the U.S. Air Force took notice.

The term "UFO" entered the lexicon following highly publicized sightings of unidentified objects in the sky by pilots, ministers, businessmen and farmers in the 1940s. The U.S. government took these reports seriously, creating investigatory groups with names like Project Sign, Project Grudge, and most famously, Project Blue Book. Started in 1952, Project Blue Book had two goals: determine if UFOs were a threat to national security and analyze the data to separate true UFO activity from natural phenomena like clouds, weather patterns, crackpots, pranksters, and liars looking to gain fame and fortune.

One of the central figures of Project Blue Book was J. Allen Hynek— an astronomer, professor, and ufologist. A trained scientist, Hynek held positions in academia at Ohio State and Northwestern, but his interests and expertise eventually led to him being hired as a consultant during the Air Force's first efforts to investigate UFOs. His cautious and conservative nature made him well suited to the work of investigating whether or not UFOs were real and, if so, what threat they posed to national security.

Hynek worked on Project Sign, then Project Grudge, and finally Project Blue Book. He was dispatched around the country to investigate unidentified phenomena like a less-attractive agent Mulder. Hynek was a UFO skeptic at heart, though the more eyewitnesses he interviewed and evidence he examined, the more value he placed on applying rigorous scientific scrutiny to the subject.

The Air Force kept an eye on these unexplained events in and around Ann Arbor, but it wasn't until the UFO sighting at Frank Mannor's farm in Dexter that they sent Dr. Hynek to investigate.

Frank Mannor was 46 years of age in 1966, a truck driver with thinning hair, a craggy complexion, and a gap between his front teeth. He was the father of 10 children. He was a simple man, and a hunter, accustomed to being in wooded swamplands.

On the night of March 20, 1966, Mannor's six dogs started barking in a way they'd never done before. He went outside to quiet them and that's when he saw what he saw—something flying through the night sky. At first it looked like a shooting star, but then it slowed, changed color, and landed in the woods, a few hundred yards from his farmhouse at 10600 McGinnis Road.

Mannor's 18-year-old son Ronald went with his father to investigate. They saw a strange brownish craft with a quilted exterior and pulsating lights moving side to side. When they got close, the brilliant white light turned blood red and the thing made a high-pitched whistle. Then whoosh, it zoomed right over their heads and disappeared.

Down the street, Bob Wagner saw the same strange object in the sky and called the authorities from a telephone at the Dexter Body Shop. Wagner described the same lights, sounds and flight pattern of the unidentified object that Mannor saw. When the cops arrived—40 men in all—they headed to Mannor's farm and searched the surrounding area for clues. They pointed their flashlights in the sky and on the trees and found weird circular marks in the grass.

Patrolman Robert Hunawill of the Dexter Village Police Department was the one who saw it first—a strange lighted object overhead. Officers climbed into their vehicles and gave chase—six cop cars and 12 cops barrelling west down Island Lake Road until the thing shot into the midnight sky. Poof. Gone.

The next night, more than 80 students at nearby Hillsdale College saw the UFO. The night after that, more reports of strange lights in the skies over Ypsilanti, Saline, Dexter, and Ann Arbor. Descriptions included: football-shaped objects, red, white, green, and blue lights, antenna, domes, a sound like sirens, a sound like the ricochet of a bullet, silence. Some said the objects floated for minutes, others saw them linger for hours. Some saw them dart around, some feared they were being chased by the objects.

Dr. Hynek stepped off the train in Ann Arbor on March 23 and was greeted by mass hysteria. He got straight to work, touring the areas where UFOs were sighted, interviewing eyewitnesses, gathering evidence. Crowds followed him everywhere.

Hynek's investigation was hamstrung from the beginning. First, it was difficult for him to meet with every eyewitness because there were so many— and their accounts differed wildly. Second, he literally struggled to speak. Hynek had suffered a broken jaw just days before his trip to Ann Arbor and was in no small amount of pain with his jaw firmly wired shut. Third, Hynek was under intense pressure from the Air Force to get to the bottom of this madness. They were sick of the national media attention, alarmed at the hysteria, and ready for answers.

Dr. Hynek took two days to investigate and on March 25 delivered a press conference to more than 60 national and local reporters. The strange lights in the sky? The hovering objects? That thing out at the Mannor farm? Not UFOs.

Hynek offered naturally-occurring explanations: moonlight, stars and the one that stuck with them all—swamp gas—also called marsh gas, bog gas, or will-o-the-wisp. Rotting swamp vegetation creating methane plumes that spontaneously combust, making colorful little flames and sometimes sounds. That was the most likely culprit for the UFO scare, according to Hynek.

Partly obscured by a cluster of microphones, Hynek tried to sell the media on his natural explanation. He looked tired behind his thick-framed black glasses, holding up sketches and referencing previously debunked UFO sightings.

His findings were not received well. The words "swamp gas" led every headline, radio, and television report. Nobody bought it.

Ann Arbor's UFO fever spread to the rest of the country with sightings from California to New Jersey. Local reports continued as well. More lights in the sky. Hovering objects. An eight-page feature ran in the April 1 issue of Life with the headline "A Well-Witnessed 'Invasion' — by Something."

Frank Mannor was interviewed and said, "I don't want no money. I'm just a simple fellow. But what I seen, I seen, and nobody's gonna tell me different. This wasn't no old foxfire or hullabillusion."

Some locals thought differently. They taunted Mannor and his family and called him a crank and a nut. They prank called his home late at night, threw bottles at his porch and his truck, and prowled the property making mischief. Mannor even chased a pair of teens off his property with a loaded shotgun after they tried to sneak into a second story window.

Local pranksters took advantage of the situation, making fake UFOs out of weather balloons and setting them aloft with birthday candles. Michigan's Zeta Beta Taus built a fake UFO on north campus that sparked a mini panic. The night sky lit up with flares and still more weird floating objects.

The situation got so bad that House Republican Leader Gerald Ford stepped in to calm the storm. "It would be a very wholesome thing for a committee of the congress to conduct hearings with responsible witnesses who have sighted these objects," said the former Michigan grad.

Hynek's investigation resulted in the Condon report, which concluded that the U.S. government's two-decade study of UFOs had contributed nothing to scientific knowledge. The Air Force shut down Project Blue Book and stopped publicly[9] investigating strange phenomena.

Dr. Hynek took his lumps and endured. He founded the Center for UFO Studies and toured the public speaking circuit, often opening his speeches with editorial cartoons lampooning his swamp gas theory. He softened his skepticism and became more of a believer. Hynek developed a classification system for close encounters with UFOs. You may be familiar with one of them—Steven Spielberg was—close encounters of the third kind, which occur when humans see animated occupants inside unidentified flying objects. Hynkek served as a consultant on the film and even appeared in an uncredited role.[10]

What became of Frank Mannor? And Ronald Mannor, Mrs. Mannor, and the nine other kids, six dogs, and that farmhouse at 10600 McGinnis? Luckily for them, by April, just as quickly as UFO fever swept the area, it was gone. Poof.

Mannor still struggled with the label of crazy guy who believed in UFOs. Every few years, ufologists or newspapermen would show up on his porch looking for Mannor to retell his tale. They were politely asked to leave.

Frank Mannor died 17 years later at the age of 64, spending his last days in the Ann Arbor VA hospital. He's buried in Forest Lawn Cemetery. The *Ann Arbor News* ran a short obituary as an excuse to recall the events in March 1966, when UFOs visited Washtenaw County. March 1966 was a moment when you could stare into the night sky and look for something spectacular and

---

9   *Publicly.*

10   He's the one with the glasses and the white goatee smoking a pipe near the landing
site.

unknown, and if you were lucky, chase those lights until they disappeared into the sky.

THE NATIONAL
MARBLES CHAMPIONSHIPS

The first contestant to advance was Leslie Hoeft, age 11, from Lincoln Consolidated School. The next day, Richard Meldrum, age 12, beat 33 other boys and girls at Platt School to earn his place in the tournament. That same week, 146 boys and girls at St. Thomas Elementary and High School battled it out until Angelo Rocco and Ernest Tomczak emerged the winners.

In the spring in 1936, seven years into the Great Depression, the entire city of Ann Arbor—age 14 and under—lost its marbles over the biggest sporting event the city had ever known. Hundreds of kids were aiming for one of 26 coveted spots in a tournament that could determine their young futures: the 1936 *Ann Arbor Daily News* Marbles Tournament.

The 1936 *Ann Arbor Daily News* Marbles Tournament pitted the best shooters from schools throughout the city against each other for an all-expenses-paid trip to Lake Geneva, Wisconsin to compete in the Western

Finals. The champion of the West would advance to the National Marbles Tournament on the Jersey Shore, and a chance at marbles immortality.

During the Great Depression money was scarce, and the game of marbles was cheap and simple to play. Regular marbles only cost a few cents apiece, except shooters, which were pricier and made of dense glass or material like flint or agate. These could set a kid back 40 cents to a dollar. Shooters were prized like a cowboy's six-shooter, and kids were really superstitious about their favorites. It wasn't uncommon to name a favorite shooter, keep them in custom pouches, and polish them to a gleam after each play.

Marbles could be played almost anywhere. Draw a circle in the dirt, 10 feet in diameter, and have each player rack 13 regular marbles in the shape of an X at the center. Players took turns crouching outside the circle, propelling the heavier shooters with their thumbs, trying to knock their opponent's marbles out of the circle. If you knocked a marble out of the circle and your shooter remained inside, you shot again. Players took turns until only one shooter's marbles remained in the circle.

Playing marbles was a big deal in 1936. The national tournament had been running 15 years, with champions as young as 11 from as far afield as Baltimore and Louisville. Newspapers across the country sponsored local tournaments to crown champions to play in the regional tournaments, hoping to back the next national champion. The *Ann Arbor Daily News* jumped aboard in 1936, sponsoring a citywide contest to pick the best shooter in Ann Arbor.

During the month of May, schools throughout the city held spirited play-in tournaments to fill the 26 slots. Local legends battled scrappy underdogs. Each day a few more spots were claimed and a few more names published in the *Ann Arbor Daily News*, which ran frequent updates, so kids and grown-ups alike could keep track of the progress.

This included coverage of 14-year-old Wayne Waggoner, who "went to town in the Dexter regional tournament, beating both the rural and village boys." There was also 14-year-old Frank Bostic, who wiped the floor with the competition in the Jones Junior High School tournament, and Carleton Coon of Mack Junior High, who bested his foes to earn an invite.

The News selected Yost Field House as the venue for the big tournament. Ann Arbor High School coach and athletic director Don A. Drake was appointed the official referee, promising to keep play fast, fair, and interesting.

On the day of the tournament, May 25, 1936, the final field of 26 paired off to play. A crew under the direction of Lorenzo D. Thomas prepared a perfect playing surface—six rings were drawn in the dirt, and they were off. William Smith of Whitmore Lake fell hard in the opening round. Frank St. Mary of Bach crapped the bed. The pressure built as afternoon turned to evening and the field dwindled from twenty-six, to sixteen, to eight, to four.

Jack Davies of Tappan emerged the favorite, mowing down opponents with ease in the early goings. On the other side of the bracket, Herman Kersey of Woodruff School in Ypsilanti annihilated his first two opponents in just two turns, barely breaking a sweat before the semis. A Davies/Kersey showdown was imminent, and the winner would go on that all-expenses-paid trip to Lake Geneva.

It would have played to script, except for a scrappy underdog—13-year-old Jones Elementary sixth-grader Marcellus Scott. Of the 22 kids pictured in the photo taken at the end of the *Ann Arbor Daily News* Marbles Tournament, 19 white faces stare at the camera alongside just three black ones. Sixth-grader Marcellus Scott was one of those three, which is significant, as no African-American kid had ever won the National Marbles Tournament.

Pitted against the titan Davies, Marcellus Scott of 616 High Street[11] whipped the favorite, then won the whole tournament, earning his way to Lake Geneva. The tournament referee pinned a gold medal to Scott's chest and posed behind him in that photo of 22 kids, left hand resting proudly on the victor's shoulder.

Marcellus and his unnamed chaperones boarded a train to Grand Rapids where they joined three other Michigan champions, took an automobile to Muskegon to pick up a fourth kid, then took an all-night boat across Lake

---

11   Because of course The *Ann Arbor Daily News* published the address of sixth-graders in the 1930s.

Michigan to Milwaukee. When they arrived, they climbed into a car for the final ride to Lake Geneva, where the team went straight to the venue to get in some practice.

Right away, things got off to a bad start for Marcellus. Among the spectators in the crowd was a Dr. Samuel Schneider of St. Louis, apparently a renowned Midwestern marbles champion in his day. The good doctor spotted Marcellus warming up and hailed the young man. Out of deference, shyness, or maybe just fear, Marcellus permitted Dr. Schneider to climb out of the stands and show the kid how he used to do it in the old days.

Dr. Schneider took hold of Marcellus' prized shooter and it turned out he was still pretty good. So good that he wiped the dirt with the Michigan boys, but not before shooting so hard that he split Marcellus' best shooter in half, then did the same to his back-up marble. The doctor apologized, dropped a dime in the young boy's palm and returned to the stands with the damage done.

Marcellus improbably lost a third shooter moments later when it plunked out of the ring and into the crowd, where it was mashed into the dirt by fans circling the action. Marcellus looked long and diligently but never did find it.

The first day of the tournament was Monday. The boys from Michigan were pitted against one another in a round robin draw until one emerged victorious to face the rest of the field in the finals. Marcellus drew Dean Miller of Muskegon to open play. Wearing a brand new sweater with "Ann Arbor" on the chest and his nickname, "Eldine," stitched on the back, Marcellus cocked his thumb with his fourth-best shooter aimed and ready.

Blammo.

Marcellus was out of the competition on Tuesday. Instead of being crowned National Marbles Champion, Marcellus had to settle for having the time of his life that week in Lake Geneva. He ate in the giant hotel dining room until he almost burst, romped in the lobby with the other boys, swam in the cold Wisconsin lakes, rode horses and bikes and sang songs around the bonfire. It was the best week of his young life.

The Michigan kids, all defeated, drove back to Milwaukee, took a boat to Muskegon, a car ride to Grand Rapids and alone again, Marcellus boarded a train back to Ann Arbor with a giant smile on his face.

Leonard "Bobby" Tyner won that tournament in Lake Geneva. Beat all the other kids to earn a trip to the national finals on the Jersey Shore during Fourth of July weekend, 1936. The 13-year-old orphan from the southside of Chicago had beaten 8,500 other children in a citywide tournament sponsored by the Chicago Parks District, just to make it to the Western Finals. There he beat the field, then boarded a plane at Midway Airport and flew to Ocean City.

When Tyner arrived, representatives from the Southern marbles coalition discovered, to their amazement, that the Western champion was black.[12] In the interest of maintaining white supremacy, they fixed the draw so the previous year's champion, the legendary (and unbeatable) Henry Altyn of Throop, Pennsylvania, would face the upstart kid from Chicago, rather than their own boy from Birmingham.

It was their hope that the heavily-favored Altyn would demolish Tyner, saving the Southern champion from the embarrassment of having to play against a Negro.

Editors from the Scranton Times caught wind of the plot. They sponsored two of the four finalists in New Jersey that summer, including Altyn, who won a version of their own tournament back in Pennsylvania. The Times editors called the Southern machinations unsportsmanlike and un-American. Rather than permit the plot to stand, they withdrew both of their champions from the tourney, leaving just two contestants remaining in the tournament. The sponsors of the boy from Birmingham had just two options—forfeit, or play the black kid from Chicago.

They opted to play, and boy, were their faces red when their white hope lost.

Leonard Tyner—the first black National Marbles Champion, won five games to two. The boy from Birmingham refused to pose with him in the

---

12   The following saga was reported by *The New York Age*, an influential black newspaper, which was produced from 1887 to 1953.

championship photo, so the "unbeatable" Henry Altyn gladly filled in.

The next day, Leonard Tyner returned to Chicago and stepped off the plane at Midway Airport—the new marbles king of America.[13]

Richard Schindler. St. Thomas Catholic schoolboy Richard Schindler kneels and takes aim in the citywide marbles tournament in 1936. (Photo by Brian Peters, original courtesy of the *Ann Arbor News*)

---

13   The National Marbles Tournament is still going today. Thirteen-year-old Jean Smedley of Philadelphia was the first girl champion, winning in 1948. There has never been another National Marbles Champion from the great state of Illinois, let alone the city of Chicago.

Marcellus Scott. 13-year-old Jones Elementary sixth-grader Marcellus Scott won the Ann Arbor Daily News Marbles Tournament to earn a trip to Lake Geneva, Wisconsin, for the Western Finals. Here he poses in June of 1936 prior to competing in Wisconsin. (Photo by Brian Peters, original courtesy of the *Ann Arbor News*)

THE MALLET MURDER

It was Sunday, September 16, 1951. Thirty-four-year-old Pauline Campbell left her rooming house at 1424 Washington Heights around 2 pm, starting her 15-minute walk to work. She was a nurse on the maternity ward at St. Joseph's Hospital[14], caring for brand new babies and the mothers who brought them into the world.

Campbell was dressed in her bright white uniform, a raincoat draped over her arm because the evening forecast called for drizzle. She carried a red leather purse that held her wallet, a lighter, and her dinner in a brown paper bag.

Around 11 pm, Campbell's shift ended, she gave her report, and she gathered her things for the walk home. It was dark now, but the walk was less than a mile. And this was Ann Arbor, not New York City.

---

14   At the time, St. Joseph's was at North Ingalls and Ann Streets, where the University of Michigan Nursing School is today.

She'd made this walk plenty of times—one of the benefits of living so close to work. She was cautious but not scared. She started back home, raincoat over her arm. The rain had held off.

She walked east towards University Hospital, turned down Observatory, then walked east to her place on Washington Heights. Her house was about halfway down the block, on the right, backing up to the Arboretum. It was nearly midnight. Campbell probably didn't pay special attention to the headlights behind her. She was hard of hearing, so she probably didn't hear the footsteps behind her. She didn't know what was happening until it was too late.

A U-M medical school student found the body some time later and called the police.

The killers were three regular boys born to three regular homes. William R. Morey, 18, Jacob M. Pell, 18, and David L. Royal, 17. They had graduated from Ypsilanti High School that spring. Morey live in Ypsilanti and was in his first week of classes as a freshman at Michigan Normal College.[15] His pal Pell lived in Ypsi too, working as a mechanic. Royal lived 15 miles away in Milan, where he worked construction. All three boys still lived with their parents.

That Sunday night in September started like most other nights for the boys. Pell borrowed his parents' two-door 1948 Chevy Stylemaster Club Coupe—a chrome-detailed monster that seated five. He picked up his friends, then the boys met a pair of girls in Milan and piled them into the backseat. They bought beer—two cases of Miller High Life, longneck bottles with gold labels. It didn't matter that they were underage—a number of taverns around Milan were notorious for selling beer to minors.

They cruised the dirt roads of Milan with the girls in the back, listening to Rosemary Clooney, Perry Como, Nat King Cole, and Tony Bennett on the radio. They pulled bottles out of the cases, one after another. Popping the tops, cracking jokes, laughing, flirting. Pell drove while Morey and Royal canoodled with the ladies in back.

---

15   Now Eastern Michigan University.

They parked at the edge of a cornfield, headlights on, radio up, draining beer after beer, chucking the empties into the stalks. The girls weren't as wild as the boys had hoped and the beer was nearly gone, so they piled back into the car and drove the girls home. It was still early, just 11 pm.

Morey would go to Ann Arbor some nights to cruise for girls. Some nights, to steal hubcaps on dark and deserted roads. One night not long before, his evening activities had become more violent—Morey had spotted a woman walking alone late at night and unsuccessfully mugged her. Ann Arbor was rife with opportunity.

That was the plan this night, after the boys dropped off the girls. Cruise, steal, or rob. They drove down by the hospital and the dark streets near the Arboretum where Morey had had luck before. Nearing the Arb, Morey told Pell to stop. He rooted around in the back seat of the car, opened the door, and stepped into the night.

In his hand he held a large rubber mallet—the kind used to bump out heavy car fenders without leaving a scratch. Pell had brought it home from the repair shop where he worked to do some auto body work over the weekend. The mallet had a 12-inch wooden handle with a 4-inch wide head. Morey tucked it into his belt and disappeared into the shadows. Pell eased the car down the dark side street, but lost sight of Morey. He parked and extinguished the lights.

There they waited. Windows down. Radio off. They could probably see the nurse Morey was following in the darkness, because of the way her all-white uniform stood out in the night.

Morey hit Pauline Campbell in the back of the head with that mallet—so hard that police found brain fluid spattered on a car door parked several feet from the sidewalk where the attack took place. The first blow knocked her to the ground. It's unclear how many more blows Morey delivered before dragging her body toward the street, hissing in the dark for his friends to help.

The car pulled up and screeched to a halt and Morey had her partway in the back seat before Pell protested loud enough to stop him. They shoved the still-breathing Campbell out of the car and onto the curb, where she lay at an awkward angle until found later that night. Morey snatched her red leather purse, climbed into the passenger seat, and Pell peeled away.

Pell drove back towards Ypsilanti, fast, taking Huron River Drive. Morey ransacked the purse. A cigarette lighter. A watch. One dollar and fifty cents. He threw the purse out the window when they hit the second bridge on Huron River Drive—right by Superior Road. They dumped the empty beer cases out the windows too.

Campbell lay in the street. She wasn't dead when police arrived at 12:20 am. Lieutenant Walter Krasny of the Ann Arbor Police Department shined his flashlight on her battered and bloody body, lying half in the street and half on the grass. Her head was shaking from side to side and Campbell was trying to speak. Krasny leaned in close. Her face was partly covered by her hair, which was caked with blood. Krasny asked her questions, but Campbell's words were unintelligible. She was rushed to the hospital, where she died that night—right around the time the three boys pulled into a truck stop in Ypsilanti, and bought 94 cents' worth of gas, along with sandwiches and coffee with the stolen $1.50.

Not that you're feeling sorry for these boys right now, but just in case— don't. Don't feel sorry for William R. Morey, 18, Jacob M. Pell, 18, and David L. Royal, 17. They didn't turn themselves in. This wasn't their first attack. Two of them—Morey and Pell—had attacked a nurse four days earlier. Morey had swung a 12-inch crescent wrench at a University Hospital nurse walking home late at night, not far from the spot where they murdered Campbell. In the earlier attack, the nurse flinched or maybe Morey just missed his mark. The blow landed, but it was glancing. The nurse screamed and ran and reported the attack to police. Morey bragged about the crescent wrench incident to a friend at Michigan Normal. It turned out that this friend happened to be on probation and could really use the $500 reward money and maybe a favor from the court.

It was this friend, Daniel Baughey, who walked into Ann Arbor police headquarters at 3 pm three days after the attack with a tip in the unsolved mallet murder. Two hours and five minutes later, police pulled up to Doran's Chevrolet in Ypsilanti and arrested Pell. Across town, police dragged Morey out of the bath and placed him in handcuffs. At the same time, Royal was arrested at his parents' home in Milan.

The suspects were questioned for four hours in Ypsi before being driven to Michigan State Police Headquarters in East Lansing for a proper grilling. Pell confessed at 11 pm, and implicated the other boys. Royal confessed 30 minutes later. Morey cracked at midnight. By 4:30 am, all three had signed confessions and were put in squad cars bound for Ann Arbor.

In the early morning hours, Pell was booked for murder at Ann Arbor police headquarters and taken to the county jail. Morey and Royal were driven to that second bridge near Superior Road—the bridge where they ditched the red leather purse while speeding back to Ypsilanti.

They stood on that bridge in 50-degree fall weather, as the rising sun burned off the morning dew. Mist shrouded the bridge—the two killers, hands cuffed in front of them, peered over the edge, pointing vaguely to where the purse may have landed. This moment may have been among the last opportunities for these tired, shivering, stupid kids to be outdoors for any substantial amount of time not surrounded by high walls, barbed wire, and men in towers with guns.

Police never found the purse. And how they tried. Investigators tossed handbags off the bridge to judge how the water may have directed Campbell's purse. Purse after purse thrown over that second bridge at Superior Road. They did find one of the empty cases of Miller High Life, stained with blood. The also found the mallet, which Pell had returned to Doran's Chevrolet on the Monday after the murder, as well as evidence of blood on the floor mat and upholstery of Pell's parents' car. There was more blood on a blanket and jacket wadded up in the back seat.

Jury selection started on Halloween 1951. There was snow on the ground. The 14-member jury—seven men and seven women, were selected after a lengthy search for people who hadn't heard about the case. All but four jurors had children of their own.

The courtroom was packed each day—the story was the buzz of Ann Arbor and made national news. Curious teenagers—former classmates of the boys—skipped school to be in the courtroom and were written up for truancy after their pictures appeared in the newspaper. The three mothers of the boys—Mrs. Morey, Mrs. Royal, and Mrs. Pell—sat in the courtroom and wept often. They had raised their sons to be good boys. They'd done their best, given their sons all they could, and were now suffocated by guilt and shame and what ifs.

The three signed confessions were probably enough to put the boys away. Add in the police testimony and the autopsy and it was a pretty open-and-shut case. The defense didn't aim to disprove guilt, it just tried to mitigate their sentences.

Morey stammered and sobbed on the stand, his voice breaking. He said he'd drunk 10 or 11 beers that night. He claimed not to have remembered the fatal blow—didn't know if the mallet made a sound when it crushed Campbell's skull, or how many times he struck her. At one point, the prosecutor held the murder weapon in his hands and asked Morey to examine the rubber mallet used to end Campbell's life. When Morey declined to take it, the prosecutor tossed it into his lap. The teen recoiled like a bag of poisonous snakes had been dumped on him, shoving it to the floor where it bounced hard, resting on its side.

The three boys were found guilty on November 14, 1951. The charge was for committing "feloniously, willfully, and with malice aforethought, the murder of Pauline Campbell."

Nine days later, Morey and Pell were sentenced to life. Royal received a 22-year prison term. None of the men finished their sentences. Pell and Royal were released sometime in the 1960s for time served and good behavior.

Morey received special attention from Governor William Milliken, who commuted his life sentence in 1970 and made him eligible for parole. Morey came before the parole board that June after spending more than half his life in prison. He had been a model inmate, earned his degree, and started a prison blood donation program. He was nothing like the kid who had killed the nurse.

Through most of his hearing, Morey smoked cigarettes and cried. He was released, a 37-year-old man who hadn't tasted freedom since Truman was president. He moved to Arizona, took a job as an accountant, and got married. That's the last we know of William R. Morey.

THE BIRTH OF IGGY POP

He was born in a hospital in Muskegon. The trailer park he grew up in was in Ypsilanti.[16] But it was in Ann Arbor where James Newell Osterberg became Iggy Pop.[17]

Ice cubes, coins, beer cans, champagne bottles, lit cigarettes—whatever would fly, flew—thrown at the stage one sub-zero February night in Detroit in 1974. The band that night, The Stooges, hired the God's Children biker gang out of Ypsilanti to keep the peace, and even they couldn't keep the crowd in check. Luckily, the stage at the Michigan Palace was pretty large, which made the band harder to hit.

Iggy Pop was running on fumes. His blood was coursing with drugs and alcohol and his body was fueled by spite. There was no joy in this performance. His face was puffy, his ribs stuck out, his shaggy hair stuck to his

---

16   Pittsfield Township, actually.

17   Shoutouts to cocaine, meth, acid, booze, pills, and ambition for their contributions.

face but those piercing blue eyes burned. He taunted the crowd, gyrated his hips and antagonized them in between songs.

"I don't care if you throw all the ice in the world," he shouted into the mic. "You're paying five bucks and I'm making $10,000, baby. So screw ya."

Iggy's usual patter with the crowd was more hostile than usual. Grievances were aired. Every insult hurled at the crowd received a return volley of ice, coins, etc. On this night, the crowd hated Iggy Pop. They wanted blood. Iggy was wise not to dive into the crowd like he usually did. This was not a night to hop down off the stage and wade into their midst, as he'd done a week earlier at a dive called the Rock & Roll Farm in Wayne.

On that night at the Rock & Roll Farm, he walked through the crowd of 120 people, mostly bikers, dressed in a skintight leotard and screaming at bikers in a way that bikers aren't used to. Shoving through the crowd with the mic cord trailing behind him, Iggy, all 100 pounds of him, came face to face with one of the biggest men in the room. The guy was 300 pounds at least, dressed in dark denim, and the colors of the Detroit Scorpions motorcycle club. Iggy gazed up at this giant. The giant looked back, then punched Iggy square in the stupid face. Iggy was on his ass. He healed quickly—in time to perform at the Michigan Palace.

The show was recorded on a reel-to-reel. You can hear Iggy yelling at the crowd—yelling at his bandmates—counting them back to the beat when they screw up.

"Gimme just the drums!" he yells into the microphone. "It's the only way you're ever gonna get it right!"

A quarter hit the Stooges bassist in the head, opening up his scalp and leaving a scar that would remain decades after this disastrous show.

The final song was an angry version of "Louie Louie" with all new lyrics—extra vulgar for the adoring fans.

"I never thought it would come to this, baby," Iggy yelled, the Stooges pounding away on their instruments.

Then, mercifully, it was over.

"Thank you very much to the person who threw this glass bottle at my head and nearly killed me," Iggy yelled after the last bass line faded. "But you missed again. Keep trying next week."

Two years later, the live recording was released as the Metallic K.O. album and it would quickly achieve cult status. Members of The Clash, Joy Division, The Sex Pistols, the Red Hot Chili Peppers, and the White Stripes would listen to and be inspired by that disastrous Stooges show. The whole mess—Iggy slurring at the crowd, taunting them, the band losing the beat, finding the beat, losing it again—would help shape music for a whole new generation.

At the time, nobody had any clue this would happen. After the set, the Stooges limped backstage, drank, medicated, then finally split. Like, split split—the Stooges were no more. That freezing cold night in 1974 was the end of a chaotic experiment, and it seemed like it might be the end of frontman Iggy Pop, who flew back to LA, his spirit broken.

But let's jump back to the birth of Iggy Pop. His first appearance was in a hospital in Muskegon. He spent his childhood years in a 50-by-20-foot Vagabond trailer on lot 96 of the Coachville Mobile Home Park at 3423 Carpenter Road in Ypsilanti. Then on to Ann Arbor. His name was James Osterberg, and he was a good kid. He was the student council president and vice president of the debate club. He didn't smoke, drink, or do drugs. He wore nice sweaters and penny loafers. He was on the high school golf team, for Pete's sake. James Osterberg—Iggy Pop!—on the high school golf team.

He was a drummer too—first in a band called Megaton Two. Then in The Iguanas—a preppy pop ensemble with matching sport coats and haircuts.

Osterberg was a great performer. People liked him, and he loved the attention. He jumped to the Prime Movers, a band with enough promise to prompt him to drop out of the University of Michigan, quit his job at Discount Records,[18] and devote himself to music. The Prime Movers were pretty good. They might go places.

---

18   Located at 300 South State Street, where Potbelly Sandwich Shop is today.

Then The Doors played the homecoming dance in 1967, so settle in for a big old digression about Jim Morrison's drunken visit to U-M.

The crowd was excited for the big Friday night homecoming dance with a special appearance by the headliner. The Doors were a big get—their debut album had come out earlier that year and "Light My Fire" was #2 on the charts.

The Doors took the stage at the U-M Intramural Building, minus lead singer Jim Morrison. The crowd expected it was all part of the act. The band played the opening riff to one of their songs and the crowd cheered. One minute passed. Then two minutes. Then five. The audience got restless and started to boo. The band stopped playing and left the stage and the crowd buzzed with confusion. A few minutes later, The Doors returned—this time with Morrison. A very, very drunk Jim Morrison who began immediately swearing loudly into the microphone. Like, a lot.

Morrison stumbled and stammered through the start of the set and the straightlaced homecoming crowd stood open-mouthed in shock. The football players blushed and their dates covered their ears. This wasn't the hippest crowd in Ann Arbor.

Morrison missed his marks, forgot lyrics, but mostly berated the audience. He was hammered and in the mood to fight—all because of a disagreement over ice cream. Earlier that day, the Doors landed in Detroit and took a car to Ann Arbor. The rest of the band wanted to stop for ice cream on the way, but Jim thought ice cream was for babies. So, while the others licked their cones like little kids, Jim bought whiskey at a local liquor store and sat in the backseat sullenly getting loaded.

Partway through the set, completely fed up, the drummer and the guitarist walked off the stage, leaving keyboardist Ray Manzarek to abandon his set up and pick up a guitar—fumbling with a few blues riffs in an attempt to salvage the totally unsalvageable night.

The crowd yelled and booed at the retreating Doors. It was an utter disaster.

Osterberg—there for the entire set—was delighted. In Morrison, he saw the intensity and aggression that he wanted to project in his own performance. Wearing leather pants, long oiled hair, with a hit record under his belt, taunting the furious crowd, Jim Morrison was a goddamn role model.

Osterberg thought, "I can do that."

A few days later, he got his shot.

Over a drug-fueled Three Stooges marathon on TV, partying at a house they rented at 1324 Forest Court, Osterberg, Dave Alexander, and brothers Ron and Scott Asheton, formed a new band. They called themselves the Psychedelic Stooges—later shortened to The Stooges. On that night, Iggy Pop emerged from James Osterberg. "Iggy" was a nickname acquired from his time with The Iguanas, and "Pop," was borrowed from Jim Pop, a local junkie.

The Stooges played their first show 11 days after the Doors were booed off the stage at homecoming. The gig was a private party on Halloween night and the set was so insane that the band's brand new manager quit on the spot and returned to teaching.

With a practice show under their belts, The Stooges booked their first public show in January, playing the Grande Ballroom in Detroit. The day before, Ron Asheton painted Iggy's guitar in Day-Glo colors for the big occasion—inadvertently painting over the pick-ups and ruining it completely. Iggy used it anyway.

The Stooges opened their set with a blender full of water which buzzed into the PA system for 15 minutes. When they finally took the stage, Iggy walked out in a full-length nightshirt, golf shoes, white mime makeup and an Afro made of tinfoil. Scott Asheton banged a pair of 55-gallon oil drums with hammers.

When they played, their music wasn't half bad.

Iggy's antics grew more and more outrageous. Before taking the stage, he annihilated a buffet of drugs and booze, and shed most of his clothes within the first few songs. He smashed himself in the mouth with the microphone, rubbed raw meat and peanut butter on his body, and carved wounds in his chest using broken glass from bottles hurled by the crowd. Iggy climbed PA stacks and lighting rigs and waded into the crowd to pick fights. Sometimes he got punched in the face by giant bikers in dive bars in Wayne.

Drunk, ice-cream-sad Jim Morrison had nothing on Iggy Pop.

When Elektra Records came to town to see the MC5, they checked out this other band everyone was buzzing about and attended a Stooges show at the Michigan Union. They liked what they saw and signed them on the spot. The Stooges finished their first album in four days—an album that would feature some of the most enduring punk songs of all time.

With the advance money, The Stooges rented a house on the corner of Packard and Eisenhower and dubbed it The Fun House. Drugs, booze, and women followed.

Iggy had no shortage of female attention, but just as his star was rising, he settled down with a groupie known as "Potato Girl." Her name was Wendy Weisberg, and she and Iggy wed on the lawn of The Fun House with Ron Asheton as best man. Instead of a tuxedo, Iggy wore a full SS uniform. The marriage lasted a month.

Live performances continued to be insane. The cult of Iggy and the Stooges grew. They recorded their second album in 1970, but unlike the debut, it bombed. The Stooges, and Iggy in particular, wore on music executives and fans alike. They skipped shows because they were too messed up to perform. Ticket sales dwindled. Elektra dropped the Stooges in 1971. The Fun House was bulldozed. The Stooges broke up—for the first time.

They reformed in 1972 thanks, in some weird way, to Pop's friendship with David Bowie. They now billed themselves Iggy & the Stooges and recorded a third album. They toured for months, but booze and drugs eroded Iggy's constitution and relationships just like the first go-round—until that fateful February night in 1974. The ice, the coins, the bottles, that whole thing.

That night was just the end of Iggy Pop's second act. There'd be a third. A fourth. And a fifth. A sixth? Who can keep track?

In 2015, Iggy Pop showed up on Anthony Bourdain's Parts Unknown, bespectacled, wearing a sensible sweater, and talking about healthy eating. Shades of James Osterberg and his days at Tappan Junior High.

At age 70, Iggy has outlived all the original Stooges and occupies a rare place in music today. He's a pioneer, an influencer, and one of the most intimidating performers of all time. He looks like hell, but he's our slice of Hades.

Muskegon can claim the hospital. Ypsi can claim the trailer park. But Ann Arbor can claim the strange alchemy that turned James Osterberg into Iggy Pop.

That's something to be proud of, right?

RIOT AT THE STAR THEATRE

The first motion picture ever screened in Ann Arbor was The Great Train Robbery. The 12-minute silent Western flickered on screen at the Light Infantry Armory[19] on September 26, 1904, shown at the end of a sold-out, seven-part program featuring singers, jugglers, and Handcuff King Fred Gay.

Between that 1904 screening of The Great Train Robbery and 1907, a trio of permanent nickelodeon theaters sprung up in Ann Arbor to show moving pictures—a growing form of entertainment at the turn of the century.

A Brief History of Cinema in Ann Arbor

The Theatorium, the Casino, and the People's Popular Family Theater—later renamed the Vaudette—all opened in succession between 1906

---

19   Located at the corner of Ashley and West Huron (not to be confused with the other Ann Arbor Armory, opened in 1911 at 225 E. Ann Street), the Light Infantry Armory hosted entertainments as far back as 1896. Not rinky-dink acts–but showstoppers like stunt equestrians, high-flying acrobats, and Del Fuego, billed as the Funniest Man on Earth.

and 1907.[20] These nickelodeons, so called because they charged five cents for admission, were lucrative side projects for existing businessmen. They were easy to set up and cheap to run. Find an open storefront, buy a projector and some folding chairs, and most of the heavy lifting was done. Hang a clean-ish sheet on the wall, get a piano or organ, and hire someone to provide the background music these new silent films required.

Along with Ann Arbor's new nickelodeons, the city also welcomed a trio of vaudeville theaters to town, showing movies along with other kinds of more proven entertainment.

The Bijou, The Majestic, and the Star Theatre all opened in 1907.[21] These vaudeville theaters weren't much bigger than the nickelodeons, but they had stages, which allowed them to host live acts, too. Singers, acrobats, trained mules, Handcuff King Fred Gay.

A typical vaudeville program might go something like this:

First act: Dancers. Second act: Theatrical opera singers. Third act: A sketch. Then maybe a fiddle player. An acrobat. A bawdy crooner. An escape artist. An animal of above average intelligence doing things to make people gasp or laugh. And, finally, a movie.

These weren't Academy Award-winning films.[22] Rather, the successors to *The Great Train Robbery* were gems like *The Dog and His Various Merits*, Over the *Hill to the Poorhouse*, *The Good Glue Stick*, and *That Fatal Sneeze*. These silent films were screened with in-house background music and, in the case of the Star Theatre, someone who narrated the action.[23]

---

20   Ann Arbor's first nickelodeon was the Theatorium, which opened in November of 1906 at 119 East Liberty—site of the old Liberty Street Video and current home to the slightly less historic Bongz & Thongz. The next year, the Casino opened at 339 South Main (the site of Real Seafood Company) and the People's Popular Family Theater set up shop at 220 South State Street, where the State and Liberty Starbucks stands.

21   The Bijou was located at 209 East Washington, where Blue Tractor and Mash are today. The Majestic was at 347 Maynard Street, which is now a parking garage. The Star Theatre was located at 118 East Washington, where Arbor Brewing Company is today.

22   The first Academy Award was presented in 1929 with *Wings* taking home Outstanding Picture. Sorry, *The Dog and His Various Merits*.

23   Silent film narration doesn't appear to have been a common thing for silent movies in the United States at the time, though it was a very popular practice in movie houses in Japan. *Benshi* were performers who provided live narration during films, sometimes advanc-

The End of Our Brief History of Cinema in Ann Arbor

This isn't a story about the cinematic history of Ann Arbor. This is a tale of another sort. And for that, we only care about the Star. Not because it was a great and historical landmark standing the test of time. Not because it was owned by a great man, or a gangster, or a murderer, or a thief, or a mad magician. No—we care about the Star because on St. Patrick's Day in 1908, it was the site of the biggest riot in Ann Arbor's history.[24]

A Brief History of the Star Theatre

The Star was a dingy single-story space with a stage 15 feet wide— enough room for acrobats, some singers, a few dancers, and comics who played to crowds of students and Ann Arbor's working class. It was run by a man named Albert Reynolds, who previously owned a billiard hall and cigar store near campus.

There's only one really good photo of the Star, in all its glory, shortly after it opened. Take a look at that photo and really take in all that's going on. A big star-shaped sign hanging over the sidewalk, suspended two-stories up by a giant iron pole drilled into the building's facade. Lightbulbs outlining the sign, as well as the word "Star" in all caps nestled inside. The front of the building plastered with cheap, mismatched wooden signs. Count them—eight in all—if you don't include the 11-foot monster towering at the curb out front. No typeface matches the one next to it, everything ALL CAPS. And the marketing! Such amazing early 1900s marketing:

---

ing the plot through description and sometimes adopting the voices of multiple characters.

24   Raise your hand, hardcore townie, if you hollered, "But what about the Battle of Ann Arbor in the summer of 1969?! That was the biggest riot in the history of Ann Arbor." Or maybe you're a clever townie and you want to talk about those handsy Naked Mile crowds of 10,000-plus. Second townie, you're just plain wrong. The Naked Mile crowds were onlookers, not brick-throwers. You, fine townie, would have an argument, that is if we were sitting in Old Town. But we're not. You're reading a book. And we can't hear you. Crowd estimates for the Battle of Ann Arbor range from 1,000 to 2,500, while crowd estimates for the Star Theatre riot range from 1,000 to 3,000. We're siding with the Star Theatre estimates and calling that the biggest riot in the city's history because 3,000 > 2,500 and, we have to assume, people were better at counting in 1909 than 1969.

The World's Greatest Moving Pictures Do Everything But Talk

Big Double Show Every Day

Yes, This is the Place Where Life is Worth Living

Cool and Comfortable Star Show

The Star doesn't look like the nicest place for a night out, nor has it been described that way. Five cents, even back then, wasn't a lot of money. So the clientele was, predictably, a little rough around the edges.

Act 1: JACOB SLIMMER DOESN'T TAKE NO GUFF

Reynolds hired tough people to work with tough crowds, and Jacob Slimmer was tough. A burly amateur boxer, Slimmer had two jobs at the Star. One was usher. Pretty straightforward. The other was to read from pre-written cards and narrate motion pictures at the Star. There's no record of whether or not he was any good at his job, but evidence suggests that Jacob Slimmer didn't take no guff.

On St. Patrick's Day in 1908, Slimmer was narrating a film at the Star for a modest crowd of students and townies. He stood at the rear of the theater as the light flickered on screen during a tense moment in the film.

"Frantically," Slimmer narrated, "the hero chews the cord that binds his wrists as he struggles to free himself and save the fair maiden from a fate that is worse than death. Will he save her?"

A voice at the front of the theater hollered, "He sure will if he's been cleaning his teeth with Rubifoam toothpaste."[25]

Slimmer dropped his script, rolled up his sleeves and walked to the front of the theater where he located the comedian. Smashed him right in the jaw with a big, meaty fist. Tenderized that young University of Michigan undergrad with lefts and rights until he lay on the floor unconscious. A

---

25   "In the morning of life when the heart is susceptible to the pure and the beautiful, one is readily attracted to rosy, fragrant charms of the dainty, delicious dentifrice, Rubifoam, the maker of pure, sweet breath and sound, beautiful teeth. Young and old should know it is wise to use Rubifoam. No age limit to its benefits." Early 1900s marketing!

classmate who jumped up to defend his friend received a similar beating.

The theater cleared, students sprinting back to campus, sounding the alarm quickly and loudly. Students ran through rooming houses, fraternities, sororities, pool halls—the cry ringing off the walls, "All out for the Star!"

One of their own had been manhandled and justice had to be served. Hordes of students coursed west down Washington, Liberty, and William, all headed for the Star Theatre, searching for Slimmer, and seeking retribution.[26]

Slimmer wasn't stupid. He skedaddled immediately after the initial fracas and was never seen nor heard from again. The first voice of Ann Arbor's silent pictures vanished forever, leaving the Star's owner, Albert Reynolds, and his wife, to manage the near riot.

Did I say "near riot"? I meant riot.

Act 2: RIOT

It didn't take long for authorities to hear what was happening. Students were tearing apart the Star Theatre. The eight-man Ann Arbor police force, plus a few special officers paid to guard city landmarks, rushed to the scene. Members of the Ann Arbor Fire Department joined them. They encountered a mass of angry—if well dressed—rioters.[27] Estimates put the number of rioters at as many as 3,000, attacking the theater in waves, bringing their own bats, but also barraging the theater with loose cobblestones and bricks, which they sourced from three wagons conveniently loaded with them at a construction site across the street.

The rioters threw every last one of those bricks. Shattered every piece of glass that could be shattered. Dented and destroyed that big star sign. They tore out the seats, smashed the organ, ripped down lights and scenery, and left the

---

26   An overreaction on the part of what was probably the majority of the U-M student body at the time? Probably, but students back then had a long history of clashing with townies. As far back as 1874, several hundred students battled police who had arrested two of their classmates during freshman rush activities. After big football wins, students would pry up the city's wood-plank sidewalks and throw them into the road. The worst was the circuses, which hired extra security, armed with tent stakes, to deal with students. Undergrads would try and rush the big top to avoid paying admission, and, if treated poorly, would sabotage the traveling carnies by throwing acid on their tents or straight up burning them.

27   The one photo from the actual riot shows a mass of gentlemen wearing smart overcoats, stylish fedoras, newsboy caps, and a maybe straw boater or two.

establishment just four walls and a pile of debris. Collateral damage carried over to nearby shops and their facades. You can't expect all 3,000 rioters to have perfect aim with a brick.

The police tried to disperse the crowd with help from the firemen's hoses, but it was a dozen versus thousands. Rioters tore policemen's uniforms from their backs, made off with their helmets. They carried the firemen over their heads before they could hook up their hoses, then took the hoses themselves, forcing the fire chief to call for a full retreat.

Poor Albert Reynolds and his wife cowered in the basement under police guard while the rioters raged above. The police managed to collar 22 of the miscreants, who were arrested and dragged down the street, but it was a drop in the riot bucket. As day turned to night and the rioters ran out of things to destroy, U-M president James Angell and law school dean Harry Hutchins strode down Washington Street to calm the crowd. Angell was a minor god in Ann Arbor and the crowd respectfully parted in his presence.

One of the students procured an unsmashed box for Angell to stand on, giving him an elevated position in front of the Star. He addressed the crowd, which fell eerily silent.

"Gentlemen," Angell began, "this is deplorable. We wish you to follow Dean Hutchins and me home and go to bed."

The rioters listened to Angell's full plea but once Angell stepped down and the two dignitaries were ushered back out of harm's way, rioting promptly resumed. Angell and Hutchins were now worried that they'd have to call the governor and request the assistance of the militia.[28]

Act 3: THE AFTERMATH OF THE LARGEST RIOT IN ANN ARBOR HISTORY

By midnight, the rioters had rioted themselves out and returned to campus, leaving the remains of the Star behind. The damage was estimated to be as high as $2,500—somewhere north of $65,000 today. As part of an

---

28   Apparently, the governor was called and the militia was marshaling, ready to intervene at the Star, but the bugle calls signaling preparations to march quickly sent the students back to campus.

arrangement with the courthouse to release 15 of the arrested, students roamed campus with tin pails the next day, collecting money to offset the cost of the damages. When they turned over $1,000, the 15 undergrads were released. Three of the remaining incarcerated pled guilty to loitering charges and were fined $4.60 each.

The Star was eventually repaired, though to what extent and how well, we'll never know. It continued to show movies and host shows until 1919 when it closed its doors for good. We could research what business replaced it, or where folks went instead for their vaudeville entertainment, but this isn't a story about the cinematic history of Ann Arbor.

Honestly, I just cared about the riot.

Star Theater. The Star Theatre opened in 1907 as a vaudeville theater. The St. Patrick's Day riot of 1908 was the largest riot in the history of the city and caused somewhere in the neighborhood of $65,000 worth of damage in today's funds. (Photo by Brian Peters, original by Brian Fulton of the Bentley Historical Library).

HENRY FORD'S STRONG RIGHT FIST

Rich, famous and powerful people have called Ann Arbor home for nearly two centuries. John Allen. Mary Sue Coleman. Bob Seger. Violin Monster.

But no Ann Arborite has been more powerful, or more feared than Harry Bennett—Henry Ford's right-hand man, enforcer, union buster and the son he always wanted.

Bennett was born in Ann Arbor in 1892 and lived in a house at 1010 Wall Street in Lower Town near today's Kellogg Eye Center. His father died in a brawl[29] when Bennett was just a baby, leaving his mother to raise him on her own. When he hit 5' 6", he stopped growing, and as a result, bloodied a lot of noses to earn the respect he desired. Those battles won and lost made him one of the toughest sons of guns around.

---

29   Apparently killed by a chair.

Bennett had a soft side too, which manifested in his love of art. He studied at the Detroit Fine Arts Academy and the Cleveland Art School, then joined the Navy at the age of seventeen—deployed to West Africa where he worked with recon teams mapping coastlines, harbors and ports up and down the continent.

In the Navy, Bennett took up boxing. He was small and muscular and could take—and throw—a punch. His compact stature made him a tough target for opponents to hit. He fought under the name Sailor Reese, throwing fists in bouts on the base and in overseas tournaments—the trips sponsored by the Navy. With cold blue eyes, a receding hairline, and a rock-hard jaw, Bennett won a lot more fights than he lost.

Around his 24th birthday, Bennett was discharged and stepped off of a troop transport ship in New York City. The stories about how he secured an audience that day with the great Henry Ford differ, but here's a good one:

Bennett was walking through the Battery in lower Manhattan when he spotted a cheering crowd. In the middle he saw two men brawling. A big galoot was pulping a much smaller sailor, who was clearly overmatched in one on one combat. So Bennett stepped in and evened the odds, efficiently dropping the bigger man. When the local constabulary swarmed in to break up the fight, Bennett was arrested.

As luck would have it, boxing aficionado and *New York Times* columnist Arthur Brisbane witnessed the entire skirmish and interceded, convincing the police to let the hero Bennett go. Impressed with Bennett's moxy, Brisbane invited the fighter to accompany him on a visit with his friend, Henry Ford.

At the meeting, Brisbane talked up the battle in the Battery, shadowboxing Bennett's rights and lefts, and impressing Ford with Bennett's bravado. "Can you shoot?" Ford asked Bennett, and the sailor fresh off the boat nodded. Henry Ford offered Harry Bennett a job on the spot.

Bennett entered Ford's employ in 1916, working in the art department in Ford's Highland Park plant. Soon after, Ford summoned Bennett to serve his true purpose and act as his driver and personal body man. Bennett wore the same thing to work every day—wearing a suit, fedora, and bow tie, rather than a necktie which could be grabbed in a fight. Bennett carried a handgun everywhere he went.

He drove to Ford's Fair Lane estate in Dearborn each morning and chauffeured the boss to the office, then completed whatever tasks Ford set for him over the course of that day and night. Bennett quickly earned Ford's trust and never let him down. Bennett was just a year older than Ford's son Edsel, but the father and son had a strained relationship.[30] In Bennett, Ford saw the son he wished he had.

In his new position of influence as Ford's personal bodyguard, Bennett met and wooed a motley crew of dangerous gentlemen on both sides of the law—police, gangsters, bootleggers and assorted hoodlums. They admired Bennett's tough attitude and respected his place beside Ford.

Bennett worked his contacts to gain intelligence on local goings-on, and used this knowledge to protect and impress his boss. Ford understood that Bennett, a man who knew things and would do anything to protect Ford's interests, was a valuable security asset.

All Ford had to say was, "Harry, can you take care of that?" and it was done.

Bennett once told a newspaperman: "If Mr. Ford told me to black out the sun tomorrow, I might have trouble. But you'd see a hundred thousand sons-of-bitches coming through the Rouge gates in the morning, all wearing dark glasses."[31]

When Ford bought 2,000 acres along the Rouge River to build a new factory, he put Bennett in charge of security. In 1917, the factory was building U-boat hunters for the U.S. Navy. Ford's instinct that Bennett was the man for the job paid off when Bennett foiled a plot by pro-German sympathizers to sabotage the Rouge works.

---

30   Henry Ford was a hard man. His only son Edsel was of slight build and liked sports cars and supporting the arts.

31   This quote makes absolutely no sense, but nowhere in this chapter will I write that Harry Bennett was clever or funny.

By 1920, Ford made Bennett the head of the Ford Service Department, the euphemistic name for what was really the Ford Motor Company's security division.

Bennett wasn't actually on the Ford company payroll. Ford paid him a small stipend off the books and gave him access to company funds, while providing him the regular perks that billionaires have at their disposal.

Bennett expanded his security detail, hand-selecting men he knew he could trust. He assembled a roster that included washed-up football players, former boxers, wrestlers, cops, convicts, mobsters and gang members all across the Midwest. They protected the plants, but also served as an internal spy detail and employee motivation squad, rooting out disgruntled workers and troublemakers.

Another of Bennett's top priorities was protecting the Ford grandchildren. The 1920s and 30s saw a disturbing upswing in high-profile kidnappings, in which criminals targeted the families of the rich and famous in the hopes of collecting huge ransoms.[32]

Ford's fear for the safety of his family turned out to be well-founded. Bennett thwarted the only known substantial plot to snatch Edsel Ford's young sons in what was planned to be a daring daylight kidnapping. The gang planned to take the boys and ransom them for $500,000. If denied the ransom, the children would be chopped into little pieces and dumped in the Detroit River.

The kidnappers diagrammed two sophisticated scenarios. If the children were playing in the sprawling backyard of the Ford estate, two speedboats would rush in and an inside man, hired as a gardener months earlier, would snatch the boys and take them to the river. One speedboat would roar away and the other would stay behind to run interference.

The second plan would take effect if the boys were driven into town by one of the security detail. A car would ram the vehicle with the kids inside, immobilizing it, and the boys would be loaded into a second vehicle, with a

---

32   The kidnapping of the Lindbergh Baby in 1932 is probably the most high profile, but kids of bankers, city officials, and prominent businessmen were also snatched throughout this period. Many of the kidnapping victims were found dead or never found at all.

third car joining the convoy to block any pursuers.

These crooks accounted for almost every detail. What they didn't plan on was Harry Bennett. Bennett had ears everywhere and learned of the scheme through his network of gangland connections. On the day the crime was meant to occur, the nine kidnappers were ambushed by police. Five were captured, the other four were mysteriously never heard from or seen again.[33]

Bennett also thwarted a planned heist of the Ford payroll—a cool $250,000.[34] Two cars loaded with a half dozen mooks toting Tommy guns pulled up to the Ford payroll office.

The front door of the payroll office opened and out stepped Bennett. He told them they'd never live long enough to spend the money. Behind him were 25 of the toughest men in the world, armed to the teeth. He explained that most of the crew would die right here, but any who might get away with the cash would be hunted to the ends of the Earth until the day his men put a bullet in their heads. The crooks huddled, conferred, then climbed back into their cars and drove away.[35]

Bennett added some very bad men to the Service Department to contend with the other bad men bent on hurting Ford and his company. Additions included :

- Former pugilist Kid McCoy, paroled into Bennett's care after a 20-year prison stint for murdering his 10th and final wife

- Serial kidnapper Joseph "Legs" Laman, nicknamed for his ability to evade the law on foot

- Chester LaMare, a Sicilian mob boss known as the Al Capone of Detroit

- New York dope king Joe Adonis

- Elmer "One Round" Hogan

33　　　Bennett knew who these men were, yet these four were never brought to justice. Hmmm. Funny, that.

34　　　Around $4.5 million today.

35　　　There's no evidence Bennett had 25 men waiting behind him. But the threat was real enough.

By the 1930s, Bennett's Service Department was 1,000 men strong. H.L. Mencken dubbed it "the most powerful private police force in the world."

Bennett's men kept strict order at Ford's plants, ensuring productivity stayed on pace and workers were kept in check. It wasn't uncommon for one of Bennett's men to beat a worker on the line for slacking off or running his mouth.

Bennett's management style was as cruel as it was corrupt. Each day he sat behind a wide, glass-topped desk in his office at the River Rouge plant, twirling a silver-handled revolver between meetings with gangsters, police, and his own men. Bennett was eventually put in charge of the entire personnel department, giving him the final say on all hiring, firing, and promotions. Want a job in the foundry? What can you offer me? Want a promotion? What can you offer me?

Ford encouraged his head of security to keep the plants productive and prevent the formation of unions at any cost. Internal factions formed, with Henry Ford and his man Bennett on one side, and Ford's son and heir Edsel on the other. Edsel was an even and fair man, liked by management and the workers, but he didn't stand a chance against Bennett, who was clearly the old man's favorite. Bennett was the power behind the throne and if the old man had anything to say about it, it would be Bennett running the company after Ford died.

The Great Depression hit Detroit hard and by 1932, thousands of auto workers were out of jobs. The ones lucky enough to stay on the payroll saw their wages cut by 50%. On a bitterly cold day in March, 1932, 5,000 marchers, many of them unemployed auto workers, paraded through downtown Detroit to the Dearborn city limits, raising signs that read "Give Us Work," "We Want Bread Not Crumbs," and "Tax the Rich and Feed the Poor." It would be known as the Ford Hunger Strike—or the Ford Massacre.

Dearborn police tried to stop the marchers at the city limits by firing tear gas into the crowd, and when that failed, beat them back with clubs. The marchers pressed on, getting within a mile of the plant when Bennett's security men arrived. The Ford Service Department workers fired pistols into the marchers, sending the crowd running in retreat.

Bennett hopped in his car and pursued, rolling down his window and firing his pistol into the crowd. Marchers pelted Bennett's car with rocks. One lucky throw managed to slip into Bennett's open window and bash him in the head. Woozy, he opened the door and emptied his pistol into the crowd while police and his own security detail rushed to save him, now firing machine guns at the marchers. In the act of being rescued, Bennett grabbed a pistol from the holster of one of his men and fired again at the retreating marchers as he was dragged to safety. At the end of the day, three marchers were dead and dozens were wounded.

Bennett's proficiencies in union busting and foiling gangland plots led to a number of threats on his own life and a few high profile attempts. Ford was concerned about the safety of his right hand man, so he purchased 152 acres of remote wooded land at 5668 Geddes Road, overlooking the Huron River to build a peaceful and safe retreat.

On that site, Ford built Bennett's Castle. The design included hidden passages in every room and secret compartments all over the place—for booze, weapons, or whatnot. The 22-room fortress had a Roman bath, horse stables, an outdoor theater, a boathouse on the water and an enclosed heated swimming pool.

For added security, they dug two 300-foot-long tunnels leading away from the property, built with twisting turns and stairs intentionally cut to different sizes to slow unsuspecting pursuers. One tunnel led to a garage and a den where Bennett kept lions and tigers, which he sometimes let roam the catacombs to prevent sneak attacks from enemies.

Floodlights illuminated the grounds at night, armed men patrolled the roof and guard dogs roamed the property. It wasn't Bennett's only residence. He had Bennett's Hideout, a concrete bunker built to look like a log cabin, just 3,000 feet from Bennett's Castle. It had a hidden door behind a fireplace that led to an attic with 360 degree gun ports.

Then there was Bennett Lodge in tiny Farwell, Michigan—smack dab in the middle of the state, which was fortified and surrounded by a moat. There was a log cabin in East Tawas too.

Even with all this protection, Bennett wasn't safe. One mobster who wasn't too happy with Bennett's heavy hand sneaked onto the property at Bennett Castle and forced his way into the house. He surprised Bennett in his living room, shooting him in the stomach and fleeing. Bennett recovered and, a few days later, received a photograph from police. It was a picture of the gangster, bullet-riddled and nearly unrecognizable. A message was written on the back:

"Dear Harry. This is the Dude. He won't bother you no more. We caught him and he tried to get away."

After the break-in, Bennett added a pair of castle turrets to the house, three stories high with a clear view to the river. Spiral staircases led up each turret to platforms where men with machine guns kept watch 24 hours a day.

Bennett's Castle was secure, but he still had to drive to work.

In 1929, while cruising down Michigan Avenue on his way to work, Bennett's car was struck by bullets from a passing vehicle. That same year, a pair of men ambushed Bennett on a country road, opening fire as he returned home from work. Bennett ducked, the bullets passing right through his windshield. He turned the car around, drew his sidearm, and confronted the killers to find out who hired them. They told.

Bennett was in the papers a lot. In the summer of 1931, he used his considerable influence to get intimately involved in a shocking case called the Torch Murders.[36] Four high school kids on a double date in Ypsilanti were beaten, raped, and shot, then dumped in their car which was set on fire. The killers were three young hoods high on bootleg hooch looking for something fun to do.

Bennett showed up at the crime scene—the only private citizen allowed past police tape, and pledged himself to solving the case. When the suspects

---

36   There's a full account of this case in this very book!

were arrested, Bennett was in the interrogation room. He donned deep-sea diving equipment to personally search the bottom of the Huron River for the gun alleged to have been used in the crime.

When a mob showed up to lynch the trio of accused killers, it was Bennett who transported them personally to the safety of the courthouse where they were tried and convicted. It was also Bennett who drove the newly-convicted murderers through thousands of angry citizens looking for vigilante justice, depositing them at the gates of the Jackson State Prison.

Then there was the Battle of the Overpass. United Auto Worker organizers planned to distribute leaflets to River Rouge plant employees as they entered and exited the building during the afternoon shift change on May 26, 1937. Nine thousand workers entered and exited the plant via a pedestrian overpass around 2 pm that day. Several of the top UAW organizers posed for a *Detroit News* photographer in front of a Ford Motor Company sign.

At the moment of the photo, a gang of Ford security thugs in snappy fedoras and suits, under the direction of Bennett, came up behind the union men and beat them senseless.

"Seven times they raised me off the concrete and slammed me down on it," said one of the UAW men. "They pinned my arms . . . and I was punched and kicked and dragged by my feet to the stairway, thrown down the first flight of steps, picked up, slammed down on the platform and kicked down the second flight. On the ground they beat and kicked me some more…"

And this is the organizer who didn't have his back broken by Bennett's men.

The Ford thugs rushed the *News* photographer to confiscate his photographic plates, but he hid them, and turned over blank ones instead. The damning photos were published and Ford and Bennett took a massive public relations hit, as well as censure from the National Labor Relations Board. It wasn't the Battle of the Overpass that forced Ford into signing a contract with the UAW three years later, but it was a major step toward union victory.

With the union under contract, Bennett's heavy hand was less needed and less desired, but his relationship with Ford was as strong as ever. When Ford's only son Edsel died of stomach cancer in 1943, Bennett was Ford's first choice to succeed him as company president.

Edsel Ford's widow blamed Bennett for many of her husband's health problems and was instrumental in rallying the remaining Fords to oppose Bennett's promotion. The patriarch acquiesced, and, in 1945, grandson Henry Ford II became the new president of Ford Motor Company. Ford II's first act as president was to have Bennett served with termination papers.

It didn't go well.

Bennett and the man with the termination papers drew pistols and narrowly avoided a shootout in the River Rouge plant. Bennett burned his private records, packed up his few belongings and left the Rouge for good. He drove home, packed up his family, and deserted their Geddes Road castle—never to return.

Henry Ford II hadn't asked his grandfather's permission before severing ties with Bennett.

"I went to him with my guard up," Ford the younger admitted. "I was sure he was going to blow my head off." But the older man shrugged and said nonchalantly, "Now Harry is back on the streets where he started."

When Bennett was interviewed in 1973 in his modest Las Vegas home, he was living off his $426 a month Ford pension—far from the rich and powerful lifestyle he enjoyed back in Michigan. In 1974, he suffered a major stroke and in 1977, died from a massive heart attack in a nursing home in Los Gatos, California.

Bennett Castle was sold in 1948 to Detroit investment broker Harold W. Stark. Stark eventually sold to Terence and Susan Liddy in the 1980s and the Liddys sold to Achla and Aneel Karnani in 1993, who put it on the market four years later for $1.5 million. Bennett Castle is still out there—now with less acreage, better decor, and an unknown tunnel status, but still full of history and secrets.

THE LEGENDARY
WEED CONTEST OF 1975

The Legendary Weed Contest of 1975 wasn't just any ordinary giveaway. It was more than a sweepstakes in which the grand prize was one full pound of Colombian smoking marijuana. The Legendary Weed Contest of 1975 was a statement. A cry for justice. A call to revolution.

Was that sarcastic enough? Do you get that I'm kidding? It was none of those things. It was like the first time a car salesman put an inflatable gorilla on the roof of his used car lot. Or the first person to hire someone to spin a sign in front of their business. It was a brilliant marketing plan hatched during a smoke-filled brainstorm among the editors of the *Ann Arbor Sun*, looking for a way to increase the paper's stagnant circulation.

The first ad for the contest appeared on the back page of the Sun on October 25, 1974. Subsequent ads with bolder calls to action and additional details appeared in issues leading up to the January 24, 1975 drawing.

Reactions fell mainly into two camps.

Camp one: Pro-contest. These included: the 5,000 or so entrants; the majority of local, regional, and statewide reporters covering the proceedings with amusement; and Ann Arbor's voting majority.

Camp two: The local and county constabulary; concerned citizens of the world—like Mr. or Ms. N. Vidito, who penned the following letter to the editor at the *Ann Arbor Sun*.

"Dear Ms. Hoffman (editor of the Sun),

I could not believe it when I read that your paper was giving a pound of the devil's weed as a first prize in a contest. The sad thing, you don't realize what you are doing. You poor girl. I can't even be mad at you. It's not your fault you are so stupid. Here in this town, I have talked to young people, a few of them admitted that starting on marijuana has led them to using stronger drugs. If god could open your blind eyes so that you might see the damage you are doing. But there are none so blind as those who will not see. I read that Michigan's cities are the worst cities in the U.S. for crime, especially Detroit, and now thanks to people like you, Ann Arbor may be able to keep pace. I wonder if you will even get to read this?

—N. Vidito, Nova Scotia"

It helps to have a little historical cannabis context to this tale. In 1971, Richard Nixon declared drug abuse "public enemy number one" and formally declared a war on drugs, directed towards eradication, interdiction and incarceration.

"By God, we're going to hit the marijuana thing, and I want to hit it right square in the puss," Nixon growled on one of the infamous White House tapes.

It was the beginning of America's War on Drugs. Penalties for the possession and the sale of marijuana could be as stiff as 10 to 20 years in prison or, for certain quantities, up to a life sentence. The country wasn't Reefer

Madness-scared of the wacky weed, but Americans were definitely cautious. It's a gateway drug, you know.

In Ann Arbor, the story was a little different. The city's $5 pot ordinance was approved the same year Nixon declared his war on drugs, setting the town in opposition to the White House[37] on this issue. The pot ordinance was repealed in 1973, but reinstated in 1974 and cemented into the city charter, making marijuana possession a $5 fine.[38]

During the Legendary Weed Contest of 1975, Ann Arbor voters supported lax marijuana laws, but the nation, state, and powerful pockets within Ann Arbor's establishment weren't too crazy about a very public weed giveaway.

There was also the newspaper itself—the *Ann Arbor Sun*. The *Sun* started in 1967 and folded—maybe—in 1976, (we'll get to that at the end) bouncing from Detroit to Ann Arbor and back to Detroit. Founded by John Sinclair[39], leader of the Trans Love Energies commune, the paper moved offices to Ann Arbor in 1968, working out of 1510 and 1520 Hill Street.[40]

The paper was the mouthpiece for the White Panther Party[41] and the Rainbow People's Party, before transitioning to operating as an independent publication that covered local topics with a left-wing view. It was DIY, erratic, and firmly anti-establishment—sometimes publishing weekly, sometimes bi-weekly, featuring headlines like "Narcs Invade Diag," "Warren Commission

---

37   This must have disappointed Tricky Dick tremendously. When he ran for president in 1960, 15,000 Ann Arborites jammed the train depot to greet him and his wife Pat. This compared to the 5,000 that greeted Kennedy in the same spot during the same campaign just two weeks prior. Et tu, A2?

38   That figure is $25 in 2017. Damn inflation.

39   Poet, political activist, and prominent member of the counterculture movement in the 1960s and 70s, he was arrested in Detroit in 1969 for marijuana possession and sentenced to 10 years in prison. Public outcry over the harsh sentence, and a visit to Ann Arbor by John Lennon himself, helped to free Sinclair in 1971. In 1972, he won a case against the United States government, in which the United States Supreme Court ruled that it was illegal for the government to use domestic electronic surveillance without a warrant.

40   Current site of the Luther House Cooperative and right near Ann Arbor's famous George Washington Park Rock.

41   Far left, anti-racist organization started in 1968. The name comes from a quote given by Black Panther Party leader Huey Newton, when asked how white people could support the Black Panthers. He responded, "Form a White Panther Party."

Frames Oswald," and "The Oil Brotherhood Plans a Lube Job on the Spirit of 76." Running a promotion where the prize was a pound of weed probably didn't surprise those familiar with the *Sun*, but still, it shook some people up.

To enter the Legendary Weed Contest of 1975, all you had to do was provide your name, address, and phone number and get that slip of paper to the *Ann Arbor Sun* offices. You didn't even have to subscribe to be eligible to win, though $2 got you four months of home delivery, and $10 got you two full years.

Hundreds of entries poured in weekly. Word got around town, raising the eyebrow of Washtenaw County prosecutor William Delhey. Delhey wasn't a man to be trifled with. A law-and-order Republican in a Democratic county, he would hold the office for 36 years, smacking down all challengers. He busted sex rings, forcibly unoccupied hippie-occupied ROTC buildings, banned indecent movies, jailed bank robbers, embezzlers, and murderers. He was the man who put John Norman Collins, Michigan's notorious Co-Ed Killer, behind bars.

"It seems inherently wrong to do this sort of thing," Delhey said of the contest. "This will expose people to criminal responsibility if it comes off, and that means both the deliverer and the deliveree."

The contest didn't much bother Ann Arbor police chief Walter Krasny, until higher-ups got involved.

"We didn't get too excited about it at first, but everyone else did, so we had to do our thing." he said.

The county prosecutor attempted to block the *Sun* from carrying out their Colombian Gold giveaway, but Delhey messed up, flubbing the process of serving the Sun staff with court papers, and the matter was thrown out immediately.

Racing to Ann Arbor's City Hall, the *Ann Arbor Sun* staff pushed through a phalanx of reporters with cameras and notepads, toting a gunny sack stuffed with 5,000 slips of paper from contestants with visions of roach clips dancing in their heads.

On hand to legitimize the drawing was Ann Arbor County Commissioner Catherine McClary, a sympathetic voice to the decriminalization movement. In plain sight of Ann Arbor's finest, McClary[42] stuffed her arm deep into the sack, pulled out a single entry slip, and clutched it tight, refusing to share the name.

The next day, representatives from the *Ann Arbor Sun* entered an unspecified University of Michigan dormitory, knocked on a door, and handed over a large bag of high-grade Colombian smoking marijuana. The winner—a U-M student—had conspired with five hallmates to stuff more than 30 entries into the contest.

The *Sun* staff were overjoyed with the attention the contest received and the absence of legal repercussions stemming from the giveaway. How could they not follow up with a bigger and better contest in 1976? That's right, the Legendary Weed Contest of 1976. The grand prize was still one pound of Colombian gold, but consolation prizes ranged from a guitar to a four-foot-long bong and a lifetime supply of Cool Leaf rolling papers. No last minute court appearances this time.

There was no third contest—at least none on record. Despite their ingenuity, the *Sun* dropped Ann Arbor from its name in the summer of 1976, moved its offices to Detroit, and then, by that fall, the trail goes cold. The Library of Congress has a question mark next to the final year of the Sun's existence and the Ann Arbor District Library archives end with the October 15, 1976 edition.

The *Ann Arbor Sun*, like the Legendary Weed Contest of 1975 and 1976…disappeared in a cloud of smoke.

---

42   Whatever became of the subversive Ms. McClary? She has held some form of office in city and county government since the 1970s, serving as Washtenaw County Treasurer from 1997 into 2017.

THE RED LIGHT DISTRICT

There was a time in Ann Arbor's not-so-distant past when a part of town was widely known as the red-light district. It included adult bookstores, topless massage parlors, prostitutes, hoodlums, and bums—and it was all just blocks from city hall and police headquarters. Cops raided the massage parlors every few months and rounded up a dozen massage workers each time, but the arrests never made a dent. In fact, prominent headlines in the *Ann Arbor News* may have even helped business by providing free publicity. Crackdowns on prostitution didn't make much of an impact either. The red-light district regenerated and persisted.

This is the story of how Ann Arbor become home to this kind of brazen adult fare.

It starts back in 1960 on the east side of Cleveland, Ohio, when Reuben Sturman, son of immigrant Russian Jews, sold his first porno magazine. Sturman had started his business innocently enough, selling comic books out of the trunk of his car and eventually earning enough money to move on to magazine kiosks. Soon he rented warehouse space and created his own wholesale operation, selling magazines and comic books across the country. Then, in 1960, Sturman realized he could make more money selling magazines with boobs in them. A lot more. By the end of the decade, Sturman was the largest distributor of adult magazines in the U.S.—and a self-made millionaire.

Sturman's operation was mostly legal, occasionally semi-legal, and sometimes very illegal. His stores and warehouses were raided in the early days by cops looking for obscene material, but Sturman managed to get wise. He forged ties with the Gambino crime family in New York and after that, a lot of his problems seemed to go away.

Around the same time, in a cornfield in Durand, Michigan—20 miles west of Flint—young Harry Mohney ran a drive-in movie theater called the Sceen Drive-In,[43] where he screened cinema classics like Swingin' Swappers and Thar She Blows to packed audiences. With the box office take from what locals called "the Durand Dirties," he invested further in smut, and bought cheap theaters and bookstores across Michigan to turn into oases of pornography. In 1966, with just his little drive-in showing dirty movies, Mohney was worth $2,000. Four years later, he was worth $6 million.

In 1970, the same year Mohney became the $6 million dollar man, Flint native Terry Whitman Shoultes visited an adult bookstore for the very first time. Shoultes was 22 and had done a stint in the Navy, so he wasn't a sheltered young man—but his face turned red seeing magazines on the rack with titles like: Peacock, Climax, and Erotic Boobs. He'd never felt this way before, and he vowed to master it. The next day, Shoultes took a job in that same shop, where he would learn from the best, owner Harry Mohney.

Shoultes soaked up as much as he could from Mohney, whose empire stretched across more than 10 states—anchored by adult bookstores and his #1 moneymaker: coin-operated peep show machines. As Mohney diversified his businesses and spent an increasing amount of his time evading scrutiny from government and anti-obscenity crusaders, Shoultes rose in the ranks. Unlike

---

43   This is a dumb name for a drive-in, we know. Just reporting the facts.

Mohney, who shunned the spotlight, Shoultes was outspoken and aggressive. In just a few years, he earned enough money to start operating businesses of his own, so he set up a base of operations on a 200-acre farm east of Lansing. It was there that Shoultes started buying and opening adult bookstores and massage parlors throughout the state, including Ann Arbor.

In May 1970, two adult bookstores opened side by side on South Fourth Avenue in Ann Arbor. The building belonged to Mohney, and though he was listed as the owner of one of the bookstores, it's hard to figure out exactly who owned what in the porn shell game.

The Ann Arbor Adult News opened at 215 South Fourth Avenue.[44] Next door, at 217 South Fourth Avenue, the Fourth Avenue Adult News opened shop.[45] Above both bookstores was the American Massage Parlor, which offered topless massages and, it was rumored, erotic services—if you had the money and knew how to ask.

It took the prosecutor's office two weeks to pull both bookstores into court, on charges of obscenity. City officials charged that certain paperbacks and magazines on the racks were "obscene, lewd, lascivious, filthy, indecent, or disgusting."

The city seized six magazine titles in which, they determined, sex was the dominant interest. These titles, "appealed to prurient interests, affronted contemporary community standards and are without redeeming social value."

In spite of the pressure, both businesses continued to operate and flourish, which sowed the seeds for the little red-light district. The bookstores attracted clientele looking to buy erotic magazines or marital aids, while the massage parlors offered more hands-on services and employed a certain kind of worker. The American Massage Parlor wasn't the only rubdown shop in town. Caesar's Retreat was just around the corner at 212 West Huron.[46] It was also rumored that you could get a $20 handjob or $45 blowjob at the Tokyo Health

---

44   Where Today Clothing is in 2017.

45   Where the Local Bike Shop A2 is in 2017.

46   Where the MLive building is in 2017.

Spa at 404 West Liberty.[47]

John Metzger, who owned Metzger's German Restaurant, would lock the doors to his family establishment each night and walk down South Fourth Avenue on the way home.

"The bums were hanging out and always the prostitutes up and down Fourth Avenue for years. I couldn't get off at 11 without one of them coming up and propositioning me," Metzger said.

The bookstores brought the massage parlors, which in turn brought the prostitutes, which bolstered the bookstores—it was an endless cycle. In just a few years, Ann Arbor developed a real and true red-light district.

Police made their first big move and raided two downtown massage parlors, the American Massage Parlor and Caesar's Retreat on October 18, 1972. After a four-month undercover operation—because investigating topless massage parlors isn't something to be rushed—six women and eight men were arrested.

The raids did little to slow business. The city wasn't sure how to react. Prostitution sweeps only created a temporary reprieve from a worsening problem. One famous police crackdown was called Smile After Dark, because, as the undercover female officers stated, that's all they had to do at night on South Fourth Street to get solicited. Police raided the massage parlors, but the workers were replaced, or the businesses closed only to reopen with new names, flashier signs, and the same old faces. Mohney and Shoultes, who ran the American Massage Parlor, got richer and richer.

Police and prosecution failed, so Ann Arbor turned to politics to effect change. In 1978, Ann Arbor City Council created City Ordinance 5:50, 'Regulations concerning adult entertainment businesses.' The ordinance defined what an adult business was: bookstores, theaters, places of personal service or any business that had 20% or more of its stock and trade in the adult business area.

---

47   Near the St. Paul Lutheran Church.

These new regulations forced the bookstores and massage parlors to obtain licenses and enforce strict rules barring minors from the premises. Despite the extra scrutiny and added red tape, Shoultes decided to expand his smut empire further in 1980, opening the Danish News at 209 North Fourth Avenue.[48] The Danish News was the first new adult bookstore in 10 years. The neighbors weren't happy.

The Danish News offered coin-operated peepshow booths, where patrons sat in gross little cubicles and watched short snippets of X-rated movies for a quarter. It also sold Shoultes' trademark adult novelties and offered a new hot-selling item, video tapes. It took the city a little over a month to drag Shoultes and the Danish News into court. The adult bookstore violated the zoning portion of ordinance 5:50 that stated no adult business could be located within 700 feet of a residential area or within 700 feet of another adult business. The Danish News was just a few doors down from its adult bookstore neighbors, and technically violated the ordinance.

At the time, Shoultes was the on-paper owner of the Danish News, and the Velvet Touch massage parlor above the other Fourth Avenue bookstores, along with five other adult businesses in the state. Shoultes told the press he raked in $2.3 million from his bookstores alone, including $22,000 from his 25-cent peep show booths and another $360,000 per year from his $50-an-hour topless massage parlors. Even before the Danish News started filling his bank account, Shoultes had the money to fight the city of Ann Arbor, and fight he did.

Shoultes was in and out of court throughout the early 1980s while he fought Ann Arbor's 1978 city ordinance. While that fight went on, he appealed obscenity laws in federal and state appeals courts. As if that wasn't enough, Shoultes was both a plaintiff and defendant a series of civil cases. One much-publicized case included a defamation charge brought by city prosecutor Bruce Laidlaw, who took umbrage at comments Shoultes made on a local radio show.

Shoultes also supported his girlfriend Karen Christy as she faced her

---

48   Where the Birkenstock store is hopefully forever.

own porn battles in Ann Arbor and Ypsilanti. Christy operated a store selling adult materials called Unique Creations at 2485 East Michigan Avenue in Ypsilanti.[49] She also had plans for a brand new adult bookstore she hoped to open on Main Street in Ann Arbor, but first, she faced the same ordinance battles as her boyfriend.

The entire time The Danish News existed, it was in a state of flux. The court would order it to close, or partially close, and then sometimes it would be fully operational. It all depended on the latest court ruling. Shoultes never stopped fighting.

"Everybody calls me brash," Shoultes said. "Well, if you look it up, brash means stupidly bold. If that means not worrying about what's going to happen to me for speaking up, then I guess I'm brash."

The city added amendments to ordinance 5:50 in 1983 to negate some of Shoultes' arguments that the original ordinance was unconstitutional. The city zoned special areas downtown where adult businesses were permitted, such as the corner of State and Liberty in the Borders building, or the Michigan Theater block of Liberty. All of Main Street, from Liberty to Huron, was open to these businesses as well. While porn magnates might have been thrilled to set up shop in the heart of downtown Ann Arbor, the rents in those zones were astronomical and the businesses rarely turned over. The city provided other options in addition to those prime locations. Adult businesses could also open in industrial zones...or the city dump. The rule that they must be located 700 feet from residences, schools, parks, and other adult businesses remained. Ann Arbor had effectively zoned new adult businesses out of the city. Police continued sweeping the red-light district and the pressure finally took its toll on the businesses. Legal fees drained bank accounts.

The Fourth Avenue Adult News was the first casualty when it closed in 1984. But the bookstores and massage parlors hung on. The prostitutes continued to ply their trade out in the open.

Local businessmen had finally had enough. A cabal of five local rich guys banded together to form the 200 Fourth Avenue Group in 1986 to put an

---

49   This address is vacant land in 2017.

end to the red-light district. It was led by real estate mogul Ed Shaffran. The group started snatching up property on Fourth Avenue with the intent of revitalizing the area.

Under pressure from the Internal Revenue Service, Mohney sold three two-story buildings on the 200 block of Fourth Avenue to Shaffran, who paid more than $1 million dollars for the properties. This put Shaffran in charge of the leases on the remaining adult bookstores on the block.

Shoultes must have seen the end coming. He attempted to negotiate and move his bookstore to other storefronts in Ann Arbor, but the ordinance worked too well against him. Shoultes continued to fight it in court, but kept losing time and money.

Shaffran honored the porn shops' leases, but waited patiently until they made a mistake. In the winter of 1988, the Danish News missed a rent payment. Shaffran immediately sued for eviction.

"Everybody wanted to rid the area of the bookstore and massage parlor," said Shaffran. "It was me who—on technicalities—got them on violations of their lease and evicted them. I had to beat him economically."

Shoultes received an eviction notice filed by the trustee of the building, J.D. Hall, who coincidentally was in the midst of battling Shoultes' girlfriend over her Ypsilanti bookstore. The Sheriff's Department threatened to forcibly evict Shoultes if he didn't clear out by February 25, 1988.

Movers arrived that cold February morning and hauled boxes and boxes of the dirty stuff out of the Danish News. Two men wearing Carhartt jackets and snapback baseball caps carefully carried the giant Danish News sign that had hung above the store to an awaiting flatbed truck and returned it to the Jones Sign Co. in Flint.

Three months later, Shaffran pounced on the last remaining place for porn, the Wolverine Adult Entertainment Bookstore—formerly the Ann Arbor Adult News—and booted them from the building for allowing the building condition to deteriorate below city standards. The businessmen had won. Well, the non-porn businessmen anyhow.

Two years later, reports of street-visible prostitution went from hundreds to zero. Ann Arbor's red-light district was dead.

Terry Whitman Shoultes died in 1998 of a heart attack at age 50. He didn't leave a will, pitching his six children into a nasty fight over his estate, which included real estate, businesses and, as you might expect, tons of porn. In his life, he'd been arrested more than 40 times on felony and misdemeanor charges, but never convicted. He filed more than 80 lawsuits fighting for his constitutional right to freedom of expression. Nearly 20 years after his death, his estate remains unsettled.

Danish News. Pornographer Terry Whitman Shoultes opened the Danish News adult bookstore at 209 N. Fourth Avenue in 1980. It was the crown jewel of Ann Arbor's red light district for eight years until Shoultes was evicted for a missed rent payment in 1988. (Photo by Brian Peters, original by Robert Chase of the *Ann Arbor News.*)

A COP KILLED IN COLD BLOOD

Just as he did every Thursday, on March 21, 1935, Ann Arbor Police Officer Clifford Stang, known as Sid to his friends, signed the station log book just before his 3 pm shift and walked a few blocks to his beat on Main Street. Before leaving for work, his wife, Jewell, asked him to buy a tie clasp for his uniform to give him a little bit of polish. So Stang made a detour to the Conlin and Wetherbee Clothing Store on Washington Street, a block away from his beat.[50] An errand that would end in murder.

Crime wasn't a big problem in Ann Arbor in the 1930s. There were occasional robberies, stolen vehicles, assaults, a riot or protest now and again. Prohibition was over and the gangsters and bootleggers had moved on. No Ann Arbor police officer had ever been killed in the line of duty. Stang couldn't have

---

50   In 2017, Arbor Brewing Company is located in the space the Conlin and Wetherbee Clothing Store once occupied.

predicted the scene developing inside the Conlin and Wetherbee Clothing Store that afternoon. He was just looking for a tie pin.

William "Shorty" Padgett stood out for a few reasons—he was 5' 2", had a large scar on his forehead, and claimed he'd grown up with Babe Ruth in a Maryland orphanage. Padgett had committed crimes all across the Midwest, serving time for armed robbery and lesser offenses.

That was before Padgett walked into the Conlin and Wetherbee Clothing Store alongside an accomplice, while the getaway driver sat in a stolen vehicle outside with the engine running.[51] Padgett's partner asked the shopkeeper, Wetherbee, if he could try on a suit coat. When Wetherbee produced one of the store's finest, the robber turned around, holding a gun.

"This is a stick up," the man said and at first, Wetherbee thought he was joking. Who robs a clothing store in Ann Arbor in the middle of the afternoon? But the man was serious. He marched Wetherbee toward the back of the store, while Padgett emptied the cash register. That's when Officer Stang walked into the store.

"Look out, Sid, it's a stick up!" Wetherbee shouted, but who robs a clothing store in Ann Arbor in the middle of the afternoon? Stang too thought this was a joke.

"Shut up or I'll blow your guts out," Padgett shouted. One of the robbers stuck a gun in Stang's ribs and took his pistol off his hip. Unarmed, Stang chose to fight. He wrestled both men, trying to disarm and subdue the robbers. During the struggle, two shots rang out. One bullet missed, later found lodged in a wooden table. The other hit Stang in the torso, pierced his right lung, and exited out his back.

The robbers fled with the money, and left Stang lying on the floor, blood pouring out of his mouth. The getaway car peeled down Washington, and a sharp-eyed taxi driver got a partial license plate number.

Officers arrived on the scene, comforting their comrade and loosening

51   Padgett was the only man ever identified in this crime, so we don't have names for either of his accomplices.

his tie and shirt collar as they waited for the ambulance. Stang never uttered a word. He was taken to St. Joseph's Hospital where he was pronounced dead.

The getaway car was found in Jackson, partially torched. Detectives believed the suspects were from Detroit and, after looking through numerous mugshots, identified William "Shorty" Padgett as one of the robbers. A nationwide manhunt began with Wanted posters distributed coast to coast.

It didn't take long for Padgett to slip up. He was arrested in Los Angeles for breaking and entering and police linked their perp to the murder of a police officer in Michigan. Nearly one year to the day of the murder, Padgett was escorted off a train in Ann Arbor and taken to the courthouse where he was convicted of murder.[52]

His accomplices were never found.

Stang's story doesn't end there. The Conlin and Wetherbee building has housed a number of businesses—today it's Arbor Brewing Company. For years, employees reported unexplained occurrences—doors closing on their own and sightings of a uniformed man spotted walking through the bar late at night.

The story goes that the owners of Arbor Brewing once invited ghost hunters to investigate the building for paranormal activity. The specialists failed to locate evidence of a haunting, but the paranormal experts and the owners posed together for a photo.

When the photo was developed, there was a faded but distinct image of a man standing behind them. Someone who looked a lot like Clifford "Sid" Stang.

---

52   Padgett was actually convicted a second time after earning an appeal due to procedural errors in the first trial. He maintained his innocence throughout, and earned his parole in 1949 after spending 13 years in prison.

A BRIEF HISTORY OF POOP

In the late 1800s, two University of Michigan medical school professors championed a new and more sanitary place to poop. It was called the earth closet. They didn't invent the thing—the earth closet was patented in England years earlier and brought to the United States to solve the issue of poor sanitation related to human waste—but they were huge proponents of it.

At that time, the standard ways of doing one's business left a lot to be desired. The earth closet wasn't perfect, but for those U-M professors, it was a step in the right direction.

Here's how it worked: the earth closet had a big wooden box to sit on with a metal hopper attached to the top. A hole was cut into the box—the perfect size for a human butt. A big pail was placed below the hole and the hopper above was filled with regular old-fashioned dirt. When you turned a handle, dirt dropped down on top of whatever was deposited into the pail, covering up your gross, disgusting, gross, dirty shame. It was essentially a litterbox for people.

The pail below was emptied every few uses, generally in and around the family garden or in a compost pile, and you added more dirt to the hopper when you needed it.

Don't judge these folks—they were doing the best they could.

The earth closet reduced contamination of backyards and waterways, which were frequently filled with you-don't-even-want-to-know-what. The earth closet could be installed inside the home, so the call of nature no longer necessitated venturing outdoors to brave the freezing cold or risk being mauled by a bear.

Poor sanitation wasn't a laughing matter. Throughout history, millions have died from cholera, dysentery, and typhoid fever as a result of contaminated soil, waterways, and gross pits of grossness where flies and other airborne beasties picked up said grossness and then landed on your face or your bagel. Ugh.

For a very long time, people dug pits near their homes and squatted over them. For indoor use, there was often a communal pot, whose contents were dumped into these outdoor pits, or chucked into the woods or something.

Rich folks had more options when it came to primitive toilets. In medieval times, people with castles could visit a garderobe—a room that protruded from a corner of the castle. These were usually built over a moat or an unoccupied area below the castle walls. People in the castle would do their business in the garderobe and that stuff would fall into the moat or trickle down the sides of the castle, making those moats and walls extra-super-gross if invading armies ever came a-conquering.

The Romans were a little better at dealing with poop, creating communal toilets in public spaces with long, bench-like seats where folks could hike up their togas up, do their dookies, and talk politics or whatever. Every once in awhile, an attendant would rinse out the area under the benches with water, flushing the mess down a little channel and away down the street.

And now back to Ann Arbor in the late 1800s, with the earth closet and these two U-M medical professors trying to save us from ourselves. At this point, most people in Ann Arbor had either outhouses or primitive indoor toilets connected to things called privy vaults.[53] It didn't matter if you were rich or poor or a gross animal or a really nice person with a decent family and a career and nice, starched white shirts. It was basically outhouse or privy vault.

The earth closet was so much better. Not the best, but better. These men from Michigan helped establish the first (and last) earth closet factory in the state, located in Muskegon. They promoted earth closets like crazy, which were cheaper than the alternatives as well as more sanitary. The drawback was having to fill the earth hopper all the time. So some concluded it was much easier to just keep chucking poop into the woods and call it a day.

In 1893, Ann Arbor began installing its first municipal sewer system. The privy vaults were sealed shut and this new-ish thing called the water closet—an early version of the flush toilet—was introduced. People liked this the best. Disease rates fell. The Muskegon factory stopped building earth closets, but stayed in the stool business, manufacturing piano stools and other non-bathroom-related furniture.

The story of Ann Arbor's very first flush toilet begins in the President's House at U-M. Completed in 1840, it's the oldest building on U-M's campus. It was constructed with a tasteful two-story floor plan, but it lacked a water closet—because the water closet hadn't been invented yet.

In 1856, U-M added gas lighting to the house. In 1863, they added a kitchen. Then they threw a third floor on there because, hey, it's the President's house.

Around 1869—just before the town was bombarded with earth closets advertisements—U-M began negotiating the hire of the president of the University of Vermont. This man would become the third president of U-M, a man named James Angell.

Before Angell uprooted his family's comfortable Vermont existence, he

---

53   Some vaults contain secret documents or gold bars. Privy vaults weren't that kind of vault. They contained something way grosser.

researched the work and living environment U-M offered and negotiated terms.

First off, Angell wanted a raise. He wanted new wallpaper and a dining room and a furnace added to the President's House. Oh, and a water closet. He explicitly asked for a water closet.

The addition of that water closet helped seal the deal to bring the Angells to Ann Arbor. They lived in the President's House for 39 years, where, through all of U-M's growth and progress in the arts and sciences, President Angell did his sweet, sweet dookies on the very site of Ann Arbor's very first not-utterly-disgusting-but-still-probably-kind-of-gross flush toilet.

President Angell's water closet was upgraded as toilet technology progressed, but I like to picture him sitting on that original 1871 water closet, pantaloons around his ankles, reading the *Michigan Daily*, scrunching up his face, gritting his teeth and really going to town.[54]

54   Happy 200th birthday, U-M! #umich200

MICHIGAN HOUSEWIFE FLIES AROUND THE WORLD

In 1927, Charles Lindbergh landed the Spirit of St. Louis on an airfield in Paris, becoming the first person to complete a solo, non-stop flight across the Atlantic. The following year, as part of a three-person crew, Amelia Earhart became the first female aviator to cross the Atlantic, earning the admiration of the nation.

Riding in a convertible next to her fellow aviators, rolling slowly down the route known as the Canyon of Heroes in Manhattan, as ticker tape rained down in celebration... maybe that's when the idea of circling the globe first popped into Earhart's head.

They were calling her Queen of the Air. She had a meeting at the White House with President Calvin Coolidge circled in her datebook. Lucrative contracts were being thrown at her feet for lecture tours, book deals, and endorsement contracts from Macy's and Lucky Strike. She hadn't even taken the controls during that transatlantic flight—just kept the plane's log.

But watching that confetti rain down from the sky—the cheering men, women and children—she must have thought about the global challenge, even if the technology to pull it off wasn't quite there.

Six years later—in 1933—a man with an eye patch named Wiley Post was first to circumnavigate the globe alone, flying from New York City to New York City in just over seven days.[55] He earned his own trip down the Canyon of Heroes.

Four years later, Amelia Earhart made her dream of attempting circumnavigation a reality. On June 1, 1937, she took off from Oakland, California with her navigator Fred Noonan, charting a flight plan that would take them around the world.[56] They made it three quarters of the way before their plane famously lost radio contact and disappeared.

Ann Holtgren was two months old when Earhart disappeared in the Pacific. She was born April 10, 1937 in Riverdale, Illinois, a suburb south of Chicago. Ann studied music at the University of Michigan and performed in the Michigan Symphony Band. That's where she met her husband Don Pellegreno. He played percussion and she played French horn. The band took three buses when they toured—two for singles and one reserved for couples. Ann and Don started out on the singles buses, but by graduation were canoodling together on the couples bus.

She graduated from U-M in 1958 and soon became Ann Pellegreno. The couple moved to Saline, where Ann worked as a guidance counselor and English teacher.

Until then, there was nothing to suggest that Ann Pellegreno would one day fly around the world. Her interest in aviation was kind of a fluke. On a visit with Don's brother, a naval aviator, she helped build and fly a gas-powered model airplane, and the Pellegrenos found that they had a marvelous time doing it. Bit hard by the flying bug, Ann and Don signed up for flight lessons at

---

55   An oil field accident in 1926 cost him his left eye. He used the settlement money to buy his first airplane.

56   This was actually Earhart's second attempt at circumnavigating the globe. She made one previous attempt on March 17, 1937, but her plane was damaged early in the journey and the plan postponed until the summer.

Willow Run. Ann took her first flight lesson in 1960 and earned her pilot's license in 1962, taking her mother up as her first passenger.

Soon the Pellegrenos invested in a plane of their own, a used Cessna 140 two-seater. They hired local aviation mechanic Lee Koepke to get it into flying shape. Koepke was an affable guy and a good mechanic who enjoyed rebuilding vintage planes in his spare time, including a Lockheed 10 Electra—the same type of airplane Amelia Earhart was flying when she disappeared. The Electra was literally a shell, having been used at Willow Run for firefighting practice. Koepke worked on it a few days a week, rebuilding it in an old Quonset hut at Willow Run.

One day, Koepke casually proposed that when he finished rebuilding the Electra, Ann should fly it around the world on the 30th anniversary of Earhart's attempt. The anniversary was five years away. The farthest flight Ann Pellegreno had flown was from Ann Arbor to Rockford, Illinois. It didn't seem like a serious proposition. She said, sure, why not.

Neither she nor Koepke thought much about it over the next few years. Ann continued flying, 100 flight hours…1,000 flight hours…and Koepke kept working on the Electra, through summers and winters, in rain or shine.

On Christmas Day 1966, Ann unwrapped a present from her husband—a book about Amelia Earhart. It reminded her of her conversation with Lee Koepke five years earlier. Ann asked him if he'd ever finished restoring that plane. He had. Together they said, sure, why not, and agreed to fly around the world.

Cue our Getting the Gang Together montage.

The pilot: Ann Pellegreno.

The engineer: Lee Koepke.

The navigator: They recruited Bill Polhemus, owner of the Ann Arbor navigation firm Polhemus Navigation Sciences. Bill supplied a lot of the expensive radio equipment for the flight, which was a nice bonus.

The co-pilot: Earhart didn't have one on her voyage, and Ann didn't want to make the same mistake. And boy, did they pick a co-pilot. Air Force Colonel Bill Payne, who set a New York to Paris speed record in 1961 flying a B-58 jet. He'd do.

The team had a lot of work to do to prepare for takeoff in June. Lee got to work on the plane. To make it lighter, he tore out six of the 10 seats and stripped the interior down to its asbestos lining, ripping out the insulation and soundproofing material right down to the metal. Giant radio racks and custom-made fuel tanks were crammed into the back of the plane.

This work was expensive, especially for a schoolteacher and an airplane mechanic, and there weren't any endorsement contracts or New York City celebrations at the end of this runway. America was already in outer space—the world's attention beyond the globe itself.

Champion Spark Plugs donated money and equipment, along with a few other sponsors whose names were stenciled on the side of the plane, but Pellegreno would need a lot more to pay for her global flight. She packed 5,000 specially-printed postcards commemorating the 30th anniversary flight. After each stop, she licked hundreds of stamps in foreign post offices, and sold them as souvenirs upon her return to America.[57] One night in Senegal, she had half the local police force licking stamps late into the night to help the crew keep to its tight timetable.

Pellegreno also gathered a box of items from everyone who donated to the flight. She tucked the box in the back of the plane, promising to return each item upon landing, so that the owners could proudly display the baseball or fountain pen or snow globe that flew with the first woman to circumnavigate the globe.

---

57   Prior to the flight she'd already sold 500 for $5 apiece.

The endeavor put the Pellegrenos $40,000 in debt—nearly $300,000 in today's dollars. That included the plane, fuel, repairs, and a pricey insurance policy with Lloyds of London.[58]

On June 7, 1967, Pellegreno and her crew took off from Willow Run for Oakland, California—Amelia Earhart's starting point 30 years earlier. The Federal Aviation Agency examined the plane and said the engines were running like sewing machines—quiet and smooth. Two days later, on a grey overcast afternoon, the Lockheed 10 Electra, codenamed Rapid Rocket, took off from Oakland heading southeast, beginning its round the world journey.

The woman the papers were calling "the pretty Michigan housewife" had never left the United States, and she was about to fly around the world. Her aircraft was sound, but still a 30-year-old plane which had retired from Canadian commercial flights, had 14 private owners, one crash landing, and countless years of being set on fire for training purposes in its history.

"I feel safer in a plane than a car," Pellegreno told one newspaper. "The only thing a car is good for is getting to the airport so I can fly."

The crew tried to follow Earhart's route as closely as possible, but deviations were necessary. They detoured to airfields offering free fuel and were forced to fly around the continent of Africa during the start of the Arab-Israeli Six-Day War.

The crew wore earplugs under their headsets to keep from going deaf. The rattle of the plane was intense. Without insulation, every sound bouncing around the flying metal tube was thunderous. That also made it very cold—and it didn't help that they tore out the heater to make more room for fuel tanks. The crew watched dozens of sunrises and sunsets from high above the Earth, eating cold sandwiches, sharing water from a thermos, and trying not to pee. A plywood bed was installed in the back where they took turns sleeping. Every takeoff was an adventure, especially blind nighttime takeoffs with no visible horizon when Pellegreno relied solely on the instruments of that old bird.

---

58   Insurance paid out $90,000 for the plane and $450,000 for the crew of four. The premium alone cost around $5,000.

They landed at some of the same airfields Earhart had visited 30 years before—remote outposts in Portugal, Italy, and Thailand. Back in Saline, Wight's Cleaners added a world map to their giant front windows, and the owners updated it daily with the flight's progress.

Ann Pellegreno wrote her husband almost every day, reporting their progress, recording receipts, or making notes for the book she planned to write. Don stayed home, fielding daily phone calls from the media. He also got a few minutes on the phone with Ann every few days when they stopped in cities with good telephone lines.

They charted a course for Howland Island—the location of Earhart's last transmission—but the airfield there was overgrown and unusable. They circled the finger-shaped island and its four-mile coastline, while Pellegreno took photos out the left side of the plane.[59]

As they passed over Howland Island, Pellegreno and Koepke headed for the rear of the plane as Colonel Payne steadied the approach. Koepke kicked open the door, turbulence kicking up like crazy, and wrapped Pellegreno in a bear hug while she leaned out and dropped a wreath out of the back of the plane—a beautiful wreath of colored leaves picked up in New Guinea to honor Earhart. It was July 2, nearly 30 years to the hour, that Earhart flew this exact route in the Pacific and disappeared forever.

Ann Pellegreno and her crew flew on, with only a few more stops until their final destination. They successfully landed back in Oakland on July 7, 1967, completing their trip around the world. They logged 31 airports, 263 flight hours, and 28,000 miles, safe and sound.

Pellegreno and the crew celebrated a few days, then took off for home, landing at Willow Run on July 11, happy but tired. They were met by 100 applauding admirers and the media.

Ann Pellegreno received her ticker tape parade, though not down Manhattan's Canyon of Heroes. Hers was through downtown Saline. Proud

---

59   She'd take 1,200 photos on the journey, publishing many in her book following the journey. The book, *World Flight–The Earhart Trail,* would be published in 1972 and was named non-fiction book of the year by the Aviation Space Writers Association.

citizens and a circling helicopter rained pink ticker tape as she and her crew paraded through Saline on July 15—which was declared Ann Pellegreno Day. She smiled and waved from the back of a convertible just as Amelia Earhart had back in 1928.

Afterward, Pellegreno wrote magazine articles, finished her book about the flight, and toured to raise money to pay back the debt she'd undertaken to fund the project. The Pellegrenos moved to Iowa in 1968, buying a 120-acre farm in Story City in 1970, on which they built an airstrip. Ann was appointed to the Iowa Department of Transportation in 1974 and continued her writing career, authoring three volumes on the history of aviation in Iowa. In 1997, they moved just outside Fort Worth, Texas, where Ann continued writing and Don rebuilt planes.

What became of Lee Koepke's Lockheed 10 Electra? The Canadian Aviation Museum bought the plane from Lee following the famous flight and shipped it back home, restoring it to its original configuration and displaying it in the Canadian Aviation and Space Museum in Ottawa. It's exhibited alongside hundreds of other vintage aircraft—but the story of the Rapid Rocket stands out.

PRESIDENTS IN ANN ARBOR

George Washington never slept here. Neither did Abraham Lincoln or Andrew Jackson or George W. Bush. Of the 45 men who've served as President of the United States up until 2017, I'm confident that 17 commanders in chief have set foot in the Ann Arbor area. Eighteen, if you count young army officer Ulysses S. Grant, who was stationed in Detroit in his late twenties. Living in Detroit with his wife from 1849 to 1850, you have to imagine they made the trip to Ann Arbor to check out the town that stole the University of Michigan, right?

Eighteen presidents—it's settled, we're counting Grant—have visited, though not necessarily during their presidencies. Some came before, some after. Eighteen of 45 is a pretty good percentage, considering Ann Arbor didn't officially become a town until the nation's fourth president was in power and Michigan wouldn't join the union until the end of Andrew Jackson's term as the seventh president of the United States.

Six Degrees of William Henry Harrison

Some presidents who never set foot in Ann Arbor are still tied to the city. The sixth president of the United States, John Quincy Adams, signed the official deed to the land that would be called Ann Arbour on March 7, 1825. He never set foot in town, but we thank him for his signature.

Ninth President of the United States William Henry Harrison slept in the White House for a single month, dying of natural causes shortly after his inauguration. Not much time to travel to little Ann Arbor, but a long enough life to create a macabre tie to our fair town.

In 1878, decades after William Henry Harrison's death, his son, John Scott Harrison, died in North Bend, Ohio, about 250 miles south of Ann Arbor. A week later, one of the Harrison family's close friends also passed away.

Harrison's son and the family friend were scheduled to be buried close to one another in the local cemetery. While arrangements were made for a fancier funeral for the ex-president's son, the family friend was buried. The day before John Scott Harrison's funeral, cemetery workers discovered the family friend's grave had been disturbed. The body was missing.

This was the late 1800s, and medical schools and hospitals around the country were in dire need of cadavers to study. Bodies obtained through legal means were in short supply, and so a lucrative black market established itself. Grave robberies were a big problem in big cities and college towns, where medical schools and hospitals would secretly pay up to $25 per corpse—close to a thousand dollars in today's money.

Ohio authorities followed a tip which led them to the Medical College of Ohio in Cincinnati. While investigating, one of the officers noticed a suspicious trap door. When they opened it, they saw a rope and a body tied by the ankles, swaying down in the hole. When they pulled it up, police were shocked. It wasn't the family friend they were looking for. It was the ex-president's son, John Scott Harrison.

Police shook down the medical school, unearthing a cadaver smuggling network involving a number of schools in the area. Bodies were being shipped throughout the Midwest in barrels marked "pickles"—some addressed to Quimby and Co. in Ann Arbor. Following the pickle connection, authorities traveled to Ann Arbor, where they eventually found the body they were looking for.

Honest Abe

The closest Abraham Lincoln got to Ann Arbor was Kalamazoo—campaigning for presidential candidate John Charles Fremont in 1856. But the Ann Arbor area boasts one of many schools in the country named for the nation's 16th president. The first of the Lincoln Consolidated Schools opened in· October of 1924 at the corner of Whitaker and Willis Roads in Augusta Township. The schools were dedicated to giving country children the same advantages of a well-rounded public school education that city youngsters had.

A fire nearly destroyed the building in 1925, but it was rebuilt and newly dedicated on Lincoln's birthday in 1927. In May 1938, a 12-foot-tall limestone statue of Lincoln weighing in at nine tons was added to the grounds, paid for by the Works Progress Administration during the Great Depression. There, Honest Abe stood proudly as progress blossomed around him. Until progress progressed too much and Lincoln started to sink. Road work and utility improvements messed with the ground beneath Lincoln's feet and around 2015, things were getting dire. Funds were raised to build a new foundation for the statue and move it 100 yards to safety. They even restored the sculpture to its natural color. Abe never set foot in Ann Arbor, but his statue here stands on solid ground.

Ronald Reagan never set foot in Ann Arbor, but the then-president did stop in Detroit to campaign for gubernatorial candidate William Lucas in 1986. The Washtenaw Community College Jazz Orchestra was recruited to play for the luncheon attendees and by all accounts, they were great.

Ann Arbor and Presidential Assassinations

Is it time to talk about murder? Let's talk about murder! I don't condone presidential assassinations. In fact, I'm against assassinations of any kind. But they have happened and at least one has an Ann Arbor tie worth telling.[60]

---

60   President William McKinley's assassin, Leon Czolgosz, has a Michigan tie, but not to

President James Garfield's assassin spent a decent amount of time in Ann Arbor, which may have influenced him on his path to murder. As a young man, Charles Guiteau inherited $1,000 from his grandfather and used it to travel from Freeport, Illinois, to Ann Arbor to attend U-M. Unfortunately, he wasn't prepared for U-M's rigorous academics and failed the entrance exam. He attended Ann Arbor High School and prepared to retake the test, but ultimately gave up, moved to upstate New York, and joined a cult. They rejected him too, nicknaming him "Charles Gitout." Poor Guiteau went on to fail at a bunch more things before setting his sights on assassination.

With borrowed money, he bought a .442 caliber Webley British Bulldog revolver—a pretty serious sidearm—paying extra for the ivory grip because he wanted the pistol to look good in a museum some day.[61]

Guiteau stalked Garfield at the train station in Washington, D.C., where he shot the president twice from behind. Garfield died 11 weeks later. Guiteau was found guilty of murder, danced his way to the gallows, shook hands with the executioner, and recited a poem he had written for the occasion entitled, I Am Going to the Lordy. His request to have an orchestra accompany his recitation was denied. They placed a hood over Guiteau's grinning face, sprung the trapdoor, and hanged him until he was dead.

"Martin Van Buren Is Not An Extraordinary Man"

Martin Van Buren, eighth president of the United States, visited Ann Arbor at least once, on July 11, 1842. He stayed for four hours, according to a letter Ann Arbor's John Geddes wrote his brother, William, who lived in Pennsylvania. John Geddes was a local businessman and politician, who ran a sawmill on the Huron River and served as justice of the peace and state representative. He was important enough that when Van Buren came to town, just a year removed from the presidency, Geddes was among the folks invited to hobnob with him.

Ann Arbor. He was born in Alpena and moved with his family to Detroit when he was five.

61   This destiny may have come true if the revolver hadn't been lost. It was recovered after the assassination, shipped to the Smithsonian and photographed, but at some point it was lost.

John Geddes might also have been kind of a jerk. When describing the visit, John wrote the following to his brother:

"Van Buren is not an extraordinary man. I had two or three short but sharp debates on Politics, and then started for home about half past twelve. As I was walking home all alone, I thought, I must endeavor to avoid these needless and foolish debates as they do no good and only aggravate, instead of convince. For my part, I don't think much of Van Buren. I think his policy is injurious to the Country and himself—no better than a leader of bandits and robbers. This is a warm day. Nothing more. Farewell."

Maybe Geddes is the reason it took another five presidents and 31 years for the next commander in chief to set foot near Ann Arbor. When that president did set foot in the Ann Arbor area, it was to visit his brother.

The Fillmore Family Reunion

Calvin Fillmore and his wife Maranda lived in a farmhouse on Dexter-Ann Arbor Road. Calvin farmed and worked construction. In fact, he helped build many of Dexter's first historic buildings, but he didn't love the work and he wasn't a very good farmer. When his brother, Millard Fillmore, was chosen as Zachary Taylor's vice president, Calvin wrote to his brother asking to be set up with a government job. Maybe customs collector or lighthouse keeper. Calvin also asked that his son be made postmaster of Dexter.

Millard was a supportive sibling. He had already taken on the mortgage to his brother's home. He wasn't ignoring his brother's pleas, but this was politics and Fillmore was on unsteady ground. These requests weren't easy to grant. Calvin kept writing and Millard kept dodging. Even when Millard assumed the presidency following Taylor's death, the letters went unanswered.

Calvin continued to struggle on the land. Millard lost his bid for a second presidential term. Calvin's declining health became the focal point of his correspondence. In 1873, he wrote that the cold weather was aggravating his diabetes and that he would like to move to a warmer climate. Ever the wet blanket, with little hope for moving out of Michigan, Calvin wrote, "I shall have to live and die here after all."

It's not clear who suggested the family reunion, but in July 1873, five Fillmore siblings gathered together in Dexter for a modest party. The New York Times wrote about it. "All were in good health, hale and hearty, and to all appearances bade fair to yet see many years of enjoyment and happiness."

Millard gifted his brother $50 and Calvin mailed him five copies of a photo taken at the event. The two continued to correspond, Millard continuing to support his brother financially and helping to pay for renovations on the farmhouse. Sadly, Millard died of a stroke the following year. In his will, the former president bequeathed his brother $500 and erased all his debts. Calvin lived for another five years before dying from complications due to gangrene.[62] Calvin, his wife, and his two sisters are buried in Forest Lawn Cemetery in Dexter.

Quick Stops and Commencement Speeches

Presidents have visited U-M for quick speeches over the years. Benjamin Harrison spoke in Ann Arbor nearly a decade after his presidency, William Howard Taft spoke twice after his time in office, and Woodrow Wilson and Theodore Roosevelt each lectured three times—none as sitting president.[63]

Four presidents have spoken at U-M's commencement ceremonies, an honor to both the university and the men speaking. U-M's 1991 spring commencement featured President George Herbert Walker Bush, and the same

---

62   It's a terrible story, really. In January 1879, the *Ann Arbor Courier-Weekly* reported, "On a recent visit to his brother, who lives in Indiana, they rode fourteen miles one very cold day, and the deceased froze his feet very badly. As a direct result gangrene set in, which soon poisoned his blood, causing his death."

63   Taft spoke twice after his presidency, making his "A League of Nations to Enforce Peace" speech in 1915 and returning in 1920 as an Oratorical Association speaker talking about "Capital, Labor and the Soviet." Woodrow Wilson lectured three times at U-M before becoming president. In 1903 on "Patriotism", in 1905 on "The University and the Nation," and finally in 1912–as governor of New Jersey–he spoke about "The Opportunity of Democracy." Teddy Roosevelt came to Ann Arbor three times over the years, once five years before his presidency to speechify about law enforcement, again two years before his presidency to talk about the necessity for fulfilling the duties of a citizen, and one final time in 1912 while on the campaign trail.

ceremony in 2010 featured President Barack Obama. Both men were sitting Commanders in Chief at the time of their respective addresses. Bill Clinton achieved the rare Washtenaw County commencement double-dip[64] by speaking at Eastern Michigan University in 2000, and speaking at U-M's spring graduation seven years later.

The most famous presidential commencement speaker was Lyndon Johnson, who stood in front of the crowd at the Big House in May of 1964— just six months after the assassination of President John F. Kennedy. U-M originally invited JFK to speak at commencement, but extended the invitation to the nation's new president, Lyndon B. Johnson, who graciously accepted. LBJ became the first sitting president to speak at a U-M commencement.[65]

Johnson didn't mail it in. In preparation, he called for his top aides and best speechwriter to join him for a little brainstorming/skinny dipping session in the White House pool.[66] He wanted to launch a "Johnson" program that would continue Kennedy's work on civil rights and Medicare but do even more. The commencement speech was the kickoff to Johnson's election campaign.

The Secret Service was on high alert. Sections of Michigan Stadium were blocked off behind the president and the stadium swarmed with armed guards. Estimates put the crowd somewhere between 70,000 and 85,000— crammed into the open sections of Michigan Stadium to hear LBJ speak.

Four helicopters landed nearby and just before 10 a.m., LBJ was rushed into the stadium where he changed into his academic robes in the visitors' locker room. Johnson walked down the tunnel and onto the field as the band

---

64   Dating back to Earle Raymond Hendrick in 1836, it has been customary for commencement speakers to receive honorary degrees from U-M. GHW Bush and his wife Barbara received honorary Doctor of Laws in 1991, Clinton a Doctor of Laws in 2007 and Obama a Doctor of Laws in 2010. Clinton received an honorary doctorate in public service from EMU for his participation in the 2000 commencement.

65   To tie a bow on the honorary degree thing, Johnson received an honorary Doctor of Civil Law degree in 1964.

66   Johnson was a notorious intimidator. He was 6-3, weighed 210 pounds, and spoke with confidence and bombast. What's more, he didn't respect personal space, was prone to swearing and spitting during heated conversations, and famously held a number of meetings while sitting on the toilet. Skinny dipping in the pool during a meeting actually seems a little tame by LBJ's standards.

played Hail to the Chief.

What would come to be known as Johnson's Great Society speech was a major success. It was 20 minutes long and he had to pause 29 times for applause. On the plane back to D.C., the president was euphoric. He'd eventually win the election, beating Barry Goldwater in the the fifth-largest landslide victory in United States presidential election history. The Big House bump.

Ford, FDR, and the Era Before Air Force One

It's common knowledge that Gerald Ford attended U-M, but when he appeared in Crisler Arena during a campaign event as president in 1976, the cheers of the crowd of 15,000 were interrupted by a crescendo of boos from people still sore about the Nixon pardon. Ford met with students, visited Bo Schembechler's team during practice at Ferry Field, and dined with the football team at the Michigan Union.

Seven years later, after failing in his bid for a second term, Ford returned to Ann Arbor with former president Jimmy Carter, who sat beside him at the dedication of the Gerald Ford Presidential Library.[67]

A number of presidents have landed and taken off from Willow Run Airport, but two notable presidential visits stand out. The first was a presidential visit to the Willow Run Bomber Plant, made by President Franklin Roosevelt in 1942, one month after the plant's completion. The Willow Run plant produced the B-24 Liberator heavy bomber, which saw significant action in the Pacific.[68]

The airfield passed into civilian control after the war and welcomed FDR's successor, President Harry Truman. President Truman landed at Willow Run in the summer of 1951, stepping off his C-54 Skymaster transport plane—

67   The Gerald Ford Presidential Library is in Ann Arbor, but the Gerald Ford Presidential Museum is located in Grand Rapids. The museum has artifacts from Ford's childhood and political career, while the library houses his presidential papers. Gerald and his wife Betty are interred at the museum in Grand Rapids.

68   More than 8,500 B-24s were built at Willow Run—one bomber built every hour during the peak of production.

the first plane put into service for official presidential use. Truman was the last president to use the Skymaster as his presidential plane and the last president to fly in a plane that didn't have the official call sign of Air Force One.

Grover Cleveland: The Most Popular Man in Ann Arbor

Ann Arbor had a huge crush on Grover Cleveland. Don't believe me? Folks wanted Cleveland to visit so badly that the *Ann Arbor Argus* wrote, "There is no man in the United States who can draw a larger audience in Ann Arbor than Grover Cleveland." This was before Cleveland even set foot in town.

When the man, the myth, the legend finally accepted an invitation to deliver the annual Washington birthday address before the U-M law school, he was met at the train depot by 2,000 adoring U-M students. He'd been out of office three years, but on February 22, 1892, no one in Ann Arbor cared.

The Ann Arbor Guard and Ypsilanti Light Infantry led Cleveland's procession to University Hall where he delivered a speech that marked the launch of his successful bid to seek an unprecedented non-consecutive presidential term.[69]

The same year as Cleveland's speech in town, Ann Arborite Charles Hauser of West Liberty Street named his seventh son Grover Cleveland Hauser. Through the County Treasurer, Hauser sent a letter to the sitting president, informing him of his namesake and asking him to act as a sponsor for the child. Cleveland wrote back:

"My dear sir, I have been informed by Mr. Gustave Brehm of the birth to your household of a seventh son, to whom you have given my name. I am also asked to act as a sponsor for the child. Supposing that in this ceremony nothing is required of me except my consent to act, I most cheerfully accede to the request. I hope that my namesake will live long in health and happiness and that he may always be a comfort to his parents. Very truly yours, Grover Cleveland."

---

69   Cleveland lost his first re-election bid to Benjamin Harrison in 1888, but rallied to win the rematch in 1892 and serve another four years in the White House.

What a guy.

Nixon vs. JFK

Dwight Eisenhower never visited Ann Arbor, but during the 1952 presidential campaign he sent his vice president, Richard Nixon, on the road to stump. Young Nixon was a decent-looking guy with a lovely wife, Pat, and a promising political career ahead of him. He presented well.

Nixon rolled into the Ann Arbor train depot during Eisenhower's whistlestop tour of the Midwest. He speechified from the back platform of the train, an American flag blowing in the breeze beside him, and Pat seated in a tasteful living room chair to his left. A nice-sized crowd came to hear Nixon speak and, though it was a brief encounter, Ann Arbor developed a Grover Cleveland-sized crush on Tricky Dick.

Nixon was back at the train station on October 27, 1960—Pat again at his side—this time campaigning for his own presidential race against John F. Kennedy. With the election just 10 days away and in full-blown crush mode, Ann Arbor made a huge deal of the visit. 15,000 packed the train depot, pushing in on the former vice president.[70]

Nixon toured Ann Arbor with his wife, welcomed at every turn by area luminaries. They shook hands with U-M head football coach Bump Elliott. and were presented with a 100-foot scroll signed by student supporters—a gift from the U-M Youth for Nixon Committee. It was a memorable visit.

A few days later, Nixon sent a letter of thanks to Ann Arbor Police Chief Rolland Gainsley, writing, "Mrs. Nixon and I shall long have the most happy memories of our visit to Ann Arbor last Thursday. We were deeply touched by the friendly welcome we received. We certainly appreciate the splendid cooperation and assistance provided us by the Ann Arbor Police. Sincerely, Richard Nixon."

The visit overshadowed another candidate's stop in Ann Arbor just two

---

70   Attendance figures from area schools were amazingly accurate in the 1960s. 3,000 of the 12,170 kids in the Ann Arbor Public School System didn't show up for class that Thursday, including more than half of the 2,092 pupils at Ann Arbor High School.

weeks prior. JFK flew into Ann Arbor around midnight on October 14, 1960 and rode with police escort to the Michigan Union on State Street where he planned to spend the night. When they pulled up to the Union around 2 a.m., they ran into a crowd of 10,000 students waiting for the candidate's arrival. Kennedy pushed through the crowd, climbed the Union large steps, and gave an impromptu speech.[71] That speech, given in the middle of the night, announced JFK's intention to form the Peace Corps—and helped inspire 220,000 Peace Corps volunteers one year later.

The next morning, Kennedy was escorted to the Ann Arbor train depot where he spoke to a more modest crowd of 5,000 from the rear of his eight-car campaign train. In less than three weeks, Kennedy would be president. The Ann Arbor bump.

Nixon. Richard Nixon's campaign train rolled into Ann Arbor on October 27, 1960 and with wife Pat looking on, he gave a speech at the train station to an estimated 15,000 people. Eventual president John F. Kennedy rallied just 5,000 at the same station two weeks prior. (Photo by Brian Peters, original by Duane Scheel and Eck Stanger of the *Ann Arbor News*)

---

71   Those famous steps at the Union were removed in 1980 to install pipes under them to melt snow and ice in the winter. When construction was done, the steps were returned to their historic place.

THE NAKED MILE

Streaking is defined as "the act of stripping off one's clothes and running naked through a public place." This may take place on a dare, as a form of protest or because everyone else is doing it.

Streaking was a common enough activity in the mid-1800s for Robert E. Lee—yes, that Robert E. Lee—to sanction streaking on the campus of Washington College in Lexington, Virginia. Lee was president of the college and viewed streaking as a male rite of passage. For that decision—and probably no other reason—Washington College was eventually renamed Washington and Lee University. Robert E. Lee went down in history as the first vocal proponent of running naked in public—and is probably not known for any other historical thing.

Streaking remained popular from antebellum Virginia, straight on into the 1970s. In fact, it was so pervasive in the U.S. that it garnered a 1973 *Time* magazine article. That was the same year the term "streaking" was coined. Before then, they just called it "running in public with your bits flopping about."

Streakers streaked across college campuses around the country throughout 1973. More than 500 people streaked in a massive nude run on the campus of the University of Maryland that fall. Notre Dame, University of Texas, Stephen F. Austin University—they all experienced surges of streakers. Momentum continued to build through the winter of 1974 and the media continued to fan the flames. Streakers were all over the place.

The University of Michigan wasn't immune to this nude peer pressure, despite Ann Arbor's frosty weather. But, Michigan's students couldn't copy what other colleges were doing. Random acts of streaking? No, no, no, that'd be too easy.

So two different student groups both organized streaking events to take place on Tuesday, March 12, 1974—the second day back from Spring Break. One event was scheduled for the afternoon, one for the evening. Posters went up. Word spread. Then on that grey Tuesday afternoon, the First Annual Ann Arbor Streak-In took place. More than a thousand lookie-loos gathered at 1 p.m. at the starting line outside Eden Foods, a notorious hippie cafe on Maynard. Just five brave streakers showed up, baring all in broad daylight and the freezing cold. The plan was to run through Nickels Arcade and down to the Diag, short and sweet. The streakers—three men and two women—didn't fare well. Two dropped out before they hit the Diag. The fate of the other three is unrecorded.

Though the first run was a bust, expectations were high for that evening's First Annual Lucky Streak, which started on the Diag. The planned course wound its way through south and west quads and back. The spectator-to-streaker ratio was 10,000 to 70. Mass chaos disrupted the scheduled start. Streakers sped off at random, running towards the undergraduate library where they basically scattered in all directions. Likely a case of cold feet, and—well, you get it.

The country was on high alert for streakers. The next month at the Oscars, a streaker rushed across the stage, interrupting a delightful monologue from David Niven. And then…that was it. The high water mark for streaking in the United States had been reached. There was no Second Annual Streak-In at U-M. No Second Annual Lucky Streak. Everyone put their clothes back on like decent folks and jogged tastefully, clad in shorts and tank tops.

Time passed. Fads faded. Then, several years later, something weird happened. Streaking came back to Ann Arbor.

In 1986, a dozen or so athletes from the U-M men's and women's track and field and rowing teams decided to streak through campus in celebration of the last day of classes. They started on Washtenaw, ran west on South University, cut through the Diag, and ended their jaunt at Regents Plaza and the Cube—just outside the administration building near the Michigan Union. Nobody paid attention. There were no arrests. No stories in the Michigan Daily. Just good, clean, naked fun.

They did it again the next year. And the next. In 1989, members of the Michigan men's lacrosse team joined in, wearing only helmets and gloves. By the following year, the now-annual event had built a little steam.

Because we can't have nice (or naked) things, everything changed in the mid-1990s. More students caught wind of what was now known as the Naked Mile. More people participated.

It was 1999 when things really got out of control. Growing numbers of women were streaking and word spread—this wasn't a sausage party anymore. Guys will go to great lengths—literally and figuratively—to see a naked lady in the wild. This was the height of the Girls Gone Wild craze, with late night TV spots hawking videos of the girl next door taking her shirt off.

Around 10,000 spectators packed campus for the 1999 Naked Mile. Local media covered it. National media covered it. Men (mostly) drove from all points to watch the action. And they weren't disappointed. Around 300 of the 1,000 or so streakers were women. Not all were entirely naked, but most stripped down. Police issued warnings that the route would be packed with cameras, camcorders, leering faces and groping hands. The internet, though not super sophisticated, did exist at this time. Photos and videos could be viewed and shared. The police warned the streakers, but few listened. The cops took a hands-off approach and just let them run.

Some streakers arrived naked, ready to run. Some stripped at the starting point. The smart ones left their clothes in their cars so nothing would be missing when they returned from the trot.

With no clear signal, they just started running, a thousand streakers strong. They moved down South University, cutting through the Diag with the crowd of spectators shouting, laughing, whistling and pressing in along the narrowing route. Ten thousand people is a lot of people. The Michigan rugby, rowing, track and field, and lacrosse teams kicked out ahead. Their fitness level made it more of a naked sprint. The more leisurely streakers brought up the rear, where the crowds pushed in closer with their cameras flashing and camcorders running. By the halfway point, the run had become more of a walk, as the streakers struggled through the tightly-packed crowd of people seeking a closer look or a better camera angle. A number of women later reported being harassed, and either fought through the crowds or fled back toward the starting line. It was a cluster.

Coverage of the event was predictably unflattering for U-M and Ann Arbor. What was a small, fun and stupid end-of-term tradition mutated into something ugly and awful.

The 2000 Naked Mile arrived way too quickly for Ann Arbor and the U-M administration's tastes. Michigan launched an intense campaign to discourage runners from participating in the first Naked Mile of the millennium. They printed flyers listing 10 reasons not to run the Naked Mile.

The list included the following:

- The Naked Mile is not sponsored or endorsed by the University of Michigan or Ann Arbor.

- You might get hit by a car.

- Photos and video could bring embarrassment to participants and their families.

The rowing, track and field, and lacrosse teams publicly boycotted the 2000 Naked Mile. But interest remained. People from outside U-M and Ann Arbor vowed to show up and run. Websites dedicated to the Naked Mile were built months in advance and featured photos and video clips from past events, promising even more to come in 2000.

Thousands showed up to watch in 2000, but when the event began just before midnight, just 400 runners streaked. They were mostly male, and many ran only half-naked or wore masks.

U-M's anti-Naked Mile campaign continued in 2001 with the slogan "The Naked Truth About the Naked Mile." The city and campus police forces finally vowed to get involved. A media company that made a name for itself by live-streaming a Madonna concert from London signed on to broadcast the 2001 Naked Mile via the internet.

"It's going to be really cool," said a company spokesman.

Helicopters and a blimp showed up in 2001 to broadcast a pack of college kids running in the buff. Only a few dozen were brave enough to face the glare of the cameras and an insanely amped-up crowd. There was cheering and screaming. Some spectators showed up drunk. Along the route, the crack of bullwhips could be heard. Everyone had a camera.

Police officers attempted to physically restrain runners. Four were arrested for indecent exposure and four others were charged after the fact.

A Troy resident who drove to Ann Arbor for the Naked Mile told an interviewer he came to "see naked chicks." He called the 2001 run "pretty lame" but said he looked forward to watching the footage he recorded and making copies for his friends.

In 2002, nearly all of the few dozen participants ran wearing underwear. By 2004, there were so few runners that they coordinated to run a night earlier than advertised. They streaked through town on a completely different route - 13 naked runners and a few people on bikes drawing almost no interest as they completed the 2004 Naked-ish Mile.

Mercifully, the history of the Naked Mile ends here. Sure, there may have been a few pockets of nude sprinters in the mid-2000s that slipped under the radar, but streaking en masse and the fabled Naked Mile ebbed just as the Internet and social media exploded.

Michigan will always have its flesh-colored past. When students braved cold, cameras, classmates and dinguses driving in from Troy. When kids streaked through campus to celebrate the end of the school year like big, dumb animals. Running naked for an entire mile, wondering the whole time if pranksters had walked off with their pants at the starting line.

THE SUICIDE SUBMARINE PARADE

A full page ad appeared in the *Ann Arbor News* on Wednesday July 14, 1943, featuring a submarine of the imperial Japanese Navy, surrounded by men in various hats, hands on hips, staring at the long steel tube.

The advertisement read:

"JAP SUICIDE SUB COMES TO ANN ARBOR"

See 38 and a half tons—81 feet of fanatical fiendishness. See one of the ships in which two of our enemies volunteer to accept death in order to blow up their objectives. See this Japanese suicide submarine and realize what a vicious, tricky, desperate enemy our boys are fighting in the pacific. Let's hit them harder. Let's depth-bomb them to the bottom of the sea. Let's show them what an aroused, all-out America can do."

The submarine in the photo—which was twice the length of a semi-trailer—wasn't a prop. It was very real. It participated in the attack on Pearl Harbor—launched from the Japanese fleet with its two-man crew knowing they would never make it home. It never struck a blow for Japan, ending up grounded, attacked, and captured. And that's how a Japanese suicide submarine ended up rolling through the streets of Ann Arbor in July 1943, stimulating the sale of war bonds.

The HA-19 submarine, designated "Midget C" by the U.S. Navy, was a two-man sub constructed in the port city of Kure in Hiroshima Prefecture—10 miles southwest of Hiroshima city. The sub was made up of four longitudinally-welded 10-inch steel ribs, reinforced by a steel frame thick enough to keep the men inside safe at certain depths, but not strong enough to withstand shelling or torpedo attack.

The submarine was built with two 18-inch torpedo tubes, each loaded with a single torpedo. Each torpedo had a 1,000-pound explosive warhead specifically designed to sink big ships.

The sub was propelled by a 600-horsepower electric motor powered by batteries that could hold a charge for about an hour when moving at top speed. Submerged and traveling slow, the submarine had an effective range of 100 miles. The only way to recharge its batteries was for the sub to dock with a mother submarine or a Japanese warship. The crew knew the deal. The sub wasn't designed to return from its mission.

Twenty-six-year-old Chief Warrant Officer Kiyoshi Inagaki and 23-year-old Ensign Kazuo Sakamaki were two of 10 sailors selected to man five midget submarines as part of the attack on Pearl Harbor. It was a high honor for both men—even if they knew it was a suicide mission.

At 3:30 a.m. on the morning of December 7, 1941, HA-19 and four other midget subs launched from their mother sub in the Pacific, 10 miles from Hawaii, just off the coast of Oahu. In four and a half hours, 360 Japanese attack aircraft would descend on Pearl Harbor to sink as much of the U.S. fleet as possible. The plan was for the subs to be in the harbor when that happened, where they could open up their own attack.

The mission got off to a bad start. HA-19 launched with a broken gyrocompass, making navigation extremely difficult. Inagaki and Sakamaki crept towards Pearl Harbor, hoping to navigate through the mouth of the harbor and wait for the main attack to commence.

Only two of the five submarines managed to successfully enter the harbor. One was spotted and sunk at the mouth of the harbor at 6:37 am. A second ran into depth charges east of the entrance, sank, and wasn't discovered until 1960. HA-19 had other problems.

With its broken gyroscope, Inagaki and Sakamaki couldn't get the sub into the harbor. They hit a reef just outside the harbor mouth three times in a row before grounding for good at 8 a.m.—just minutes after the first wave of planes attacked. At 8:10 a.m. the battleship USS Arizona took a direct hit and sank in nine minutes, prompting ships from the U.S. fleet to rush for the mouth of the harbor and flee for the open sea. The destroyer USS Helm broke through the flames and smoke and spotted HA-19 hung up on the reef at 8:17 a.m. The Helm turned towards the sub, shelling at full speed.

The Helm's big guns missed, but the concussion blasted the sub off the reef, knocking Sakamaki unconscious. The grounding and shelling damaged the hull, one of the sub's torpedo tubes collapsed and water seeped in. Sea water shorted out some of the sub's batteries, which gave off toxic fumes.

Inagaki pushed the sub into a dive, and attempted to escape the Helm but again it hit the reef. He reversed and tried again. And again. Six attempts and six failures. The deadly fumes filling the small space. The Helm fired one last time before heading out to sea—the impact collapsing HA-19's final torpedo tube, crushing the periscope and rendered Inagaki unconscious as well.

When they awoke, it was night, and the sub was poking out of the water, grounded on a reef off the shore of Waimahalo, 10 miles from Pearl Harbor. The engine was dead. The mission was over.

As they were trained, the team set explosives to scuttle the sub, and planned to swim for shore. Inagaki was too injured to do much, so Sakamaki set the charge. They swam for shore. It was dark. Inagaki, wounded and exhausted, soon slipped beneath the waves. Sakamaki managed to swim to safety but when charge didn't go off, he returned to the sub and dove down to investigate. He had overestimated his stamina. The waves pulled him under and Sakamaki sank beneath the waves as well.

Eventually, Sakamaki washed ashore, waterlogged but alive, and was discovered by a Hawaiian soldier. He was taken into custody and became the United States' first Japanese prisoner of war. Sakamaki begged to be allowed to commit suicide, but his captors refused. Inagaki washed up dead the next day.

Sakamaki was shipped to the mainland where he remained a prisoner until the end of the war. They used an Army tractor to pull his submarine out of the surf, and transported it to a secret location where it could be searched and studied.

Then someone had a great idea. Why don't we parade the sub around the country as a trophy and sell war bonds? They stripped HA-19 of anything sensitive or dangerous and reassembled it without the periscope, motor, you know, the functional stuff.

They outfitted it with dummy air tanks made of wood and sheet metal, attached faux torpedo warheads, and cut six-inch-wide and six-foot-long plexiglass windows so people could see inside the hull. For the finishing touch, they put two mannequins at the controls, dressed like Japanese naval personnel.

Next, they strapped the submarine to a custom-built trailer, pulled by a truck from the Bigge Drayage Company out of Oakland, California. The trailer included a clever design that allowed the sub to tilt on its side so it could clear low railway bridges and overpasses on its travels.

The tour started in San Francisco in the fall of 1942 and was an instant success. According to one official, roughly $22,000 was raised for every 60 minutes the sub was on public display. The tour continued, and by the summer of 1943, the suicide sub was being paraded through the Midwest. On July 17 of that year, it rolled through downtown Ann Arbor.

Picture the scene: It's a sunny Saturday afternoon on Ann Arbor's west side. What is called a midget submarine, but is still a giant, weighing in at 38.5 tons, and stretching to 81 feet of fanatical fiendishness, slowly moves into view, led by two crack platoons from the local ROTC marching in formation.

People lined up along the sidewalks, 10 people deep in some places. Folks elbowed one another for a better view, toddlers sat on parents' shoulders, kids rode their bikes alongside the submarine, swarming like pilot fish. Cheers erupted as the scuffed, dingy, black trophy of war moved slowly by, tilted at a 45-degree angle to avoid hitting overhead wires.

The submarine spectacle rolled east on Huron Street, slipping under the railroad bridge, and turned south on Main Street to William Street, where it headed east to State St., then north to Huron St., finally stopping on Fourth Street where it stayed on display until 10 p.m. that night. Temporary catwalks were erected so people could peer into the plexiglass portholes and see the interior of the suicide sub and the scarecrow enemy sailors seated at the controls. This was a chance for the American public to reach out and touch the cold steel that crossed the Pacific to wage war with the United States.

Booths staffed by members of the Zal Gaz Grotto and Daughters of Mokanna did brisk business selling war bonds all day. A Navy official escorting the sub said he'd never seen a parade route packed with so many people per block.

Nearly 10,000 climbed the catwalks, pressed their faces to the plexiglass, and touched Japan's secret weapon. They bought $15,000 worth of war bonds—which is about $210,000 today. Military officials stayed the night in Ann Arbor, leaving the sub parked across from the courthouse on Fourth Street—an overnight guard on duty, just in case.

That Sunday, the submarine moved on to Adrian, then through the streets of Tecumseh, and on to the next town, and the next. After the tour, the sub was taken to Navy Pier in Chicago, where it stayed on display until the end of the war. In 1947, it was trucked to Key West and displayed there.

In 1989, the sub was declared a U.S. National Historic Landmark. In 1991, it became part of the National Museum of the Pacific War in Fredericksburg, Texas, where it remains today.

In 1991, Kazuo Sakamaki, America's first Japanese prisoner of World War II, flew to Texas to reunite with HA-19, the suicide submarine that couldn't be sunk. It had crossed an ocean only to be pulled out of and paraded around the United States to raise money for the war effort. The 72-year-old Sakamaki, a lifetime removed from Pearl Harbor, approached his old submarine, touched its flat black steel, and wept.

Sub. In the summer of 1943, a submarine captured in the attack on Pearl Harbor rolled through the streets of Ann Arbor on the back of a truck to stimulate the sale of war bonds. Curbs and sidewalks along the parade route were packed with thousands, while kids rode their bikes and ran alongside the machine of war. The sub was tilted slightly on its side to avoid hitting low hanging bridges or snagging overhead wires. (Photo by Brian Peters, original by Eck Stanger of the *Ann Arbor News*)

THE TORCH MURDERS

On a hot August night in 1931, four teenage lovebirds sat in a parked car on Lover's Lane in Ypsilanti, doing what teenage lovebirds do after they've lied to their parents about where they're headed for the night.

Thomas Wheatley and Harry Lore, both 17, were the evening escorts for two young girls from Cleveland—15-year-old Vivian Gold, who was Harry's cousin, and 16-year-old Anna May Harrison. Thomas and Vivian canoodled in the front seat of his dad's two-door Willys sedan, while pal Harry and Anna May spent time in the back. It was around midnight, the windows were down, the radio turned low. Ypsi's Lover's Lane was a popular spot for teens down at Peninsular Grove[72] where the warm summer breeze blew off the Huron River.

It was then that two men stepped out of the darkness, guns drawn, and told the teens to raise their hands.

---

72   Now Peninsular Park, not far from the Peninsular Paper Company.

Around 5:15 am, police received a call from a farmer in Ypsilanti, reporting a car on fire near his property on Washtenaw-Wayne County Road—now Rawsonville Road—southeast of Ypsilanti . Police and firemen rushed to the scene to find a two-door sedan ablaze. They pierced the gas tank to prevent an explosion, but it was nearly empty, then extinguished the flames as the sun broke the horizon, revealing a grisly scene.

Badly-charred bodies were piled in the front and back seats of the torched interior. Police roped off the crime scene and tried to make sense of the brutality.

The four nearly-unidentifiable bodies were removed from the car, which was pretty clearly intentionally set on fire. A nearby ditch revealed evidence which suggested a murder scene. Police found signs of a struggle—bushes and reeds trampled and streaks of blood visible in the grass. A blood-stained high heel shoe lay nearby.

Police traced the license plate to Thomas Wheatley's father, who was brought to the morgue to identify the bodies. He recognized two keys his son always carried, as well as a belt buckle worn by his son's friend, Harry. Thomas had borrowed the car that night, telling his parents he and Harry were attending a Young Masons meeting in town. At Harry Lore's home, his cousin Vivian and her friend Anna had told his parents they were headed to the movies. The four teens met up and were last seen around 8 pm Monday night.

Police began one of the biggest statewide manhunts in history, even going so far as to allow the head of security at the Ford Motor Company, Ann Arbor native and resident Harry Bennett, to put his own men on the case.[73] Bennett's crew of questionable employees included murderers, kidnappers, and henchmen of every stripe, but law enforcement officials were so desperate to find the killers—and quickly—that they gave Bennett full access to the case. They allowed him to investigate the crime scene, read all the reports and eventually become a key player in the interrogation room.

The first break in the case came that same Tuesday afternoon. A

---

73   Bennett has quite a story of his own. If only someone would write about that. Oh, wait! Look for the chapter "Henry Ford's Strong Right Fist" in this very book!

traveling vacuum salesman spotted a blood-spattered purse in the middle of Tuttle Hill Road near the village of Willis, Michigan—a few miles southeast of Ypsilanti and just nine miles from where the torched car was found. The purse belonged to Vivian Gold, one of the victims. The working assumption was that the purse had been tossed from a moving vehicle either headed towards or away from the crime scene.

Suspects were rounded up throughout the state and interrogated, but no solid leads developed. It wasn't until the following night that police had their first good suspect. Otis Oden, a black man who ran a rooming house in Ypsilanti's colored district, turned over a .38 caliber pistol one of his boarders had left behind as a rent payment. Oden identified the renter as David Blackstone, a 26-year-old tamale vendor and ex-con on parole from Illinois State Prison in Joliet.

Oden said Blackstone arrived at the rooming house at 5 am Tuesday in a frantic state. Oden confronted him about liquor Blackstone had stolen the night before while drinking with some friends. They shouted at each other and then started fighting. Either the .38 fell out of Blackstone's jacket and he offered it to Oden to settle up what he owed or, following the fight, he offered it up out of the blue. One way or another, Oden was in possession of a .38 that, after what were now known as the Torch Murders, seemed highly suspicious.

Oden must have hated Blackstone, or been really tempted by the $2,000[74] in reward money offered by the *Detroit News* and *Detroit Times*. It was 1931 and Oden, a black man on probation himself, was involving himself in the brutal murder of four white teenagers. It was also more than a decade into Prohibition and Oden's rooming house included a not-so-secret speakeasy, serving bootleg whiskey and all kinds of illicit hooch.

The revolver cracked the case wide open, but Oden didn't escape unscathed. His rooming house was raided by police three days after he turned in the revolver, police firing shots at boarders who fled in terror. Oden was arrested and charged with breaking parole and violation of Prohibition law. It's unclear if he did any time, or if he got his cut of the reward money, but Oden definitely suffered for his civic duty.

---

74   Roughly $30,000 today.

Police took the .38 to Detroit where they ran ballistics tests trying to match the gun to bullet wounds found in the autopsies. In the early hours of Thursday morning, the results came back. The gun was a positive match for the weapon used in the Torch Murders. Further evidence connecting Blackstone to the crime came from a pawnshop in Detroit, where Blackstone had hocked a watch for $6. The watch that belonged to Vivian Gold.

Thursday morning at 7 am, a little over 48 hours after the car was discovered, police arrested Blackstone. They brought him into the interrogation room and tried to work a confession out of him. The only solid leads they generated were the names of two men he'd been with the night of the murders—Fred "Curly" Smith and Frank Oliver. Police knew Smith—a 22-year-old farmer from Ypsilanti who was on parole for armed robbery and car theft. Oliver was new to them—a 19-year-old from Ypsi with no previous criminal history. They arrested Smith that morning and arrived with guns drawn in Ypsilanti where Oliver was on a ladder painting a house.

The three men were brought to the jail at City Hall in Ypsilanti where "due process" was carried out. The suspects were grilled in the jail one by one—the police taking extreme liberties to get at the truth. Hundreds gathered outside City Hall once they learned the suspects were inside—one of them a black man. They hollered at police to release the killers to the mob, stringing nooses over trees in front of the building to signify their intent. Police let the suspects know what was waiting for them outside and promised to protect them if they confessed. They promised a lot of things, including more of the same extreme liberties if the men didn't admit to their crimes. One by one, the men cracked.

Smith agreed to tell the cops everything for guaranteed protection from the angry mob. Blackstone said he'd prefer mob justice over life in prison. Blackstone admitted to nothing. To break him, police sicced Bennett and his Ford security men. These were men who had no problem beating up workers at the Ford plant who complained of long hours and bad pay, men who fired bullets at unarmed union protesters by day, and slept like babies at night.

The trial was hastily arranged for that Thursday night. Smith and Oliver admitted to everything while Blackstone didn't testify. He didn't speak because he probably wasn't able to. Bennett and his men had resorted to drastic measures to make him talk in the interrogation room. Rumor has it Blackstone was told to stand up in the interrogation room full of goons and his pants were pulled down. His penis was laid on the interrogation table and an unidentified interrogator smashed it with a billy club, over and over again, until he told them what he did that night. And when they heard all the details, they beat him some more.

This was the story pieced together from the killers' confessions:

Blackstone, Smith, and Oliver met at Oden's boarding house in Ypsilanti, where they drank homemade liquor late into the night until they got bored. Blackstone proposed they swing by Peninsular Grove and look for young lovers spending the quiet evening together and do a stick up. Oliver drove. They saw a single car parked near the river. Oliver cut the lights and Smith and Blackstone got out, each holding a revolver. When they got to the side of the car, they told the kids to stick 'em up. A startled Harry Lore looked up from inside the car and saw his childhood friend Fred Smith pointing a gun at him. They were neighbors and as children used to play and go fishing together. Now Smith held Lore at gunpoint and the situation went sour.

Blackstone was enraged. Smith was paranoid. All four teens were forced into the back seat of Wheatley's dad's two-door Willys sedan. They yelled for Oliver to join them and made him sit in the front seat and hold a gun on the teens. Blackstone climbed in back and sat between the four kids, also armed. Smith took the wheel and they drove, unsure of where to go or what to do. They headed south, driving for about 30 minutes until Smith pulled over on Tuttle Hill Road. The girls begged the men to let them go.

"If we let you go, you'll give us a ride to the jug," Blackstone said.

They parked and the bandits got out of the car. Smith ordered the girls to join them. Anna Harrison climbed out but Vivian Gold refused—she told the men with the guns that she'd rather die. Blackstone fired his revolver four times. He might have been drunk or just a really bad shot, but the bullets only hit one of the teens in that back seat, killing Lore almost instantly. The girls were dragged into the grass where Smith and Blackstone beat their heads in with rocks they found on the ground. One of the killers used a wrench. Thomas Wheatley was dragged out of the car too, covered in his friend's blood. His head was caved in by one of the men wielding a huge rock, which police found, splattered with blood and brains. Blackstone dragged one of the girls into the grass and raped her. She was alive, but he likely didn't know that.

Blackstone and Smith did all the damage—Oliver watched the monsters do their work. They debated what to do with the bodies—ended up throwing them in the back seat. Then drove the 20-plus minutes back to Peninsular Grove to get Oliver's car, the bodies piled like wood in the back.

They stopped and picked up Oliver's car and he followed Smith, who was at the wheel of the teenagers' sedan with Blackstone riding shotgun. Then, they just drove. They turned and circled, unsure of what to do. Maybe they were still drunk or exhausted from the adrenaline rush. Smith and Blackstone were covered in blood, and had four bodies piled in the back seat, rigor mortis slowly setting in.

They took River Road toward Ann Arbor, crossed to Packard, turned east towards Ypsilanti, drove past the Washtenaw Country Club. It was late, but these were very public streets. They drove down Michigan Avenue and First Street, where Blackstone got out and grabbed a shovel. They drove like this for hours, mutilated bodies in the back seat, blood drying, limbs stiffening. They took U.S. 23, drove past the airport, then down a deserted stretch of Washtenaw-Wayne County Road—now Rawsonville Road— and parked.

Blackstone grabbed the body of the girl he hadn't assaulted at the initial crime scene, dragged her into the ditch, and raped her. Though violently attacked hours earlier, the coroner's report later concluded she too was alive when Blackstone raped her, though Blackstone likely didn't know that. When he was done, he carried her body back to the car, and dumped her in the front seat.

The men siphoned gas from Wheatley's dad's sedan, doused the floorboards and bodies, and lit a handkerchief, tossing it into the vehicle.

Flames lit up the night. They squeezed into Oliver's car and sped back to the rooming house in Ypsi. The farmer spotted the flames and called the police.

The trio confessed around 5 pm on Thursday in City Hall. A trial was hastily convened at the Washtenaw County Courthouse in Ann Arbor. The accused were whisked out the back door, right under the noses of the lynch mob outside, and driven to Ann Arbor, where a much larger crowd awaited.

Their trial began at 7 pm. Guilty pleas were entered and the whole thing took 30 minutes. All three were found guilty beyond a reasonable doubt. Sentencing took place at 10 pm. The judge handing down four consecutive life sentences to each man, one for each victim. These were the longest prison terms in Michigan history.

By this time, the crowd outside had grown to 12,000 screaming people, pounding on the courthouse doors, calling for blood. The National Guard was called in to protect the building and the prisoners, but even they didn't like their odds.

Around 10:30 pm, courthouse officials made the call to transport the criminals, despite the angry mob outside. National Guardsmen fired tear gas into the crowd to hold them at bay as a convoy of cars led by Harry Bennett himself rolled up onto the steps of the courthouse. Guards rushed the guilty men out of the building and into the chaos. Shots rang out—at least one was aimed at Blackstone. Several shots came from National Guardsmen firing their rifles into the air.

Smith and Oliver made it to the car and Bennett peeled off, but Blackstone and his guards were swarmed—the prisoner's shirt ripped from his body. They retreated back into the courthouse and escaped out the back door, evading the mob, and jumping into a waiting car. The two cars transporting the criminals met up on the road, and proceeded, keeping watch for barricades that were rumored to have been erected by vigilantes hoping to stop the cars on their route to the prison in Jackson. However, the trip was uneventful.

At 11:33 pm, the cars arrived in Jackson and Blackstone, Smith and Oliver began their lives in prison. They each spent a week in solitary confinement before being shackled and packed into cars, which were part of an 11-officer contingent transporting the men to Marquette Branch Prison on the shores of Lake Superior. There they began the longest prison sentences in the history of the state. Only one of them would ever be a free man again.

Fred Smith died of a heart attack in his cell at the age of 68. The official cause of David Blackstone's death in 1950 was listed as a heart attack, but that's not really how he went. Blackstone's fellow inmates stuffed him into a rock crusher in the prison yard in Marquette, where he was pulverized to bits.

Frank Oliver entered prison at age 19. When he turned 56 he was granted parole by Governor George Romney, who reluctantly commuted Oliver's four life sentences. He traveled to Washington state where he worked in a nursing home, found love, and eventually married. His ultimate fate is unknown.

The Torch Murders scarred Ypsilanti. Police launched an investigation into rumors that the three killers were part of some larger gang of thugs— robbers targeting teens heading home from dances or nights out, or parking in secluded areas like Peninsular Grove. The Grove itself lost all romantic value. The town imposed an informal curfew for teenagers for many years after, fearing men like David Blackstone, Fred Smith, and even clean-cut kids like Frank Oliver, wary of more devils in their midst.

THE GHOST OF FIRST METHODIST

There are surprisingly few ghost stories for a town as old as Ann Arbor. In the late 1950s, the congregation of the First Methodist Church in Ann Arbor was convinced they had a ghost on their hands. Caretakers heard footsteps late at night, but never spotted anyone in the church. Boxes of crackers and leftovers from Ladies Auxiliary potluck dinners went missing from time to time. Matches, blankets and pew cushions also went missing over the years. Some blamed sticky-fingered Boy Scouts whose troop met at the church weekly. But others were convinced it was a ghost.

What was the spirit's business?

In June 1959, a church volunteer arrived before dawn to prepare for a banquet and saw a shadowy figure standing in the kitchen. It wore a small hat, gloves, rumpled pants, and a dark shirt. The woman screamed and fled. Six police officers searched the church but found no sign of an intruder. It wasn't the first time the cops had visited First Methodist. They'd received calls to this address before—reports of prowlers on the property, shapes in the windows, or sounds coming from inside the building. Despite repeated investigations, they'd never found a thing.

Items continued to go missing, and mysterious footsteps continued to echo through seemingly-deserted halls. The church finally called the Sanford Security Agency which dispatched a nighttime security guard named William Edison to keep an eye on the place. Late in the evening on August 30, 1959, not long on the job, Edison heard footsteps in the church. He called the cops, who showed up in the pre-dawn hours and checked every room in the giant church yet again. Patrolmen Norman Olmstead and Ritchie Davis were last on the scene. Once again, no one found evidence of anything natural...or supernatural.

But on the way out, Olmstead spotted a steel door at the top of a ladder. The patrolmen climbed it and swung the door open onto a flat section of roof above the north wing of the church. Across the roof was another door, this one leading to the rafters. The caretaker produced a key to the door, which they unlocked and carefully opened, training their flashlights on the 40-foot long space. It was hard to see—the sun wouldn't be up for another hour. One of the beams of light revealed a jar of instant coffee ... a box of crackers ... a makeshift bed of pew cushions. They walked carefully on the wooden rafter boards high above the church and stepped into a makeshift home. The bed, someone's belongings, and in the corner, curled in the fetal position, a body.

Officers Olmstead and Davis trained their flashlights on the form. Davis unholstered his weapon and pointed it at the thing, which rose and put its hands up when asked. It was feral. Long, uneven hair hanging off its head. Shirtless, it wore a pair of filthy swim trunks. It glistened with sweat. It wore a wristwatch. It was a man named Cheng Guan Lim.

Lim, known to his friends and classmates as David, wasn't a ghost—he was a University of Michigan dropout. After he was arrested and taken to the station, Lim told police his tale. How he came to the United States from Singapore to get an education, sponsored by the same Methodist Church he had "haunted" for four years. How he transferred from Albion College to the U-M in 1952 and enrolled in the College of Engineering. He got good grades, up until 1954, when he didn't. Lim had trouble in math and physics and, at the end of the school year, had failed multiple classes. He wanted to transfer into another program but his grades were too low. He feared he was on the verge of being expelled. Lim had already taken out a number of loans, his funds were nearly dried up, and his part-time job as a janitor at the First Methodist Church wasn't making enough of a difference. He was too proud to accept more aid, and too humiliated to return to Singapore.

"So many people helped me," Lim said. "I failed them all."

He didn't return to classes that fall and gave up his living quarters. He stayed off campus in places like the Arboretum, the railway station, and city parks and he used his key to sneak into the First Methodist Church when the weather got foul. From working there as a janitor, he knew the church inside and out, and found it easy to slip in, sneak a bite to eat here or spend a rainy night indoors there. The only thing that brought Lim out in the public was his beloved Michigan Wolverines. He loved college football and never missed a game, buying tickets to Michigan Stadium and catching away games on a little portable radio.

On October 8, 1955, Lim sat in the stands with 97,000 other fans and watched Bennie Oosterbaan's Wolverines beat an unbeatable Army squad, 26-2 on an unseasonably warm fall day. Following the game, he walked out of Michigan Stadium, blending in with the fans streaming to their cars and into the streets. He bypassed downtown, keeping his head down just in case, and headed for a secluded section of the Huron River. There, he told officials, he tossed his passport and some clothes into the river, faking his suicide[75], and packed everything but the clothes on his back and an earphone radio, into one big suitcase. He stored that in a locker at the bus station.

It was dark now. No one saw him walk up Huron towards the First Methodist. Unlock the door. Slip inside. Climb up the ladder, open the metal

---

75   Apparently this was a lie, though it makes for a pretty dramatic red herring.

door, climb out onto the roof, unlock one final door, and hide in the rafters, 12 hours before the Sunday congregation would arrive.

He stayed for four years. Lim lived in the rafters, never speaking to another soul. He never left the church. Ever—until that August morning, in the presence of Officers Olmstead and Davis, with the sun below the horizon and his hands cuffed behind his back.

Four years of foraging for food—at the mercy of church function leftovers and the odd box of snacks. Which wasn't bad. He ate well—that we know. Lim weighed 10 pounds more when he left the church than when he arrived. After he was arrested and examined by physicians from the University Health Service, they concluded that he'd been receiving adequate amounts of Vitamin A, C, and D. His muscle tone was good and his teeth were in fair shape.

Lim hadn't neglected his body in seclusion. He brushed his teeth, using the ends of kitchen matches and baking soda. He jumped rope late at night or early in the morning when he knew no one was in the building. He shaved regularly with two sharpened pennies, cut his own hair and bathed in the church bathroom. He read books and magazines by the light of a tiny Christmas bulb taken from the church tree, listened to his earphone radio, catching newscasts, and rooting for the Wolverines during football season. He also rooted against the Tigers from the spring and into the fall.

"The Tigers annoyed me because of their optimism," Lim said. "Each spring they said this was the year. But it never was."

He also slowly went mad.

His living quarters were basically outdoors. In the rafters of the A-frame building, temperatures easily reached 100 degrees on hot summer days and dropped below freezing during the winter months. Snow and icy wind whipped through gaps in the roof during storms. He carried as much water into his hideout as he could each night for fear that any movement during the day would reveal him. Paranoid, Lim would lie still all day long, afraid to make a single move lest a board creak or a footstep become audible.

Time was all he had. Lim wound his wristwatch every day so he'd know exactly what time it was. In the years that followed, it started to lose its function, but Lim reset it every night, matching it with the clocks in the church.

He also screamed. Literally screamed. There was a closet downstairs that, when the door was closed, was nearly soundproof. Some nights, he'd creep into the closet, close the door, and sing at the top of his lungs. Some nights he'd yell and thrash and scream to hold the breakdown at bay. The nights when no one was in the church weren't bad. But the days were very hard.

Lim got careless. He wanted to get caught and started exhibiting more brazen behavior. Like the morning he was spotted by the volunteer in the kitchen. Like the night he made too much noise and alerted the church's new patrolman.

In jail, he learned some bad news right away. Lim's father had died of cancer months earlier, before having a chance to complete a planned trip to Ann Arbor to look for his missing son. Everyone had looked for Lim when he vanished; classmates, university officials, church members.

Coming out of hiding, Lim expected the worst. Instead, he received all the help he would need. U-M was quick to accept him back into the fold, re-enrolling him and placing him in the Literary College. He received letters from across the country and around the world, many of them containing checks or offering financial assistance. A Texas oil man sent money. A retired business woman in Pennsylvania and a Brooklyn schoolteacher each sent checks. The First Methodist Church too offered to finance his education and pay his expenses.

The university gave Lim a new identity to escape the nationwide attention—changing his name, giving him a new haircut, and putting him up in a house close to campus with an unlisted address and phone number.

Weeks later, he was back in class. Just another junior studying history. After a time, he said, no one seemed to recognize him. He mostly got good grades—good enough to graduate with a bachelor's degree on June 17, 1961, blending into the graduation crowd at commencement listening to an address given by journalist Edward R. Murrow.

After graduation, Lim's trail goes a little cold. A short newspaper article mentions him on December 5, 1961. Typical *Ann Arbor News* clickbait—a small item reporting that Lim was hit by a car while riding his bicycle near the corner of Stadium and Industrial, receiving slight injuries. His address is given and he's listed as a graduate student at the U-M.

Every other media account mentions him returning to Singapore in 1961. It seems he never married and he kept his head down the rest of his life. In Singapore in 1986, Lim suffered a fatal heart attack and died at the age of 55.[76]

The First Methodist still stands, closing in on 200 years of active service.[77] And in all those years, after all those funerals and boy scout meetings—still no ghosts. Unless you count the stealthy footfalls of the shut-in, Cheng Guan Lim.

---

76   The one American Lim kept in contact with after returning to Singapore was Reverend Eugene Ransom, director of the Methodist ministry at the U-M. Ransom and Lim corresponded off and on after Lims graduation, though Lim was always evasive in his responses. Still, Lim never missed sending Ransom a Christmas card during the holidays.

77   The first sermon was preached there in 1825.

THE HOTTEST GAY BAR
IN ANN ARBOR

Ann Arbor's longest-running gay bar didn't intend to be. A gay bar, that is. But fate's wheel started turning on April 30, 1949, when the Cupid Bar rebranded as the Flame Bar, transforming a modestly popular downtown student watering hole into a slightly more popular downtown student watering hole at 115 West Washington Street.[78] Neither the Cupid Bar nor the Flame started out as gay bars. In those early days, both bars were run of the mill student hangouts doing brisk business right off Main Street.

The Flame wasn't anything special. Other than a giant print of the painting Custer's Last Stand behind the bar, the most memorable thing about it was bartender Harry Tselios. Born Christos Pasaportis, he served in the Greek merchant marine following World War II, visiting ports of call around the world. Pasaportis arranged a 29-day shore leave to America in 1950 to visit his two uncles who lived there. First he spent some time in New York City, then

---

78   Where the fancy restaurant Logan is in 2017.

visited the second uncle in Michigan. He never left the Mitten. Young Christos Pasaportis took the name Harry Tselios, married Theresa Talaske in 1952 and worked his first shift at the Flame on April 14, 1953—hired through a cousin who worked as a waiter.

Stories about the Flame in those early days offer lots of different details, but the one constant was that Tselios was a great bartender and a good friend. Always polite, always smiling, Tselios was the king of the buyback.[79] He showed no prejudice and played no favorites.

Business stayed strong through the 1950s as Ann Arbor's population grew and the Main Street district thrived. Then two things happened, and there's a date assigned to only one of them. The first thing is that the Flame was sold in 1959 to a man from Dexter named Harvey Blanchard. The second thing is that the Flame became a gay bar.

There was a gay bar a stone's throw from the Flame called the Town Bar—a cocktail lounge and the go-to hangout for Ann Arbor's gay community around the late 1950s and early 1960s, until the owners added live music. This brought in a new clientele who weren't comfortable with the regulars and vice versa. Fights broke out. The new atmosphere kind of sucked. The displaced regulars needed a new bar to call their own and right down the block was the Flame—and it had this nice bartender who didn't care who you were or who you loved. It wasn't too crowded. It didn't have live music. And, again, it was right down the street. So the Flame became, pretty quickly it seems, the new gay bar in Ann Arbor—a pretty common fact to anyone living in the city in the 1960s.

The Flame wasn't a nice bar. It was actually kind of a dive. A lot of the credit for that ambiance can be laid at the feet of Blanchard, who, it seemed, was happy to stop by and raid the till, but didn't much care for upkeep or general cleanliness. He thought the dirt on the walls added character.

The Flame's big windows facing Washington Street would have

---

79   A buyback is when a bartender rewards a regular customer with a free drink every once in awhile. Maybe it's a shot on the house or that fourth drink free. The reigning Ann Arbor King of the Buyback is Andy Garris who, at the time of this book's printing, is holding things down at Nightcap on Main Street. Tell him Retyi sent you.

revealed a dark, dirty, smoky interior, but there wasn't much of a view in or out. The window sills were cluttered with pots of long-dead plants, a rainforest of dried-up vegetation, coated in nicotine from the countless cigarettes over the years. Further obscuring the windows were yellowed newspaper clippings taped to the glass, old posters, junk nobody got around to taking down.

Inside, the bar itself was basically one big box. A long bar ran more than 30 feet from the door down to the end of the building, the back lined the whole way with liquor bottles. A big, long room to the back, and a side door opening into the alley. There was no dance floor, no upstairs. Booths had jukeboxes, some of which actually worked. Outside, a big neon sign burned bright with the words "FLAME BAR" and "LIQUOR" and a big arrow pointing to the door.

The utter lack of cleanliness is what most people remember, and love. The Flame's filth is mentioned in every account of the place. The last significant investment Blanchard put into the bar came right after he bought it—new barstools purchased by his second wife as a wedding present to her hubby. Those same stools, installed in 1959, were still there the day the bar relocated more than 30 years later.

If Blanchard didn't spend money keeping up the place, install amenities like a dance floor, or spring for better glassware, it's because he didn't have to. As Ann Arbor's only real gay bar, the Flame had a ready clientele. It wasn't the kind of place everyone went. In the 1950s and 60s, it catered more to older gay men and women rather than students or professionals. Some faculty members at the University of Michigan were afraid of being spotted at the Flame and would travel to Detroit or Toledo to socialize instead.

It wasn't until the 1970s, when the town became a little more progressive and cultural change started to sweep the country that the gay student population, and eventually faculty and staff, looked past the dead geraniums and wilted newspaper clippings and walked into the Flame.[80]

---

80   In the 1970s, local gay and lesbian groups used the Flame as a meeting place. These activist groups formed to advocate for equal treatment and to end state morality laws that, at the time, made it not only illegal to engage in homosexual activity, but illegal to even *ask* anyone to engage in homosexual activity.

The Flame also had a reputation for being friendly to underage drinkers, as well as having the latest last call in town. You could catch last call at the Del Rio and pop over to the Flame for at least one more. Some said it was also the only bar in Ann Arbor where you could light up a joint and no one would say a thing.

The Flame lived hard. Paint peeled, glasses broke and weren't replaced and the dirt stuck to the dirt stuck to the dirt. Other gay bars sprung up—better bars, to be honest—with dance floors, and DJs, and good music and color on the walls. But they weren't the Flame. They didn't have Tselios. Or the broken bar stools, splintering booths or dead plants in the window. This was truly the Flame's gross golden age.

In 1973, a review of the Flame read:

"The city's gay bar. There is no music there, but the drinks are relatively cheap."

That's it. That was the review. Even Mr. Flood's Party got 100 words.[81] But the regulars loved it.

Then, in August 1983, high tide receded. Blanchard died of a massive stroke. Without its owner and in financial disarray, the bar closed while Blanchard's estate tried desperately to sell. The estate wanted to dump the Flame, "as soon as legally possible," but it still took a year for paperwork to be signed and the doors to open once again. Former patrons and even Tselios put together offer sheets, but the family sold to local businessman Andy Gulvezan. Gulvezan had a good business reputation around town, but Flame regulars didn't care about business—they'd been family for three decades.

Gulvezan's first move was to build a close relationship with Harry Tselios. The pair got along well and, by the end of the 1980s, Gulvezan even went so far as to create two unique brews in Harry's honor, called Harry's Lager and Harry's Light, bottled at the Joseph Huber Brewing Company.[82] For a time,

---

81   Mr. Flood's Party was a legendary Ann Arbor watering hole located at 120 West Liberty where West End Grill is in 2017. They featured live music seven days a week in their heyday in the 70s and 80s.

82   Located in Monroe, Wisconsin, it happens to be the second oldest brewery in the United States.

Harry's was the only beer served at the Flame. Reviews ranged from "disgusting" to "it sucks."

Gulvezan also made some changes, some of which long-time Flame patrons didn't like. He fixed the place up, cleaned a bit and added colored lights—minor alterations but massive changes from the Blanchard-era. People missed their dark and dirty home. Gulvezan also talked about adding a dance floor—but that never happened.

Then, Gulvezan did the second-most dramatic thing he could. In 1995, squabbling with the owner of the building over the lease, Gulvezan moved the Flame, one block away to a building he owned at 112 West Liberty Street—the site of a former Gulvezan bar, Kitty O'Shea's—and where Alley Bar resides today.

Patrons barely had time to steal keepsakes. The Flame held a blowout in the old location on April 18, 1995, before opening their doors the next day at the new location. The scene was apocalyptic—Gulvezan's crew moved things through the alley from the old bar to the new digs, while inside the old Flame, the party raged. Local Jim Rees captured the scene for his blog:

> *"The place had been going downhill in recent months. The windows were broken, the neon tubes removed from the sign. The individual jukebox control boxes at each booth disappeared a couple of years ago. This last winter, the furnace broke and wasn't fixed, so they moved in a kerosene heater. On the coldest nights customers would huddle around the stove, laughing and drinking. Last week the booths were removed.*
>
> *But last night the place was jam packed. There was cake, food, and beer, a drag queen beauty show, and an auction of memorabilia. There was a group of bartenders from the Old Town, waitresses from the Bella Ciao, and musicians from all over. As I sat at the bar chatting with a Fleetwood waitress, the beer bottles piled up, the staff not bothering to remove the empties."*

The final night on Washington Street was chaotic. They pried the old booths from the floorboards and walked them to the new location. But they didn't take the dead plants, or the wedding gift barstools. The dirt stayed too. Through the alley to Liberty Street went Tselios and whatever patrons were willing to follow.

In April 1995, the new Flame opened its doors, but it was never the same. That chemistry, that special magic of the old place on Washington—how can you recreate that? How can you carry that down the alley along with everything else?

Harry Tselios retired two years after the move and everyone showed up for one more huge party to see him off. The following year, April 11, 1998, Gulvezan did the most dramatic thing he could—and closed the Flame for good.

Andy Gulvezan died on Valentine's Day in 2010 due to complications from a bone marrow transplant to treat a recurrence of leukemia. He lived a good life, opened a ton of successful businesses, and many credit him for making Main Street what it is today.

Harry Tselios died on June 16, 2015 at home with his family by his side. He was 85 and had poured drinks at the Flame for more than half his life. His memorial service was well attended.

The Flame's demise wasn't Andy's fault.[83] The Flame just ran out of oxygen. The Liberty location was replaced by Babs', which was replaced by Alley Bar, which, under new management, exists in the space today.

There's still a piece of the the old Flame alive at Alley Bar—the booths. Those booths were nailed to the floor on 115 West Washington back in the 1950s and made the move to the the new location in the 1990s, where they were cut to fit a narrower floorplan. They're lined up against the wall one block from where they supported the derrières of Ann Arbor's gay community for all those years.

Those booths that have seen so much, lived so hard, and are here to tell the tale.

---

83   Well, maybe it was a little bit Andy's fault.

The Flame. The Flame Bar was one of Ann Arbor's longest-running gay bars. Originally located at 115 West Washington Street from 1949 until 1995, when it moved to 112 West Liberty, before closing for good in 1998. This photo shows a snowy January night at the original location back in 1991 (Photo by Brian Peters, original with special permission from Jim Rees—thanks Jim!)

ANN ARBOR'S
TOP 10 ASTRONAUTS

This is the countdown to the countdown:

#1: An astronaut is a person trained to travel in a spacecraft, but they don't always get to make the trip.

#2: The main reason there are enough Ann Arbor astronauts for an actual countdown is the University of Michigan Aeronautics program—the first of its kind in the United States. It started way back in 1914, 11 years after the first sustained, manned flight took place at Kitty Hawk. To date, more than 6,000 aeronautical and aerospace engineers have graduated from the program. It has made Ann Arbor a premier destination for pilots interested in rockets and spacecraft, as well as space, earth and flight nerds—some of the best nerds out there.

#3: Until 2004, astronauts were sponsored and trained exclusively by governments, either by military or civilian space agencies. Classes of astronauts were recruited every few years. NASA Group 1 was recruited in 1959 and dubbed Mercury 7, while NASA Group 4 (brought onboard in 1965) were dubbed The Scientists. Many of our Ann Arbor astronauts came up together in these classes.

#4: This list is accurate as of the fall of 2017. There's still time for Ann Arborites to get their butts in space and crack our top 10 when *"The Book of Ann Arbor II: Even More Book"* comes out in the summer of 2019.

Now for the countdown.

#10   THEODORE FREEMAN

Theodore Cordy Freeman, born February 18, 1930 in Haverford, Pennsylvania

Some kids muck stalls in exchange for horseback riding lessons. Freeman did the equivalent at his local airfield, doing grunt work in exchange for flying lessons, earning his pilot's license at age 16. Freeman had big plans to join the Navy and fly jets, but a freak blow to the jaw in a high school football game knocked his teeth out of alignment, which caused him to fail the Naval Academy physical.

Freeman underwent painful surgery to correct the problem, which involved grinding down his teeth and anchoring them with heavy braces. His teeth slowly straightened to Navy standards and in 1953, he was accepted to the academy. Freeman earned a bachelor's degree in science at the Naval Academy, then graduated with his master's in aeronautical engineering from U-M in 1960, all while flying as a test pilot and rising in the military ranks.

Freeman was part of NASA Group 3[84] in 1963. He'd finally made it. Sadly, just one year into his NASA training, he was returning to base after a practice flight when his jet hit a goose midair. The jet crashed, killing him.[85] He was buried with full honors at Arlington National Cemetery.

---

84   Group 3 was nicknamed The Fourteen and, tragically, four of them would die before they could fly to space.

85   The first two NASA men at the scene of the crash were fellow astronauts Jim Lovell and Pete Conrad. They'd been out goose hunting near the air base when they saw a crowd gathered around a smoking crash site. They recovered some of the surviving instruments and estimated the location of the mid-air collision. When they arrived at where they suspected the mid-air collision occurred, they found two things. The smashed plexiglass windshield of the jet and a very dead Canada goose.

#9   KARL HENIZE

Karl Gordon Henize, born October 17, 1926 in Cincinnati, Ohio

Henize served as the observer for the University of Michigan Observatory from 1948 to 1951 and earned his Ph.D. in astronomy from U-M in 1954.[86]

NASA selected him as a scientist-astronaut in 1967[87] and he served on support crews and in simulations for nearly 20 years until he got his first shot at space travel in 1985—right before his 50th birthday. Henize blasted off aboard the Space Shuttle Challenger as part of the Spacelab-2 mission, conducting a range of experiments. After 126 orbits of the Earth, he returned with 188 space hours under his belt.

Henize later accepted a position as senior scientist in the NASA Space Sciences branch, where he continued studying humans and space travel. In 1993, at the age of 66, he climbed Mount Everest to test a NASA device measuring how the body reacts to radiation at extreme elevations. By the time he reached Advanced Base Camp, about 21,000 feet up the mountain, he was struggling to breathe. His lungs filled with fluid due to high altitude pulmonary edema and help arrived too late. He died on the side of the mountain.

#8   ANTHONY ENGLAND

Anthony Wayne England, born May 15, 1942 in Indianapolis, Indiana

England was born in Indiana but grew up in Fargo, North Dakota. He earned three degrees from Massachusetts Institute of Technology in Earth and Planetary Sciences and was made a scientist astronaut in 1967 at just 25 years old—the youngest recruit at the time. England was on support crews for Apollo 13 and 16 but got tired of sitting on the bench and left for the U.S. Geological Survey in 1972. NASA lured him back to Johnson Space Center in 1979 and finally sent him into space with our pal Karl Henize on the Skylab-2 mission.

---

86   He worked in several observatories around the world, including South Africa, Australia and the Smithsonian Astrophysical Observatory in Cambridge, Massachusetts, primarily focused on astronomy and solar physics.

87   NASA Group 6 - The Excess Eleven. Love these names!

His Ann Arbor connection? England served as associate dean for academic affairs in the College of Engineering at U-M and as of 2017 is the Dean of the College of Engineering and Computer Science at the U-M Dearborn.

#7   A PICTURE OF ED WHITE

Edward H. White II, born November 14, 1930 in San Antonio, Texas

The story of the Voyager Golden Records is amazing. NASA contracted with astronomer Carl Sagan in the 1970s to create golden records which would be affixed to the Voyager 1 and Voyager 2 space probes. Both probes were shot into space on predetermined paths to planets and their moons, but should alien life forms ever encounter or recover the probes, it was thought that including a message from humanity would be a good idea.

Sagan assembled a committee to create a collection that included various sounds from nature, musical selections from different eras and cultures, spoken greetings in 59 languages and 115 images.[88] Some of the images were scientific in nature—mathematical definitions and diagrams of human anatomy—but a good portion were photos of humans doing human things. The activities portrayed included eating, looking through microscopes, breastfeeding and walking in space.

The space walker in the photograph was Ed White, a 1959 U-M graduate and the first man to walk in space. He's the only truly identifiable person included on the golden records, and his image is currently hurtling through space well beyond Pluto. This image of this amazing man has been traveling farther and farther away from Earth for the last 40 years, waiting to be seen by aliens unknown.

The two Voyager spacecraft have enough power to operate their scientific instruments through 2020. By 2025, we'll likely lose communication with them as they drift through interstellar space. But they'll still be carrying that handsome picture of Ed White—and a recording of Johnny B. Goode.

---

88   The United States' musical contributions included Navajo chanting, some gospel, blues and "Johnny B. Goode".

#6   JAMES A. MCDIVITT

James Alton McDivitt, born June 10, 1929 in Chicago, Illinois

McDivitt attended high school in Kalamazoo and went to college at Jackson Junior College[89], then joined the Air Force, flew 145 combat missions in the Korean War, and returned to school in 1957 to finish first in his aeronautical engineering class at the U-M in 1959.

McDivitt became a test pilot and in 1962 NASA made him an astronaut,[90] putting him in command of his very first flight, Gemini 4.[91] Along with co-pilot Edward White (whose picture you're well acquainted with), the crew spent four days in space in 1965. While White made humankind's first spacewalk, McDivitt was the photographer for the image immortalized in golden record form.

McDivitt blasted back into space on Apollo 9 in 1969 and commanded a 10-day mission in which the Lunar Module was first used. He rose in the ranks at NASA, and was eventually offered the position of Shuttle Director, which he turned down to go into the private sector.

He's in the U.S. Astronaut Hall of Fame, the National Aviation Hall of Fame, and even appeared as himself on the frickin' Brady Bunch.[92] He also picked up an honorary Doctorate in Aeronautical Science from the U-M in 1965.

Not enough? How about named places. At the intersection of South and East University on U-M's campus is McDivitt-White Plaza, right near the Engineering Arch. Guess who that's co-named for?

McDivitt also has a conference room named after him at the U-M aerospace building. For the record, it seats 40 and has a 65-inch TV with HDMI hookups.

---

89   Now Jackson College.

90   Part of NASA Group 2 known as The Nifty Nine.

91   Another first: McDivitt was the first Roman Catholic to fly into space.

92   In the episode, called Out of This World, Peter and Bobby think they see a UFO, which is actually a hoax being played by Greg. The trick backfires when Peter and Bobby take pictures, which leads to a government investigation involving James McDivitt, playing himself.

#5   JACK R. LOUSMA

Jack Robert Lousma, born February 29, 1936 in Grand Rapids, Michigan

This member of our countdown grew up right here in Ann Arbor. He attended Angell Elementary, Tappan Middle School, and graduated from Ann Arbor High in 1954. Like a good Ann Arbor kid, he went to U-M, earning a B.S. in aeronautical engineering in 1959, then joined the Marine Corps.

Lousma became a NASA astronaut in 1966[93], supporting three Apollo missions, including the famous Apollo 13 flight. During that mission, Lousma was the person at Mission Control who received the famous, "Houston, we have a problem," message.

His own first trip to space was a doozy—a 59 and-a-half day mission on Skylab-3 where he served as pilot on the three-man crew. They made 858 revolutions of the Earth before splashing down in the Pacific.

Lousma returned to space a second time in 1982 as commander of STS-3, the third orbital test flight of the Space Shuttle Columbia. He spent another eight days in space before returning safely.

What do you do with the rest of your life after spending more than two months in space? Well, first you accept your honorary doctorate from U-M, and then you run for office! Mayor? Heck, no! Congressman? As if!

Lousma ran for U.S. Senate in 1984 against Democratic incumbent Carl Levin. He lost but received a respectable 47% of the vote, blaming the defeat on a recording that surfaced right before the election in which he told Japanese auto workers that his family owned a Toyota. The tape didn't play well in Detroit.

Lousma entered the private sector and, after 52 Michigan winters, moved his family to sunny Texas. He too is in the U.S. Astronaut Hall of Fame.

#2   THE APOLLO 15 CREW (THREE-WAY TIE)

James Benson Irwin, born March 17, 1930 in Pittsburgh, Pennsylvania

David Randolph Scott, born June 6, 1932 in San Antonio, Texas

---

93   Part of NASA Group 5, one of the largest classes with 19 astronauts.

Alfred Merrill Worden, born February 7, 1932 in Jackson, Michigan

This is the famous all-U-M Apollo flight, so let's establish those Ann Arbor credentials right up front. Irwin and Worden earned their Master's degrees from U-M in 1957 and 1963 respectively, adding honorary doctorates in 1971 after— spoiler alert— they blasted into space and were the first to drive the frickin' Lunar Roving Vehicle on the surface of the moon. Scott attended U-M for one year, studying engineering and joining the swim team, but left for West Point and didn't earn a U-M degree until that sweet honorary doctorate came his way in 1971.

Scott was called up to NASA as part of Group 3 in 1963, while Irwin and Worden joined with NASA Group 5 in 1966. The old dog of the group, Scott went up in Gemini 8 and Apollo 9 before getting the call to command Apollo 15. The mission was the last trip to space for Scott and the only trip to space for Irwin and Worden—for reasons we'll get to later (that don't involve death).

During the mission, as Irwin and Scott did donuts on the surface of the moon in the rover, Worden orbited the rock, earning a Guinness World Record for being the most isolated human being ever. While on the dark side of the moon, Worden was 2,235 miles away from the closest human being. Meanwhile, on the surface, Irwin and Scott roared around in the rover for 18 hours.

The crew spent a little over three days up there, collecting samples and conducting experiments, and returned to Earth under a cloud of controversy and rumor.

First, there was the stamp incident. Without permission, the crew stashed 398 pre-stamped commemorative postcards in the module to sell as space souvenirs upon their return. Though NASA had turned a blind eye to this practice in previous missions, they decided to crack down on the crew of Apollo 15 and none of the astronauts ever flew to space again.

There were also some U-M related rumors about the flight. Is there a Block M flag on the moon? Probably not, though the crew did stash 20 miniature U-M flags in their gear with the intention of giving them out as gifts when they returned. There was also a rumor that Scott and Irwin dropped a document on the moon's surface establishing a U-M Alumni Association chapter.

Irwin retired right after the mission, forever changed by his experience on the moon. "I felt the power of God as I'd never felt it before," he said. Irwin spent the next 20 years as an ambassador of peace for Jesus, launching several expeditions to Mount Ararat in Turkey looking for Noah's Ark. Irwin's spirit was strong, but his health was failing. He suffered three serious heart attacks from 1973 to 1991, the last one fatal.

Scott stuck with NASA until 1977. In June 2017, he turned 85. Worden took some of the money from the sale of the space postcards and funded an unsuccessful bid for congress in Florida. He too turned 85 in February of 2017.

#1   EDWARD H. WHITE II

Edward H. White II, born November 14, 1930 in San Antonio, Texas

After White graduated from West Point in 1952, just a tenth of a second shy of earning a spot on the U.S. Olympic team in the 400-meter hurdles, he flew NATO jets in Germany for three years. In 1959, he came to Ann Arbor and picked up his Master's from U-M. Three years later, he was in NASA. Three years after, he flew into space on Gemini 4 with fellow alum McDivitt.

It was on that four-day mission that White popped the hatch on Gemini and floated in space for 20 minutes. McDivitt had to beg him to come back into the capsule.

"It's the saddest moment of my life," White said upon returning to the craft.

U-M conferred honorary doctorates on both astronauts upon their return to Earth, but White was the rising star, selected for the new Apollo program and chosen to be the senior pilot of Apollo 1 in a crew with experienced astronaut Gus Grissom and space-newbie Roger Chaffee.

The launch was scheduled for 1966 but was pushed back to early 1967 as the astronauts trained. During a simulated launch countdown procedure just a month before liftoff, a fire broke out in the cabin, killing all three men. The flaws that caused the fatal fire were located and fixed, allowing the Apollo program to safely complete 16 missions to space.

White was buried in West Point Cemetery and awarded the Congressional Space Medal of Honor. In addition to an exhaustingly long list of achievements, White's memory is further preserved by an impressive number of namesake locations. His name graces at least nine elementary, middle, and high schools throughout the country, along with a bunch of parks and streets, a library, a West Point dormitory, the aforementioned McDivitt-White plaza at U-M and an honest-to-goodness hill on the surface of Mars.

Edward White: The first man to walk in space. Part of the Nifty Nine NASA Group 2. 1959 U-M graduate, almost Olympian—a man with the rightest of right stuff.

NAZIS VS. EVERYBODY

Ann Arbor police spotted the Nazis and their rented U-Haul on the edge of town—two hours before they were expected to arrive. Members of the Nazi S.S. Action Group out of Westland—three squished cheek to cheek to cheek across the front bench seat and 12 more packed into the back, their butts, shields and jackboots bouncing after every pothole.

The Nazis issued a statement earlier in the week announcing their intention to rally at Ann Arbor City Hall at 1 pm on March 20, 1982. It was a rally to speak out against the growing threat of communism in the country and also to give Ann Arborites a white power sales pitch.

Two counter-demonstrations were planned as a response that day. There was a polite and respectful one organized by The Committee on the Affirmation of Human Dignity and Freedom, supported by the Jewish Community Council and the Interfaith Council for Peace. This rally about peace and acceptance and dignity was set to take place at 1 pm at the Federal Building on Liberty Street.

The other counter-demonstration had a slightly less turn-the-other-cheek vibe. It was organized by the vocal and less-bureaucratic-than-it-sounds Committee to Stop the Nazis. This group planned to demonstrate at noon at Ann Arbor City Hall and would include speeches and music to whip the crowd into a frenzy of force as the Nazis rolled into the city for their 1 pm demonstration.

The *Ann Arbor News* tried its best to soothe a predictably nervous populace, which feared an onslaught of Nazis goose-stepping down Huron Street—but the media also wanted to lessen the potential for massive riots. The *News* published several articles, with the prevailing sentiment captured in this headline: "Let Nazis march in splendid misery."

"Let the neo-nutsies march, let 'em holler and chant and let 'em make fools of themselves. They'll tire of it soon enough. When they don't draw a crowd or provoke a response, they'll quit. They'll go back to whatever rock they crawled out from."

From Captain America to Indiana Jones to present-day heroes walloping alt-right assholes, the United States has a long and proud history of punching Nazis in the face. The *News* had its work cut out for it preaching peace.

The Nazi U-Haul cruised past City Hall two hours earlier than expected, and one hour before the Committee to Stop the Nazis demonstration was scheduled to start. Still, a sizeable "Stop the Nazis" crowd was already gathered in front of City Hall, so the Nazi wheelman audibled, hung a left, and cruised past the Federal Building to scope out that location. Taking in the Federal Building's older, more manageable and docile-looking assembly, the Nazis parked nearby and changed their rally point on the fly.

One by one, 14 neo-Nazis climbed out of the U-Haul, stretched their legs in the parking lot of the Federal Building and smoothed their clothes. The driver stayed behind in the getaway vehicle. Most wore black uniforms tucked into scuffed jackboots. A few wore fatigues and sneakers—practical urban battle attire. They wore the visors on their black motorcycle helmets down, partially obscuring their baby faces beneath. Most were teenagers—a few reported to be as young as 15—but they looked intimidating. Some clutched shields fashioned out of old stop signs with giant white swastikas painted on black and gripped long black clubs. Some carried spray-painted signs on white poster board reading "Reds Get Out of Central America" and "Smash Red Treason."

When the Nazis rounded the corner, they surprised the hundred-odd people setting up for their peaceful 1 pm rally. The Nazis didn't waste much time. They gathered in front of the glassed-in lobby of the Federal Building and their spokesman took charge. He began a long and rambling speech about the evils of communism. His voice cut in and out thanks to the defective bullhorn pressed to his lips. His words bounced off the buildings across the street, and news of the Nazi arrival traveled quickly to the demonstrators awaiting them at City Hall. The Committee to Stop Nazis rally had just begun. One by one, then 10 by 10, then 50 by 50 and 100 by 100, the estimated crowd of 2,000 anti-Nazi demonstrators thundered the two blocks towards the Federal Building, arriving at speed.

The crowd swelled and packed in close, their voices drowning out the Nazi and his defective bullhorn. Chants of "go home" and "eat shit" rose in volume and fervor. Police were scattered amongst the crowd, pulling riot helmets over their ears and holding batons and shields of their own to protect the Nazis and control the crowd. The constabulary were vastly outnumbered.

Someone got the idea of throwing a snowball at the Nazis. Someone brought tomatoes. Those who forgot to pack projectiles picked up rocks. Some found bricks. The crowd let loose. The Nazis held up their shields, the sound of rocks and wet fruit mixed with the shouting, further drowning out the Nazi bullhorn. The barrage backed the Nazis up against the plate glass doors of the locked Federal Building. They were cornered and as the crowd advanced, skirmishes broke out on the edges. Clubs were swung and fists were thrown. Police tried to push through but the crowd was packed too tight.

It looked really bad for the Nazis, trapped between an angry crowd and a hard place, when someone from the crowd hurled a brick, missed, and shattered the plate glass door of the Federal Building. The Nazis now had an escape route.

Their natural instinct was to retreat into the now-accessible building, but that's when things got really scary. An armed guard inside the Federal Building stepped forward and leveled his weapon at the frantic Nazis, ordering them out of the building. The Nazis panicked, caught between a gun and 2,000 angry Ann Arborites.

Fortunately for them, the crowd also saw the weapon. Someone yelled "GUN!" and everyone within earshot reacted, ducking, diving and fleeing for cover. The police took advantage, and 45 cops rushed forward with batons and shields up to protect the hysterical Nazis and calm the shaken Federal Building employee.

Police formed a protective corridor and hustled the Nazis along the face of the building toward safety, their shields deflecting many of the missiles that the crowd once again starting tossing. They reached the parking lot where the U-Haul was parked—and it was gone. Federal Building guards had ordered the Nazi driver to move the vehicle 30 minutes earlier.

Police regrouped and formed a phalanx, hunkering down and radioing for a Washtenaw County Sheriff's Department bus, which arrived 10 very long and very tense minutes later. Heads down, the Nazis loaded in, pressing their shields against the bus' windows as yet more rocks and bricks broke the glass. They drove to Sheriff's Department headquarters on Hogback Road, where the Nazis were reunited with their U-Haul and escorted out of town.

The Nazi leader, Ted Dunn, blamed the near riot on Ann Arbor's communist element and reported that his men suffered nothing more than scrapes and bruises in the fracas.

"I didn't even get a chance to swat one of those Reds, even though I wanted to," Dunn said.

Dunn claimed the event was a success. He credited it with adding a new recruit to their ranks, one who was, "young, single and white."

Maybe we'll make this a yearly event, like Hash Bash or May Day, Dunn told reporters.

One Year Later. March 20, 1983.

The headline read: *"All Right, Ann Arbor, Let's Do It Right This Time."*

One year to the day of the Nazi rally, *Ann Arbor News* columnist Don Faber appealed to the city's fairer nature as the media tried once again to get Ann Arbor to ignore the incoming Nazi visitors.

"Let them holler and chant and make bloody fools of themselves," Faber wrote. "When they're tired of it and find they aren't drawing a response, they'll go back to whatever rock they crawled out from."

In anticipation of the Nazis' return visit, Ann Arbor police spent $27,000 on baton training and gas masks, and earmarked $14,535 for police overtime.

Many of the same 15 neo-Nazis who visited the year before arrived at the northeast edge of town around 11:30 am, carpooling this time in several vehicles and a battered, windowless rental truck. They'd announced plans for a noon rally at City Hall to celebrate, among other things, the 50th anniversary of Adolf Hitler's rise to power. Police cruisers met the Nazis at the edge of town and escorted them to the *Ann Arbor News* parking lot off Ann Street.

The Nazis, once again clad in black uniforms and fatigues, carrying shields and clubs and signs, headed to City Hall. They faced a crowd of hundreds of counter-demonstrators—who caught sight of them pretty soon after they got out of their vehicles and ran full speed at the Nazis, throwing rocks, batteries and baby jars full of ammonia. Police formed a protective shield and, just like the previous year, hustled the Nazis back to their vehicles and out of town.

The counter-demonstrators cheered in the streets. This time, the Nazis had boots on the ground for, at most, six minutes. Surely they would never come again.

Another Year Later. March 17, 1984.

Same black uniforms. Same fatigues. Same black helmets. Same long black clubs with grip tape on the handle. Same stop sign shields with big white swastikas on the face. This time the Nazis were two hours late. It wasn't their fault. They'd parked in Dearborn the previous night following a rally, and all four tires on their van were slashed and the motor damaged. Plus they had taken a wrong turn on the way over. But here they were at 3 pm in front of the good old Federal Building, where most of the protesters who'd gathered two hours earlier to meet them had already gone home.

An anti-Nazi crowd of 75 or so remained at the Federal Building when the Nazi S.S. Action Group arrived. Only 11 Nazis had made the trip this time. Their uniforms looked a lot shabbier than in past years. Spokesman John Reich launched into his lecture on the communist conspiracy.

Reich spoke for a minute or so before a man powered through a line of reporters, screaming "You're a goddamn killer," and tackled Reich to the ground. The rest, frenzied by the attack, jumped the 10 remaining Nazis as police tried to step between the groups. Batons and fists clashed again. A counter-demonstrator smashed Ann Arbor Police Detective Richard Anderson above the right eye, opening a nasty gash. Patrolman Craig Mason was hit in the head by something thrown from the crowd.

Police arrested the man who jumped Reich and four other demonstrators, while the Nazis huddled behind police for the third time in three years. Not knowing where the Nazi van was parked, police led the cowering crew to a Sheriff's Department bus nearby. The Nazis were hustled on board, and, in a cruel twist of logistics, the arrested counter-demonstrators were also led onto the bus.

An attorney on scene vehemently argued with police that the arrested protesters shouldn't be kept with the Nazis. After being warned that if he charged the police lines one final time, he'd be arrested, he did and he was.

Officers kept the groups separated on the bus until it arrived at Sheriff's headquarters on Hogback, where the protesters were led into the building and the Nazis escorted to their van.

The Nazis didn't come back a fourth time. Not formally, like they had each March before. Ted Dunn and John Reich and the rest of their fascist buddies didn't disappear, but they stopped thinking they could rally in Ann Arbor without consequences.

Captain America. Indiana Jones. And Ann Arbor. Upholding the proud American tradition of punching Nazis in the face.

Anti-Nazi Gathering. A crowd of counter-demonstrators gathers near the Federal Building on East Liberty Street on March 18, 1984. (Photo by Brian Peters, original by Robert Chase of the *Ann Arbor News*.)

Neo-Nazis Retreat. On March 18, 1984, 11 Nazis marched to the Federal Building on East Liberty Street to educate Ann Arbor about the communist conspiracy. They weren't welcomed with open arms. (Photo by Brian Peters, original by Robert Chase of the *Ann Arbor News*.)

Neo-Nazi Brawl. This was the scene on March 18, 1984 in front of the Federal Building on East Liberty Street moments after a counter-demonstrator (center, kicking the man on the ground) jumped on John Reich, a neo-Nazi who had been holding an impromptu press conference. At left, another neo-Nazi raises a club while in the center of the photo, City Police Detective Richard Anderson (leather jacket, beard) grimaces after being punched over the eye by a counter-demonstrator (head down). (Photo by Brian Peters, original by Robert Chase of the *Ann Arbor News*.)

IT'S LOVELY TO DIE TOGETHER

The two girls were peculiar, even for Ann Arbor in 1971. They looked like college kids with a hippie vibe to them. Nothing outwardly weird, but something definitely strange. They stood a few feet apart, face to face, on the corner of State and Liberty. Witnesses said they stared at the moon. Others said they just stared at each other. Stared for hours and hours that cold November night. Something about them wasn't right, so someone called the cops, who pulled up in a squad car and saw two girls staring at each other. Calm. Expressionless. Normal, but not normal.

The girls climbed willingly into the back seat and rode silently to police headquarters. Remained silent during lengthy questioning. They had identification—20-year-old Anita McQueen from Livonia and 26-year-old Raelle Weinstein from Skokie, Illinois. They seemed like a pair of typical hippie drifters passing through a college town.

The girls weren't on drugs. They weren't drunk. But they didn't speak.

Didn't say why they were in town. What they were doing on that street corner. Where they were staying.

The cops called the City Attorney and County Prosecutor requesting that the girls be committed to a mental institution for 48 hours of observation. The request was denied. The women appeared neither homicidal nor suicidal. They were forced to let them go—that was the rule. The girls were dropped off at the same street corner where they were picked up. The patrol car drove away. The girls wandered the streets, somehow ending up at an apartment at 517 South Division—the home of three University of Michigan co-eds.

No one's sure why the students let them in. Maybe it was cold. Maybe the co-eds were nice Michigan girls doing strangers a solid. But they let them in and allowed the strange girls to stay the night. But just one night, they told them. Then they'd have to leave. Out the door. That's it.

But when the next day came, the co-eds didn't have the guts to tell the strange pair to leave. They too sensed that something wasn't right. Something peculiar, even for Ann Arbor in 1971. Rather than kick the two girls out, the co-eds left and spent the night with friends in the building next door. Left the two girls alone. To stare at the moon. Or each other. Or do something far worse.

This isn't a happy story. There's no fun twist or witty "And then one of those girls grew up to be," trivia nugget to share later tonight. You should probably stop reading right here. This is where it goes really bad.

Around 4:30 am, early Wednesday morning, all alone in the apartment, Anita McQueen and Raelle Weinstein found two rolls of white wrapping paper. They went into the kitchen and sat cross-legged on the cold linoleum. They wrapped themselves from head to toe. Then they set themselves on fire.

They used no gasoline or accelerant. Only paper and clothing and hair and flesh. The flame must have taken coaxing to blaze into a proper fire, to pass from paper to clothing. To build to a pair of infernos that would scorch more than 30 percent of Raelle's body and 20 percent of Anita's. It must have been slow. It must have been excruciating.

The police got a call at 4:40 am reporting a fire at the apartment. A call presumably made from the co-eds in the next building. They saw flames. Heard women screaming. Smelled burning hair. Officers and firefighters rushed to the scene, kicked in the front door, and saw the two girls engulfed in flames, still sitting cross-legged across from each other. Screaming. Screaming, but making no effort to save themselves. Rescuers grabbed blankets off the sofa to smother the flames and used knives to quickly cut away the burned clothing which stuck to their flesh.

They were put on stretchers and hurried to the ambulance outside. Loaded in side by side. One of the girls—they were too badly burned for paramedics to know which one—reached out and touched her friend's hand.

"It's lovely to die together," she whispered.

The ambulance arrived at U-M Hospital and the girls were rushed to the burn unit.

"We wanted to die together," one of them said while nurses and doctors worked to save their lives. Police and fire officials found no evidence of drug use. No evidence of alcohol.

The girls remained in critical condition for a month. They didn't say much. At least nothing recorded. It's unlikely the girls saw each other.

With Christmas approaching, Raelle's condition worsened. Her kidneys failed and she went septic. On December 19, she died in her sleep. Anita remained in critical condition—there's no record of her state of mind, nor her thoughts on her dead friend.

Two months later, February 24, 1972, Anita's condition was upgraded to fair.

That's it. No redemption at the end. No explanation for why the girls did it. That's all we know about what happened to Anita up to February, 1972.

Some stories don't make a lot of sense. Some weeks are just more peculiar than others, even Ann Arbor in 1971. Creepier than creepy. Worse than bad.

THE BALLAD OF SHAKEY JAKE

In 1973, an accounts payable clerk at the University of Michigan named Fred Reif booked a musician named Jake Woods to play the Ann Arbor Blues and Jazz Festival.[94] Reif had spent time in Saginaw and was familiar with Woods—a popular street performer who dressed like a million bucks and played the blues (sort of) on his guitar all over the city.

On stage at the festival, in front of close to 10,000 people, Shakin' Jake (as he called himself) smiled for the crowd. Wearing a suit, bowtie, white scarf, and a straw hat on his head he leaned into the microphone:

"I'm gonna do my thing. I'm gonna do it my way. So here it is."

Shakin' Jake played a four-minute set. Musically, it was terrible. His

---

94 The festival was a big deal back then. B.B. King headlined the first Ann Arbor Blues Festival in 1969. When jazz was added to the festival in 1972, Ann Arbor welcomed performers including: Miles Davis, James Brown, Etta James, Count Basie, and Al Green.

guitar was out of tune, his strumming pretty random. You, dear reader, could have played better.

But his style, charisma, and gravelly-voiced lyrics won over the crowd. He played like drunks walk, and sang like a man who did a shot of hot sauce each morning, a shot of bleach each night, and smoked 1,000 cigarettes in between. The crowd cheered. Shakin' Jake doffed his hat and exited stage left.

Rumor has it ladies flocked to Shakin' Jake backstage, thinking he was a bona fide blues legend. He turned to someone and said, "I ain't never goin' back to Saginaw." And just like that, Ann Arbor became his new home.

For the next 34 years, the legend of Shakin' Jake—better known as Shakey Jake to the people of Ann Arbor—grew and grew and grew.

This ballad of Shakey Jake Woods is a story of fact, fiction, and outright lies. Shakey told so many tales to so many people that sometimes it's hard to tell the difference between reality and myth.

Take the story of his birth. Shakey Jake said he was born on Halloween night on River Street in Little Rock, Arkansas in the year 1900, which would have made him 73 years old when he stepped on stage at the Ann Arbor Blues and Jazz Festival. Not likely. Even less likely was his assertion that he was born a little person, but when the doctor left the room, he grew six inches.

He got his first guitar when he turned one—also the year he claimed to have started smoking. When he was two, he left Little Rock, hitchhiked to New Orleans, and hooked up with some of history's legendary bluesmen. He lived above what is now the Gold Mine Saloon on Dauphine Street. Played his guitar in bars. Made friends everywhere he went.

Shakey Jake traveled the world. 66 times to be exact. Every state, most cities. He hitchhiked everywhere, never riding on a plane to cross continents—only boats. He'd visited China. Hong Kong. Everywhere you can name. Always on the move. That was his catchphrase: "I'm on the move." He'd shout it to passersby when hustling from one Ann Arbor street corner to another, his guitar case bouncing wildly, looking like it would burst open any minute.

Shakey Jake always doing his thing. Always his way.

He found his way to Saginaw, playing his guitar on street corners, singing in a voice worn ragged with smoking. His guitar was always out of tune, sometimes strung with only three strings. Sometimes two. Occasionally one.

That didn't bother Shakey, who was supremely confident in his blues ability.

"Who ever had the ridiculous idea that blues needed 12 bars and three chords?" Jake asked. "Probably white people with guitars. Now you know better."

Not that Jake couldn't play the guitar—at least according to him. "There's 88 notes on a guitar. I know 'em all," Jake said.

He moved to Ann Arbor, sometimes couch-surfing, sometimes renting cheap apartments around town. Always up early, moving from one spot in town to another. Through rain, snow, sleet, and heat. Chasing the sun from South University through campus to State Street and on to William, Liberty, Main. He settled into a lot of regular haunts.

Shakey Jake always wore a suit. Big bowtie. Straw hat. Dark sunglasses. Had an array of moth-eaten coats (fake fur, sheepskin) a scarf around his neck, a carnation in his lapel. Rings on his fingers. A smile on his face. Fifteen invisible bodyguards always close by to protect him from the devil.

A streetsman. A bluesman. A raconteur. A philosopher, a poet and a preacher.[95] He slept just two hours a night.[96] Was never arrested.[97] Told people he knew the exact date of Judgment Day. Dispensed wisdom to young and old—but especially young—in need of it. Jake was always trying to save the next generation from danger, from sin, from the graveyard.[98]

One night in 1974, he streamed through the crowd at Hill Auditorium during a talk by gonzo journalist Hunter S. Thompson. Nattily dressed in a suit

---

95   "I can't read nothin', not even my name, but I make it work every day." - Shakey Jake

96   "Sleepin' is a waste of time. Never been sick a day in my life." - Shakey Jake

97   "I go by the older rules. The rules of 1909. Those were the days. There weren't no police stations, no city hall, no killins. Your mother and dad were the jury. The teachers took more time with the kids. So did the mothers." - Shakey Jake.

98   "You know what's wrong with the world? A lot of people forgot how to smile. They don't know how to enjoy life. I laugh at 'em when they get mad." - Shakey Jake

as always and with a guitar slung on his back, Jake clambered on stage—
Thompson took his hand and helped him up. Jake played an impromptu set for
the crowd, then Thompson helped him down from the stage and the event
resumed.

Shakey Jake was the unofficial mayor of Ann Arbor through the 1980s.
He once modeled for a class at U-M's Taubman School of Architecture. They
liked him so much that the school commissioned a life-size clay statue of Jake
and displayed it in a hallway.

Jake was the grand marshal of Michigan's 1984 homecoming parade.
He sat next to the homecoming queen and waved to the crowd packed along
the parade route.

When he wasn't strumming on corners and talking to the people, he
was working at the Ann Arbor Music Mart[99] or as a general handyman, fixing
TVs and refrigerators, running wire, that kind of thing. He shoveled snow,
raked leaves, sold copies of the Ann Arbor Sun and played his unique style of
the blues in bars all across town. Shakey Jake was always on the move.

Eventually his legend grew so big, they monetized it. Made t-shirts,
bumper stickers, postcards, cassette tapes, and CDs. Half of Ann Arbor had an
"I Brake for Jake" bumper sticker on their fender.

He got a little slower in the 1990s, but still stayed on the move. Took a
cab downtown each morning at 6 am. Grabbed breakfast at the Bagel Factory
on South University.[100] Or maybe his usual—oatmeal and wheat toast—at
Afternoon Delight.[101] Picked up his messages at Peaceable Kingdom. Checked
in at Lucky Drugs, Espresso Royale, Bimbo's, the Cloverleaf. Got his hair cut at
the State Street Barbershop. Had drinks at Old Town or the Del Rio or any of
the dozen or so places in town where bartenders or townies were willing to buy
a round for Ann Arbor's famous bluesman.

---

99   Wazoo Records now.

100   Inventors of Ann Arbor's famous Fragel.

101   "I like all kinds of foods. I don't have no favorites. Never had no special woman
either. I likes to be around the ladies, but I ain't never been married. Never had time." - Shakey
Jake

They'd ask him if it was true he wrote "Swing Low, Sweet Chariot." Or "Sweet Home Chicago." If he knew B.B. King back when he was just B.B. Prince. Or Miles Davis. All the greats of jazz and blues.

Ann Arbor was good to Shakey Jake. People pitched in to help him pay for his peddler's license, ponying up to help him afford city insurance to strum his guitar and dispense his wisdom from the street corner. The city embraced him from the very moment in 1973 when he climbed onstage and first opened his mouth.

"I've built a thing here," he said, in 1999. "I'm going to stay and I'm going to live forever. Ann Arbor is nothing but a playhouse for me."

He died on September 16, 2007. He was probably 82 years old. He claimed to be 107. His memorial service drew 500 people, who paraded through the streets of Ann Arbor visiting his favorite haunts, singing songs and playing instruments.

There will never be another Shakey Jake Woods, Ann Arbor's most famous bluesman who couldn't play a lick of music.

Then again, who ever said you need 12 bars and three chords to play the blues?

Shakey Jake Downtown. Shakey Jake Woods was an Ann Arbor institution from the day he took the stage at the 1973 Ann Arbor Blues and Jazz Festival. Here he poses downtown in 1990 with the snow-sculpting team at Winterfest. 'Hey, I'm gonna make you famous, you just wait and see!' Jake told the team when this photo was taken. Welcome to the book, Laura and Andy Adamson and Lesli Watson! (Photo by Richard Retyi, original by Colleen Fitzgerald of the *Ann Arbor News*).

Shakey Pinball. Shakey Jake spent a lot of time downtown and on South University, playing his guitar and singing on street corners, his voice ragged from smoking. Here he poses in front of the old Pinball Pete's on South University in October of 1998. (Photo by Brian Peters, original by Leisa Thompson of the *Ann Arbor News*).

THE GIRLS IN THE BAND

"And now, ladies and gentlemen…the marching men of Michigan!" Back in the day, that was the standard intro that boomed from public address systems as the University of Michigan Marching Band took the field, Drums booming, horns blowing, piccolos piccolo-ing. The Michigan Marching Band gave its first public performance in 1897 and stepped onto the football field for the first time in 1898. You've probably heard of them.

The band named its first official drum major in 1914. He was a military school graduate and saxophone player from Portland, Oregon named George Olsen. Olsen had experience leading drum and bugle bands, and used those skills to drill the Michigan Marching Band daily, turning them into a well-oiled machine. When Olsen led the band onto Ferry Field for the first game of the 1914 season, the crowd went wild. Who was this man leading the band, dressed differently than the rest, twirling a giant baton? Caught up in the excitement of it all, Olsen tossed that baton over the crossbar of the field goal uprights and caught it in stride, inventing a new marching band tradition.

Olsen, and every drum major since, has been tasked with leading the band in practice and on the field. Through verbal cues, hand gestures, and a handy whistle, the drum major works with the band director to keep the group's rhythm and timing, ensuring things are structured and organized.

Over the years, drum majors have added more traditions alongside the baton toss, like high stepping through the formation, and the back bend at the beginning of the pre-game performance. This backbend is when the drum major plants their feet on the 20 yard line, leans back, and touches the turf with the big maize feather affixed to the top of their puffy white drum major hat. The real showoffs remove the hat, tuck it under their arm and touch the turf with their bare heads.

Drum major is a physical job. A high-profile job.

Clearly, a job for a man.

Women had no place in the Michigan Marching Band until 1972, not even during World War II, when it was slim pickings when it came to male euphonium players. By the late 1960s, the all-male status of the band was even a badge of honor among some. But times change. On campus, women were, shockingly, asking for equal rights. The dean of the Music Department dropped the all-male status of the band in 1971, but no one really found out about the change until tryouts were over. It would be a year before the first Michigan women would have a chance to make the squad.

Band director George Cavender didn't think women could handle the strenuous physical effort required of Michigan Marching Band members. It was too demanding. A more vigorous activity than would be proper for a lady. Women couldn't be expected to be excused from rehearsals if they had "female problems." Girls should be interested in dolls and Girl Scouts and other activities. Why bother with the rough and rugged world of college marching bands?

Women on campus thought otherwise and made a big push to try out for the band in the summer of 1972. Many auditioned. Ten made the final cut.

They fought through the intense heat of summer practices just like the men in the band, and none quit. By the opening game on September 16, more than 70,000 fans in Michigan Stadium saw the first women in the history of the Michigan Marching Band take the field.

Cavender wasn't happy having women in the band and expressed his displeasure with a special halftime performance. The band opened with "There is Nothing Like a Dame" from *South Pacific*—a song that includes the lines:

"There ain't a thing that's wrong with any man here … That can't be cured by putting him near … A girly, womanly, female, feminine dame!"

Then the halftime performance got less subtle. The band struck up "The Stripper"—yep, that song—and the band formed the shape of a woman wearing a skirt while the stadium announcer hooted to the crowd, "All those in favor of raising the 1972 skirt length higher, say 'aye!'"

The crowd yelled "aye!" The band called back, "HIGHER," and slowly, slowly the bandmembers, including those 10 brave women, shifted formation, making the skirt rise higher and higher. The stadium announcer broke in, in falsetto:

"Wait just a minute! There'll be no exploitation of sex on the football field. Let's lower that skirt, boys."

Classic Cavender humor, one of the female clarinet players said afterward.

The ten women stuck it out. Even more women tried out the next year. Thirty-eight were accepted. More the next year. And the next. Until women joining the band was no longer something to remark on.

The fight isn't over. Women are still vying for equal footing on two fronts. In more than 100 years, a woman has never held the position of director of the Michigan Marching Band.

The next highest profile position, drum major, has only twice been filled by a woman. The trailblazer was Greenville, Michigan-native Karen England, who served as drum major in 2001. She had one chance to lead the team onto the field before the 9/11 attacks. Her second time at the head of the band was during an emotional September 22 pre-game performance. When England touched the turf with her hat during the backbend, you could hardly hear the band over the roar of the crowd.

Fifteen years later, Ann Arbor saw the second woman ever to wear the distinctive drum major shako[102] with the proud maize plume. In 2016, McKenna Thayer of Hillsdale, Michigan led the band onto the field. The physicality wasn't a problem. Thayer played volleyball, ran track, and spent three years as drum major for her high school marching band. As part of the Michigan Marching Band, where band members compete weekly to see who gets to play on the field, she marched in every game her sophomore and junior years, playing alto sax.

She auditioned twice for the role of drum major, earning it her senior year. The *Ann Arbor News* interviewed Thayer before her big debut and she downplayed the significance of being only the second female drum major in Michigan Marching Band history. Her actions spoke louder than words.

When she led the band out of the tunnel and onto the field for the opener against Hawaii, Thayer executed her baton toss flawlessly, kicked the clouds with her high step, and, at the end of the M Fanfare, nailed her back bend on the 20 yard line—removing her big white hat, tucking it under her arm, and touching the turf with her head like a true showoff.

Take that, Cavender.

---

102   My editor, some kind of band and word purist, requested I use the proper term for this headgear, instead of my preference, "weird giant awkward showoff hat". Happy, Sara?

SANTA'S #1 HELPER

Everyone knows Santa lives at the North Pole. There, the big man and Mrs. Claus reside year-round, surrounded by an army of elves and a herd of immortal reindeer. What's less clear is where Santa's Helpers live. Those mall Santas, those sidewalk Santas, those SantaCon winter drunks dressed in road-salt-and-barbecue-sauce-stained Santa suits, leaning against telephone poles or vomiting gin behind alley dumpsters. There are always a few bad apples in the bushel—but most of Santa's Helpers are great people. As it turns out, Ann Arbor had one of the best.

Ann Arbor's Santa's Helper was so good that four U.S. presidents praised his work. So did governors, senators, congressmen—essentially any elected official looking to shake hands and smile into a camera around Christmastime. Our Santa's Helper was once presented the key to the city of Ann Arbor. Then the key to the city of Detroit. Then he was honored with the key to Washington, D.C. I told you! He was a big deal. Newspapers, magazines,

TV—he received media coverage coast to coast, including a two-page spread in Life Magazine in 1956.[103]

His name was Albert F. Warnhoff. He lived at 1315 Franklin Boulevard in the Fourth Ward on Ann Arbor's south side, just a quick sleigh ride from Pioneer High School. It was there in his basement workshop that Warnhoff toiled most nights and weekends, making toys for sick and handicapped kids in Ann Arbor and the surrounding communities.

We're not talking a few dozen toys, or even a few hundred. Over 58 years, Warnhoff built more than 41,000 toys by hand, all in the name of old Saint Nick—hand-delivering them to children all over the state.

But why?

Ann Arbor's Santa's Helper has a murky origin story. Warnhoff was born March 5, 1890, in the Netherlands and moved to Ann Arbor when he was one. By all accounts, he was a nice kid, good at working with his hands. When Warnhoff was somewhere between 12 and 14 years old—accounts vary—the plight of a curly-haired little five-year-old neighborhood girl got his attention.

She was sick with diptheria—a nasty affliction that causes severe sore throat, fever, a terrible barking cough, and, in some cases, can affect the heart, nerves, and kidneys. Even today, the fatality rate for the disease can be as high as 20% for children 5 years and under.

Things didn't look good for the little curly-haired girl, and Warnhoff wanted to do something. His dad suggested he buy her a doll. Or he could make her one. Come on, Albert! You're pretty handy. So that's what the young man did. This was the first of more than 41,000 toys Warnhoff would make in his life, and the experience changed him forever. The little girl's appreciation bowled him over, as did a doctor's assertion that around the same time she received the gift, the sick little girl began her road to full recovery.

From that moment on, Warnhoff started making toys for sick kids. He

---

103   The cover story that week was the seven sacraments, with a photo of a baby being baptized on the cover. Journalism has changed a smidge since 1956.

made a handful in time for Christmas that very year. And the Christmas after that, and the Christmas after that.

Decades passed and Warnhoff continued toiling in his little workshop in relative obscurity. He made the toys by hand and personally delivered them to ailing children. It was just a few dozen at first, which he made on Sundays, his only day off from his $3-a-week job at the Fingerle Lumber Company. For every year Warnhoff worked at Fingerle, the pay got better and the hours kinder. That meant that every year, he could expand his Santa operation a little more.

It's unclear if Warnhoff's wife, Ethel Swarthout Lohrke, knew what she was getting into when she married him on August 18, 1937. Her husband's hobby must have been mildly annoying in the early days—since he spent most nights and weekends leading up to Christmas in the workshop, cranking out toys. I say "mildly annoying" because these were the early years, before Ann Arbor really knew who Warnhoff was.

His secret was revealed on December 2, 1939. The *Ann Arbor News* published an article headlined "A Christmas Story for Children." They profiled Warnhoff, with a photo of him working in his tiny basement workshop.[104] The 49-year-old Warnhoff had, just that year, made more than 60 toys, which he planned to deliver to sick kids at U-M's University Hospital.

"Although Mr. Warnhoff has managed to keep his name out of the newspaper, he isn't going to get away with it this year," the story read.

The media coverage lit a fire under Warnhoff. Production increased. Like, a lot.

Four years later, in 1943, The *Ann Arbor News* checked in on Warnhoff again, this time at 722 Packard Street. He was putting the finishing touches on 376 toys for little girls and boys. The country was at war and raw materials were scarce, but Warnhoff's work was so well known that he was given special treatment. This included supplementary gas rations so he could make the drive

---

104   That year, Albert's workshop was in the basement of his home at 311 1/2 South Fifth Ave, where Earthen Jar is located in 2017.

to Ypsilanti that Christmas to deliver toys to kids at the Rackham School of Special Education.

It was around this time that Warnhoff and his family moved to 1315 Franklin Boulevard in the Fourth Ward on the South Side, where he really got down to work. He went from making hundreds of toys to producing thousands. He built rocking horses, intricate wooden models of churches and schools, pull-toy ducks with big wooden wheels, crank-operated windmills, and endless amounts of doll furniture. Warnhoff had a system. He mass-produced a single kind of toy until he hit a self-imposed quota. Then he switched to another toy model. This focus on efficiency allowed him to turn out an average of 1,500 toys a year over the next decade.

Even Santa's Helper needs some help. The public donated many of the tools needed to run his Santa's Helper workshop: power saws, band saws, a jigsaw, a drill press, mechanical dust collectors, and swivel chairs, which he went through every few Christmases.

Supportive citizens delivered raw materials to 1315 Franklin Boulevard year round. Girl Scout troops and women's clubs sewed everything from blankets to doll clothes to accompany Warnhoff's creations. Soon Santa's Helper's workshop was a year-round endeavour. The toys didn't all fit in the workshop, so he packed them in Chef Boyardee and cake mix boxes and piled them five feet high in his living room, hallways, the bedroom.

Warnhoff claimed the basement looked lonely when it wasn't stacked with toys, so he made sure the work never stopped.

Mrs. Warnhoff was supportive of her husband's calling, despite the workshop taking up most of her husband's free time and most of her liveable space. But Warnhoff wasn't a young man anymore. He was in his late 50s following World War II and began to talk about finding a replacement.

By 1950, he was still making 1,000 toys a year, but at age 60, his health began to fail. Warnhoff suffered a series of heart attacks over the next few years and in 1955, at the age of 65, something had to give. He retired from Fingerle

Lumber. Warnhoff's wife got sick, and he spent more time taking care of her. His agility in the workshop began to diminish as well, leading to a few serious accidents, including one involving an electric saw and his thumb.

Though his days at Fingerle were over, Warnhoff still got out of the house five days a week, working as a crossing guard at Seventh and Pauline, guiding schoolchildren across the street. It still gave him plenty of time to make his toys.

In 1956, at the age of 66, Warnhoff produced 1,800 toys. That was the year he was featured in *LIFE* magazine—photos spread across two pages—one in his workshop, one with Warnhoff next to smiling kids, one sharing a moment with his wife in their breakfast nook, another lugging a giant sack of toys up the steps of a Lansing school.

Each time he was profiled, Warnhoff mentioned the search for that successor. Probably everyone knew he never intended to slow down, never mind retire as Santa's Helper. In 1960, Warnhoff set a personal record, topping 2,000 toys. At age 70, he was still loading sacks into the trunk of his car and hauling them up the steps of area hospitals, just to see the smiles on all those faces and maybe set them on the road to recovery.

Albert Warnhoff died on August 15, 1962, at age 72. The community rallied to help out in those final years, raising thousands of dollars for medical bills. With Albert and Ethel living in assisted care in 1961, the Kiwanis Club of Ann Arbor Eastern jumped in to carry on his work that Christmas, dubbing it Project Warnhoff.[105]

But it just wasn't the same.

---

105   An elevator fire around Thanksgiving of 1962, just weeks before Christmas, destroyed many of the toys built by Project Warnhoff. The community helped clean and refurbish toys damaged by water and smoke, while members of the Elk's Club 325 and Western Kiwanis Club donated toys they had gathered for separate Christmas projects.

Albert and Ethel Warnhoff are buried together in Fairview Cemetery. Their three children gave the Warnhoffs at least 13 grandkids, but his work touched the lives of countless children in Ann Arbor and Southeast Michigan.

Albert Warnhoff was definitely one of Santa's Helpers, and one of the good ones. Maybe even the best.

Albert Warnoff. Albert Warnhoff wasn't just Santa's No. 1 helper, in 1955, he also served as a public school policeman (crossing guard), helping kids cross the street at Seventh Street and Pauline Boulevard. (Photo by Brian Peters, original courtesy of the *Ann Arbor News*)

THE METEORITE HEIST

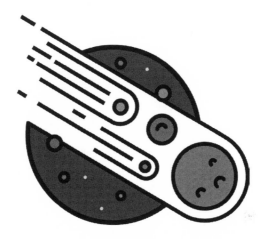

There haven't been a lot of heists in Ann Arbor's history. A few bank robberies, hold-ups, and sure, thousands of stolen hearts[106], but true and proper heists? Only one.

Our story begins 50,000 years ago—not in Ann Arbor but in what would eventually be known as Arizona. The United States didn't exist. Ann Arbor didn't exist. Pretty much nothing existed. If a meteorite falls in present-day Arizona in the Paleolithic Age and only a woolly mammoth and a giant sloth are there to hear it, does it make a sound?

The answer is probably. Probably a very loud sound.

That's what happened. 50,000 years ago and halfway across the continent, a giant asteroid fell from space. Half of it burned up on the descent. The rest—about 300,000 tons, traveling 30,000 miles per hour—hit the earth

---

106   See Tom Brady, University of Michigan (1996-2000)

with the force of 500 atomic bombs. Most of the asteroid vaporized on impact, creating a hole almost a mile wide and 50 stories deep. Space rock fragments were blown up to five miles away from the impact site.

Native Americans considered the crater cursed and avoided it. European settlers documented its location sometime in the 1800s and in 1853, an engineer surveying the site named it "Diablo Canyon Crater." By 1905, meteorite fragments from the crater were being shipped and sold throughout the world.[107]

These weren't the first space rocks sold in the U.S., but the Diablo Canyon Crater and its meteorites were special. The crater had that reputation for being cursed and the meteorites taken from it cursed as well. For some reason, people pay money for cursed things from space.

Nobody's sure when or how one of the meteorites from the Diablo Canyon Crater ended up at the University of Michigan Museum of Natural History. The meteorite had been there so long no one remembered when it first arrived. It was just...there.

I imagine it arrived by truck and a few burly men wearing sensible shoes were called to help. They placed the big wooden crate full of straw on the ground and someone fetched a crowbar to pry it open. They took the space rock out of its box and someone decided to put it on the fourth floor, behind glass, held up by a thick metal wire to make it easier for patrons to see.[108] You can imagine the crowds that gathered those first few months to catch a glimpse of the new exhibit. The cursed rock from outer space.

The meteorite was on permanent display for as long as anyone could remember, the glass case growing slightly more opaque with age, the wire gathering dust, teeny tiny spiders spinning teeny tiny webs. People took the meteorite for granted. Then one steamy night in August 1998, it vanished. It

---

107   The largest meteorite recovered was called the Holsinger Meteorite and weighed 1,400 pounds. Most of the meteorite fragments were much smaller. It's estimated that 30 tons of specimens were recovered around the crater, not counting the estimated 8,000 tons of fine-grain iron ore in and around the crater.

108   It doesn't look like you might expect. It isn't round like an asteroid or even semi-oval, really. It's jagged. Smaller than you'd expect—more like half a jawbone of a medium sized rhino than a rock from outer space.

wasn't removed for cleaning or to make way for a newer, cooler space rock. It vanished in a rare proper heist.

No signs of forced entry. No fingerprints. No witnesses. The wire securing the meteorite was neatly snipped and the meteorite was gone. Zero clues. The museum wouldn't have a surveillance system for years, so there wasn't security tape to review. The heist was a near impossible case for Detective Kevin McNulty of the U-M Department of Public Safety to pursue.

You don't hang "Lost Meteorite" posters around the neighborhood when your cursed space rock goes missing. McNulty and an employee at the museum did the next best thing—they put a missing meteorite post on the internet, which was still a pretty new thing at the time. Miraculously, they got a reply.

Since meteorites were first bought, sold, and displayed, there's been a thriving black market for space rocks. People pay hundreds of dollars for small chunks of extraterrestrial ore—even if they're stolen. Meteorites are a rare commodity and new ones are nearly impossible to find, so specimens as small as a pound fetch thousands of dollars.

A rock dealer in Cayuga, New York, saw the missing meteorite post on the web. In fact, he saw the actual Diablo Canyon meteorite. It was sitting right in his living room. The man bought it just the other day from someone claiming to be from Michigan. The rock dealer contacted Detective McNulty with the name, address, and phone number of the meteorite seller and the detective drove to the address just outside Ann Arbor and knocked on the door. What are the odds that the person who sold a stolen meteorite would be dumb enough to give their real name, address, and phone number to the buyer?

Steven Collins—a man dumb enough to give his real name, address and phone number. Steven Collins wasn't a good liar. He answered the door (probably in a stained bathrobe) and admitted to Detective McNulty that he traded the meteorite to the rock dealer in New York State. Traded it for $100, a prehistoric crab fossil, and a 250-pound slab of amethyst. Collins denied stealing the meteorite from the museum, first telling police that he bought it from a man he met in prison.

Then, he changed his story and said he met a man in a bar who had similar interests in rocks and fossils. After a few drinks, that man invited Collins to his car, where he popped the trunk and showed him a meteorite he just happened to have.

No one but Collins really knew the truth. If he did steal the meteorite, he was a much better thief than seller of stolen goods. The authorities had no hard evidence that Collins had stolen the meteorite, but they did have plenty of evidence that he left the state of Michigan with stolen goods. Poor, dumb Steven Collins had one month of parole left when he crossed the border and drove to New York. One condition of his parole was to remain in the state. Collins was incarcerated in state prison in Jackson for violating parole and charged with interstate transportation of stolen property and selling stolen goods across state lines—good for a nine-month stint.

Collins was never charged with stealing the actual meteorite. Police lacked proof and Collins wouldn't admit to the heist. Detective McNulty took the cash, the prehistoric crab fossil, and the 250-pound rock Collins had and drove seven hours to Cayuga, New York, to recover the meteorite. He spent the night in Cayuga, maybe watching bad TV in a roadside motel and keeping all his receipts, then drove back to Ann Arbor with the precious rock from space.

It didn't return to public display right away, but when it did, the meteorite was briefly popular again—until it was passed over for newer, cooler rocks. Then they just said screw it, removed the case, and mounted it in the open for all to see and touch, letting a whole new generation of cursed space rock fans run their grubby paws over a piece of Ann Arbor history.

THE EMBASSY HOTEL

It was a hot June day in 1988 inside the ground floor manager's office of the 105-year-old Embassy Hotel. The hotel manager, his wife, and their two children knelt on the carpeted floor and, one by one, pressed their foreheads to the feet of the man sitting in the manager's chair. This man was dressed all in white—flowing robe and pristine turban. His eyebrows were thick, his eyes dark and his beard full. This was His Holiness, Baba Hardev Singh Ji, considered by the millions of followers of Sant Nirankari to be God's prophet.[109]

His Holiness had come at the behest of the hotel manager, who was having a spiritual and life crisis. The hotel manager begged the prophet for help, and here he was. His Holiness toured the building, visited some of the rooms and then blessed the Embassy Hotel, telling the manager that this was where

---

109   Major thanks to Ami Walsh, who is responsible for a lot of the source material for this story. She wrote about Baba Hardev Singh Ji's visit in the Ann Arbor Observer in 1990 and refers to him as Lord Master—though I could only find one use of that term vs. many more calling him His Holiness.

the man and his family were to complete his life's mission.

If you haven't seen the Embassy, I can tell you it's no special wonder. The exterior is covered in dull grey siding, the signage is old, and its clientele wouldn't be welcomed with open arms at many other establishments in Ann Arbor.

What made the Embassy worthy of a visit from His Holiness?

You can see the building that houses the Embassy Hotel on a map of Ann Arbor from 1853—at 200 East Huron Street, right on the corner of South Fourth Avenue. The Slawson & Geer grocery store occupied the ground floor, while the second and third floors served as apartments back then.

In 1910 the building was sold to a man named Caspar Rinsey, who changed the name of the grocery store but little else. Two years later, Rinsey turned the two floors of apartments into hotel rooms, calling it the Central Hotel. It didn't go well. The hotel closed just a year later and the rooms were leased as apartments again.

In 1928, right before the Great Depression, Greek immigrants Charles and Peter Kokkales rented the building from the Rinseys and once again tried the hotel concept—opening the 21-room Huron Hotel. They converted the ground floor into a restaurant, and then—at the end of Prohibition—served alcohol as well and called it the Huron Hotel & Cafe. The hotel and bar started out as a classy Ann Arbor destination, doing decent business despite the tough economic times. But as the Great Depression dragged on and on, fewer guests came to town, room rates had to be lowered, and a very different clientele took over.

The Depression hit Ann Arbor hard in the 1930s. The Kokkales family lost their home and moved into a room on the second floor of the hotel to keep their heads above water. The whole family now worked at the hotel to cut costs—cooking in the kitchen, serving in the bar, cleaning rooms and splitting shifts at the front desk 24 hours a day.

The Kokkales family never despaired, welcoming guests with open arms and offering a room or a bite to eat to those who were the most down on their luck. Colloquially, the hotel was known as Charley's Place, after the family scion Charles Kokkales. If you were passing through Ann Arbor and needed a friendly face, Charley's was where you went. The family made it through the Depression and World War II, but the Huron Hotel & Cafe never regained its former glory. The Kokkales family closed the business in 1951.

The Compass Hotel Company leased the building and renamed the hotel the Embassy, trying to class the place up again. They paid to cover the battered brick exterior with fancy-at-the-time vertical Kaiser aluminum siding, and turned the restaurant and bar into offices.

The attempt to bring the corner back to its pre-Depression splendor never took. The hotel mainly housed itinerant workers and lower class folks passing through town. Later, it would put a roof over the head of a number of Ann Arbor's homeless population—becoming one of the few places in town to accept shelter vouchers.

Partway through the Compass lease in 1957, the Rinsey family sold the building to real estate speculators Wendell and Ruth Hobbs. The Hobbses had plans to redevelop the property—that part of town was already heavy with hotels. The Allenel hotel was directly across the street and the St. James was a block over at Huron and Main. But as the other hotels were leveled and replaced, the Embassy remained untouched.[110]

The Embassy ran as usual on the top two floors, while ground floor offices were rented out to a number of tenants, including congressman Marvin Esch. When Esch closed his office in the late 70s, the Embassy expanded to the ground floor to ease its chronic overbooking problem, adding four guest rooms, a new office and a larger apartment for the hotel manager.

The Embassy Hotel was smack dab in the heart of Ann Arbor's red light district in the 1970s and a popular hourly retreat for prostitutes who plied their trade right on the street next to Fourth Avenue's adult bookstores and

110   The Allenel, named in honor of town founder John Allen, was demolished in 1964 to make way for the Ann Arbor Inn. In the 1990s, the city took ownership of the property through tax foreclosures and sold it to a company to develop senior apartments—calling it Courthouse Square.

massage parlors.[111] The business was available and the price was right for Dr. Ranjit Bajwa and his wife Harlivleen,[112] who leased the Embassy Hotel around 1974 along with one of Dr. Bajwa's colleagues at Eastern Michigan University. The couple also opened an Indian restaurant called Raja Rani in 1976, located at 400 South Division.

Harlivleen had a sister, Meena, who lived in India with her husband, Gobind Singh. The family was well-to-do and could have lived comfortably, but Meena chafed at the traditional female roles imposed on her in India. She craved the freedom her sister talked about in the United States. Meena begged Gobind to visit America, so in 1974, they flew into New York City and made their way to Ann Arbor, staying with Harlivleen and Ranjit.

The Singhs underestimated the cost of traveling throughout the United States, so Meena and Gobind mostly stayed in Ann Arbor, spending most of their time eating American food, taking long walks and watching TV. They also applied for green cards and began planning to put down roots in this new country.

Soon, the Bajwas entrusted Gobind and Meena to run the Embassy full-time. The couple earned a combined $500 a month, plus commissions on each room they rented. The Singhs eventually brought their son to America to join them, and moved the whole family into room 204 at the Embassy— eventually taking over room 104 after the renovations in 1977.

Gobind took English as a second language and business classes at the University of Michigan and Washtenaw Community College, using his time on campus to tack up posters advertising the Embassy. While on campus at U-M, he'd walk up the hill to the hospital and tell staffers to recommend the Embassy to the families of loved ones spending long stretches in the hospital.

The Singhs saved as much as they could, subsisting on cheap pizza and takeout and spending most nights in—too tired and busy for much of a social life.

In 1981, Gobind and Meena bought out the Bajwas to own business

---

111   There's a whole wonderful story about Ann Arbor's old red-light district in this here book!

112   Also known as Loveleen.

outright, and in 1987, they bought the whole building.[113]

The Embassy remained a place for Ann Arbor's struggling class, filled with folks staying indefinitely. Simple rooms—a TV, phone, bed, desk and a chair. Shared showers and bathrooms. A/C units in some rooms—for others, it was bring your own fan. The walls were thin and you could hear voices, noises and TVs any hour of the day.

Despite their success, these were trying times for the Singhs, who worked constantly to keep everything running smoothly, while raising two young kids in a town that was a lot rougher than today's Ann Arbor. Gobind turned to religion to see him through, and begged His Holiness aba Hardev Singh Ji for advice. In 1988, His Holiness did him one better and paid a visit to Ann Arbor.

It wasn't as much of a stretch as it might seem for the leader of a global spiritual movement followed by millions to bless Ann Arbor's second-cheapest hotel.[114] Gobind Singh had connections. His father was a revered preacher in India—considered a spiritual second-in-command to His Holiness. During His Holiness's world tour, Gobind's father, his wife, and their bodyguards paid a visit to the Embassy. And had a lovely time.

The Singhs ran a tight ship through the 1990s and into the new millennium. Visitors were rarely allowed in the rooms and those who were permitted to pop in got five or 10 minutes before they were asked to leave. Doors to each room had to remain closed and kids weren't allowed to play in the hallways. Gobind frequently patrolled the halls, citing infractions, and threatening to kick people out if they couldn't stick to the rules. Everyone had to pre-pay for that night by 11 am or risk being tossed on the street.

One short-term resident likened it to living in jail. But it was a lot better than the street.

The Singhs still run the Embassy and their son, Gurvinder, works

---

113   The building was valued at $200,000 in 2012.

114   A single room at the Embassy ran you $28.56 in 1990. A room at the YMCA was just $20.76.

locally in the hotel business as well. They put in 70-hour weeks and have stuck it out through good times and bad, allowing the Embassy to continue filling the role it has filled since the 1930s. A place where the less fortunate can come in out of the cold and rain. Have a bed to call their own. Afford to live day-to-day in a town that's not so affordable.

And it doesn't hurt that the building might be the only one in Ann Arbor blessed by God's own prophet. So they've got that going for them.

Embassy Hotel. The location of today's Embassy Hotel was first used to room guests in 1912 and though the building and businesses have changed hands over the years, 200 East Huron Street has been a hotel of some sort for more than 100 years—surviving fires (the one pictured in the winter of 1974), floods and the steady march of progress. (Photo by Richard Retyi, original by Cecil Lockhard of the *Ann Arbor News*).

ANN ARBOR
CAGES PUBLIC ANIMAL #1

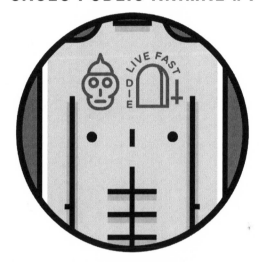

Dozens of cities tried—hundreds of lawmen failed. Ann Arbor was the only city in the world that could cage punk rock's most anarchic, violent, and revolting personality. He was more combustible than Jerry Lee Lewis.[115] More punk than Sid Vicious.[116] Ten times weirder than Marilyn Manson.[117] Sort of an Iggy Pop crossed with Charles Manson—he had the voice of Randy "Macho Man" Savage, and enough of a connection with serial killer John Wayne Gacy to develop a father-son bond.

He was the man, the legend, the infamous Public Animal #1: GG Allin.

115　　Was a notorious wild man on stage, married seven times, including to his 13-year old cousin, and was once arrested outside Graceland after allegedly traveling there to shoot Elvis.

116　　Could barely play bass, but was a pretty good punk vocalist. Probably stabbed girlfriend Nancy Spungen to death and died of a heroin overdose before the case went to trial.

117　　Mostly just really good at makeup and making parents angry.

The first time GG took a shit on stage was at the VFW in Peoria, Illinois, on July 31, 1985. Defecation became a staple of his live shows, so much so that when Geraldo Rivera interviewed him on TV in 1993, it was one of the first questions he asked.

"Why did you defecate in front of a live audience?" Geraldo asked.

GG's response: "My body is a rock and roll temple and my flesh, blood and body fluids are a communion to the people. Whether they like it or not. My rock and roll isn't to entertain but to annihilate."

Crapping on stage was just one layer of the GG live-show shit sandwich. He pissed on stage too. Jerked off sometimes. All his front teeth were fake—smashed out years ago after repeated self-inflicted blows with microphones and his own fists. His head was crisscrossed with gashes—most self-inflicted. Regularly brawled with his audiences, trading punches and kicks, dragging spectators out of the crowd by their hair and beating them on stage. He swung microphone stands and threw chairs into the audience.

At a gig in a little classroom at NYU, GG unpeeled a banana and crammed it up his ass. When some of it smushed flat, he threw the mess at the crowd and licked his fingers clean.[118]

GG's shows rarely lasted more than a few songs before club owners cut the power or the police showed up. Crowds knew what to expect. Nobody went to a GG Allin show by accident.

GG's brother and bandmate Merle once said, "We never plan on finishing the whole tour. There's two reasons. Prison or the hospital."

GG spent plenty of time in hospitals and claimed to have been arrested more than 50 times, but through all the blood, broken bones, shit and violence, only one city was able to stop his nihilistic musical tornado of destruction.

Ann Arbor.

(Hold for applause)

GG was born Jesus Christ Allin in Lancaster, New Hampshire in 1956.

---

118   The venue thought they were booking Henry Rollins, not GG.

He earned the nickname GG as a baby—given to him by his three-year-old brother, who couldn't pronounce Jesus.[119]

GG got into music at an early age, fronting band after band, each more violent and extreme than the last. As the bands got crazier, so did GG—wild on booze, heroin, and any drug offered to him for free.

That night at the Peoria VFW in 1985 was still early in GG Allin's career. He was a month shy of his 30th birthday and hustling to make a name for himself. He took a bus from Chicago to play the gig and was paid next to nothing to sing in front of a crowd of a few hundred hardcore punks and straight edge kids.

He wore a satin robe that night, draped over a jockstrap with the words EAT ME and an arrow pointing to his crotch. GG was nuts, but he was also a showman. Shitting on stage wasn't some accident or spur of the moment idea. GG planned it. He ate a box of Ex-Lax hours before the show and had to clench as hard as he could not to prematurely erupt.

When the set started and he crapped all over the stage, chaos broke out. The punks in the audience, many of them underage, lost their minds and ran. The old vets who looked after the VFW ran too—towards this maniac ruining their hall. They tore out of the kitchen and leapt over the bar to kick GG's ass, but when they got close, GG started scooping handfuls of liquidy poo off the stage and rubbing the filth on his nearly-naked body.

The smell was described as "incredible." Hundreds of disgusted punks streamed out of the hall and into the parking lot while GG continued the show, yelling into his shit-stained microphone, tossing handfuls of poo at the remaining onlookers.

When things got too hot, GG beat a hasty retreat, climbing into a van and speeding into the night just as the cops arrived. GG got drunk and passed out in a sweltering, roach-infested apartment in the suburbs, taking the bus back to Chicago the next day.[120]

---

119   His mom renamed him Kevin Michael Allin after she split with his very insane father and took the kids with her.

120   The VFW still stands today. Stop by on Taco Tuesdays for $1 tacos and 75 cent Bud

That's essentially every GG Allin show ever. Whether you saw GG and the Jabbers, or GG and the Scumfucs, GG and the Toilet Rockers, the Disappointments, or GG Allin & The Murder Junkies—it was GG mostly naked on stage, playing with his dick, crapping and/or pissing on stage, punching fans, smashing himself in the face with the microphone, and, oh yeah, singing.

GG Allin showed up in Ann Arbor in April, 1989 with his bandmates T. Ricky Insult and Big Bad Bob of the Disappointments. They crashed for a few nights at the apartment of Leslie Marie Morgan at 717 N. Fourth Avenue. Morgan was either a friend, groupie, or short-term girlfriend of GG's. The band met her a week before in Muskegon and she offered them a free place to stay if they were passing through. These details will become very important in a minute.

On April 12, 1989, GG and the Disappointments played a gig at the University of Michigan. They didn't schedule the show—they barged into a snackbar/theater called The Halfway Inn at East Quad and took over the stage during the East Quad Music Co-Op's weekly open mic night, which usually featured acoustic guitar performances and poetry readings. GG and the Disappointments pushed everyone off stage and played—GG bashing his face and head with the microphone, covering himself and the stage in blood. Then he whipped out his penis and masturbated on stage before attacking the booing members of the audience. He kicked a female U-M student in the stomach and hit another with a chair. They played for about 15 minutes until the Co-Op kids killed the power and campus security swarmed the place. GG and the band fled into the night and a warrant was issued for his arrest. One count of indecent exposure and two counts of assault and battery.

Ann Arbor's finest never found GG, who left town two days later, though the warrants remained active while the band toured the Midwest. This was good news for GG, who wanted to avoid incarceration as long as possible so he could deliver on a promise made to *Maximum Rocknroll* magazine earlier

Light drafts.

that year. GG wrote to the magazine, vowing to kill himself on stage on Halloween night that year. He didn't offer specifics and most readers were skeptical that he'd actually go through with it, but GG seemed serious. His bandmates worried that he'd take a few people with him.

GG played Chicago in May and Columbus in June and on September 9, 1989, the car he was riding in was stopped by Secret Service agents on the southside of Chicago after he withdrew money from an ATM to attend a Rolling Stones concert in Wisconsin. GG was on the White House's radar after writing a letter to John Hinckley, the man who attempted to assassinate President Ronald Reagan in 1981.

Allin had a thing for convicts and serial killers. He wrote Hinckley because he was curious about the shooting. He had a fascination with John Wayne Gacy, who he corresponded with and eventually visited on death row in Illinois where Gacy was waiting to be executed after killing 33 young boys. GG spent six hours with Gacy, but said it felt like 10 minutes.

"He's a good guy. He's my father figure. I don't care what he did." said Allin.

The Secret Service ran GG's name and his warrants in Ann Arbor popped up. They transported him back to Ann Arbor, where GG faced a new criminal charge—assault with intent to do great bodily harm less than murder. The victim: friend, groupie, or short-term girlfriend Leslie Marie Morgan of 717 N. Fourth Avenue. GG pled not guilty to the misdemeanor assault and indecent exposure charges stemming from the open mic invasion, but demanded a preliminary investigation into Morgan's felony claims.

Beating up college kids and pulling his penis out in East Quad were the least of GG's worries. The new felony charge brought a maximum sentence of 10 years in state prison and $5,000 fine.

There are two sides to Morgan's story, which we'll review in a second. Know that the court reduced the charge to assault with a dangerous weapon in exchange for a plea of no contest. GG was sentenced to 18 months in the state prison in Adrian and fined $2,000.

"I somehow feel that I'm getting tried for my reputation, not my crime." GG said afterward.

Court documents stated that over the course of six days and five nights in that apartment on N. Fourth Avenue, a lot of very bad things happened to Leslie Marie Morgan. The injuries described by the hospital physician were numerous. Cigarette burns on her face and the bottom of her feet. Several cuts on both cheeks, cuts down the middle of her abdomen, deep cuts in a half moon shape around both breasts and a four inch by four inch third degree burn on her left leg that required skin grafts. Morgan spent nearly two weeks in the hospital, including five days in intensive care.

Morgan said GG orchestrated a week of physical and mental torture that resulted in her injuries. She alleged that GG was an animal. Took great delight in hurting her. Told her he was painting a masterpiece while he cut her flesh. She told police she was convinced she was going to die.

GG didn't dispute most of the injuries, but he told a far different story. He said he and his bandmates arrived on Sunday night, April 9—three days before the East Quad show. They drank hard and partied hard as Morgan's guests. GG said Morgan was in love with him, constantly asked him to marry her, and wanted to have sex with him and watch him masturbate all week. GG said she asked him to cut her clothes off with her own butterfly knife, then cut her flesh. GG said Morgan acted crazy, punching out windows and rolling in glass. The burn came one night when Morgan was passed out and GG tried to wake her up.

" I'll admit that using a lighter was not the smartest thing we should have used to wake her," GG said.

GG said she only went to the cops because him and his bandmates wouldn't have a foursome. The proceedings dragged through September and into October, making it pretty clear that GG wouldn't make his Halloween date with destiny. He was furious at police and the doubters who said he'd never actually kill himself on stage.

GG was locked up December 8, 1989 and spent the next 18 months in prison, keeping a daily journal of his experiences, which he'd later publish, while also corresponding for the first time with John Wayne Gacy.[121] He was visited by friends and random fans, including a young Kurt Cobain, who was in Ann Arbor to play a show at the Blind Pig. Cobain idolized GG, so before Nirvana headed to its next stop on their tour, he and future Flaming Lips drummer Nathan Roberts stopped by the prison to say hi.

"After we told him who we were and that we were big fans, GG cursed and spit at us and kept yelling that we were 'just a couple of Kansas City faggots who want their dicks sucked," Roberts said.

GG was released on parole on March 26, 1991 and immediately said "fuck you" to his parole officer and left the state to record his next album and begin touring again. A young filmmaker from NYU named Todd Phillips contacted GG and asked him if he'd be interested in having a documentary made about him. GG agreed and for the next few months, Phillips shot "Hated: GG Allin & the Murder Junkies." The cult classic includes footage of GG on stage and in action, shitting, cutting, brawling with fans, and pondering life and his ambitions.[122]

"I have one pair of pants. A jacket. A shirt. Pretty much everything I own will fit in a paper bag," GG said. "I'm the type of person who always has to get out of town. The whole thing was supposed to last a year or two, but as the thing escalated, there was so much more to do. I said, fuck it, let's take over the world."[123]

The plan once again was to kill himself on stage on Halloween night.

---

121   GG and John Wayne Gacy hit it off pretty quickly and remained pen pals until Michigan prison officials eventually stopped their correspondence. John Wayne Gacy didn't know why GG stopped writing all of a sudden. It hurt his feelings.

122   A portrait of GG was commissioned for John Wayne Gacy and used as the movie poster and VHS cover. GG was kicked out of the screening of his own documentary, but apparently liked it. Phillips went on to direct Old School and the Hangover movies.

123   Other than living with his mom in New Hampshire, I never uncovered a single address for GG in all my research. He seems to have roamed the country exclusively staying with friends, bandmates and fans.

The grand finale would be caught on tape. GG & the Murder Junkies only completed a handful of shows that winter before things got out of hand on February 18, 1992—a little less than a year after GG was released from prison.

The band played a gig at the Cavity Club in Austin, Texas, and true to form, GG stripped naked but for a black dog collar and black gloves, bashed himself bloody with the microphone and crapped on stage and threw it at the audience. Someone in the crowd took offense and maced him. The fumes filled the club and drove everyone for the doors in a panic. When Austin police showed up, GG was covered in blood and shit and in obvious respiratory distress.[124] He was taken to the hospital and booked, where his parole violation in Michigan popped up. GG was shackled and transported back to Washtenaw County where he served the rest of his term in the state prison in Jackson. GG once again spent Halloween behind bars, and the voices of his doubters grew louder and louder, making him angrier and angrier.

GG meticulously planned his comeback tour from prison. He wrote his brother Merle constantly, sending him lyrics to new songs they'd include on the new album, booking shows and radio appearances, sketching t-shirt and sticker designs and even negotiating a recording deal with punk label Enigma Records. On March 11, 1993, GG's prison sentence was complete and he was ready for the Murder Junkies spring/summer tour.

"This tour is gonna be the most violent tour yet," Merle Allin said. "We're basically out to get everybody in our fuckin' way."

GG & the Murder Junkies hit the ground running, playing shows from Boston to L.A. and every point in between. They returned to Michigan one more time, playing the Marquee in Detroit on June 6, 1993. These shows were rougher and rawer than before, with momentum building toward Halloween as the summer wore on. Would GG finally make good on his word?

The answer is no.

GG didn't kill himself on stage in 1993. Three weeks after the gig in Detroit, GG played an all ages show at the Gas Station in New York City, for

---

124   Google the arrest report for this incident. It's amazing.

which, it seemed, nobody was prepared. GG was already covered in blood and feces by the second song of the set when the owners cut the power to the place. An enraged GG destroyed the club before taking to the streets, still coated in blood and shit, leading a crowd of a hundred punks down East 2nd Street, shouting and smashing their way through Manhattan.[125] GG was elated at the carnage he had caused. He ended up at an apartment on Avenue B, drinking and doing a bunch of heroin to celebrate. GG fell asleep on the floor, snoring loudly as everyone drank and did drugs long into the night. In the morning, everyone noticed that GG hadn't moved. He was dead.

GG's funeral was held back home in New Hampshire on July 3, 1993. For the wake, his bloated, unwashed and make-up-free corpse was dressed in a leather jacket and jockstrap, with the words "Eat Me" written on the codpiece. In one hand, they jammed a microphone and in the other, a bottle of Jim Beam. GG's new album played full blast on the stereo as mourners got hammered, did drugs, and messed with GG's body, Weekend at Bernie's-style. They drew on him with Sharpies, pulled down his jockstrap, shoved pills in his mouth, wrenched the bottle of Jim Beam from his arm and took big, sloppy swigs.[126]

Before closing the casket for good, Merle placed headphones over his brother's ears and pressed play on a Walkman, playing a copy of GG's Suicide Sessions album on a loop. They lowered GG into the ground next to his grandparents in St. Rose Cemetery.

GG's tombstone bore the epitaph "Live Fast Die". It immediately became a destination for curiosity seekers and hardcore fans, who frequently vandalized the grave with cigarette butts, liquor bottles, drugs, urine, and feces, until GG's mother had the tombstone removed to make the grave harder to find.

That was it. GG didn't get the chance to take himself out in front of a live audience on Halloween night. Instead, he died a typical rock star death. GG never forgot or forgave the Ann Arbor cops for taking years off his career—

---

125   Google this too. There's video.

126   Pictures and video of the wake and funeral exist. The internet is seriously amazing.

nor for twice killing his plans for a glorious public suicide. It took the little town of Ann Arbor to finally cage Public Animal #1: GG fucking Allin.

THE DICTATOR COMES TO TOWN

Throughout Ann Arbor's hospitable history, visiting heads of state, dignitaries and geniuses have dined at the opulent Michigan League. Among them Presidents Ford, Carter, and Bush the elder—luminaries like Leonard Bernstein and Chinese ambassador Zhang Wen-Gin have dined on sumptuous spreads while guests in Ann Arbor.

On September 19, 1966, then-President of the Philippines Ferdinand Marcos and his beauty queen wife Imelda partook in a lavish luncheon at the League, dining with the Governor, sitting University of Michigan President and assorted special guests.

Ferdinand Marcos was the newly-elected president of the Philippines— son of a politician, a former lawyer and a young and inspirational politician. He was athletic, charismatic, sharp as a tack, and a decorated war hero. He was also married to one of the most beautiful women in the country, who was herself from a prominent aristocratic Filipino family.

Ferdinand and Imelda met during recess at a Congress of the Philippines budgetary session. He was a member of the House of Representatives and she was attending with a friend. It was a classic meet cute. They locked eyes across the room and Ferdinand recognized Imelda immediately as a recent contestant in the Miss Manila and Miss Philippines pageants. He approached, made some small talk, and then asked her to stand back to back with him so they could compare heights.

Thus began what would come to be known in the Philippines as the Eleven-Day Whirlwind—the period of less than two weeks in which Ferdinand aggressively courted Imelda. She was a talented singer, one of the most beautiful women in the country and also from an influential family. Ferdinand was already dreaming of the presidency, and Imelda would make the perfect first lady. He showered her with flowers and gifts. Every day, he showed up at her door with a marriage license in hand, begging her to sign. On day 11, she did.

Together they wooed the country while Ferdinand rose from the House to the Senate—eventually running a populist presidential campaign, which promised massive infrastructure projects, new jobs, and independence from outside interests. Marcos swept into office in 1965.

Marcos began an aggressive round of infrastructure improvements that included the erection of a number of expensive monuments. He also slowly edged the Philippines into involvement in the Vietnam War—contrary to his election promise to stay out of the conflict. The Filipino voters adored their charismatic new head of state and mostly forgave him for this policy shift. The U.S., however, was overjoyed, viewing the Philippines and Marcos as a valuable ally in Southeast Asia.

To build even closer relations with the Philippines, the U.S. government invited the Marcoses to visit America, arranging a 16-day trip to the United States beginning September 14, 1966, in Washington, D.C. Just before the visit, the Philippines deployed 2,000 military advisors and army engineers to Vietnam to support the U.S. By the end of the war, the Philippines would commit more than 10,000 men to the conflict.

Rain washed out a meticulously-planned welcome ceremony[127] on the South Lawn of the White House. Instead, President Lyndon Johnson and wife Lady Bird greeted Ferdinand and Imelda indoors with the sound of trumpets bouncing off the White House walls. Johnson, 6'4", and Marcos, 5'7", made an incongruous pair sitting side by side on a small couch chatting in English. Former beauty queen Imelda, impeccably dressed in a soft pink dress, sat opposite, quietly considering the conversation. That night, at a black tie state dinner, LBJ danced with Imelda, who wore a gorgeous canary ballgown, while Ferdinand spun Lady Bird across the dance floor.

Interviewed by reporters at the White House, Marcos said, "The United States is a nation on which we can depend for the salvation of mankind."

Three days later, on September 19, Ferdinand and Imelda Marcos walked down the gangway of a U.S. Air Force 707 jet at Willow Run airport. They were greeted by a small but enthusiastic crowd that included Michigan Governor and First Lady George and Lenore Romney and a contingent of media and VIPs. A U-M student from the Philippines handed Imelda a giant bouquet, while the U-M Philippines Student Association president stepped forward and shook Ferdinand's hand.

It was 11:15 am and the Marcoses were in for a whirlwind one day visit that included a convocation ceremony, a luncheon, a tour of Ann Arbor, and plenty of chit-chat. A convoy of vehicles drove straight for the Clements Library for the invite-only convocation, where Marcos received an honorary doctorate of civil law degree from the university.

In a citation accompanying the honorary degree, Marcos was likened to President John F. Kennedy, who had been assassinated just three years earlier. The comparison—at that time—wasn't far off. The Marcoses were seen to be kind, well-spoken, and beautiful people, beloved by their country. Local and state officials showered them with admiration, which Ferdinand returned in a warm, off-the-cuff speech, in which he praised the United States and his so-far

---

127   It would have included a red carpet and a 21-gun salute.

brief trip to Ann Arbor. He also spoke of his country's commitment to democracy and his support for the ideals that made America great.

"If Vietnam is the testing ground of the new weapons of communism, then the Philippines is the testing ground of whether or not democracy can succeed in an underdeveloped country."

After the convocation ceremony, the Marcoses were taken to the Michigan League for a 1:15 pm luncheon in the Vandenberg Room. There they ate with the Romneys, a handful of lucky U-M dignitaries, and a few U-M students from the Philippines. The students were particularly starstruck by the handsome Ferdinand and beautiful Imelda, who looked even more glamorous than she did on the cover of that week's Life magazine.

Following the meal, Ferdinand and the men retired to Inglis House to talk, while Imelda left for a personalized tour, riding through the streets of Ann Arbor to see the city in the fall.

When Imelda's bus returned to Inglis House, Ferdinand and his wife reunited and slipped into cars that took them back to Willow Run. With San Francisco, Los Angeles, and Honolulu still on the itinerary, the Marcoses didn't get much of a chance to see the rest of Ann Arbor. They climbed the steps of the plane, Imelda carrying her bouquet and Ferdinand with a hand on her lower back, and settled in for the flight to the West Coast. The plane rose into the air at 4 pm as Michiganders on the ground waved goodbye.

A storybook visit from the new Philippine president and his pretty wife.

The world wouldn't find out until 2011 that the United States had been storing nuclear weapons in the Philippines since 1966 and the beginning of the Marcos presidency, in direct violation of the Philippine constitution.[128]

Marcos hid this fact from the rest of the country and continued to support the U.S. in Vietnam, in exchange for tens of millions of dollars in aid to help fund Marcos's public and personal projects.

---

128   The deployment of nuclear weapons at U.S. military bases in the Philippines was part of a much larger Pentagon program in which nearly 13,000 nuclear weapons were deployed outside the U.S. in case of a major nuclear war.

Through Marcos's first term, the economy grew, infrastructure projects like new roads, bridges, and public buildings were moving along, and the Marcoses looked radiant in every public appearance. Ferdinand won an easy re-election in 1969. His opponents warned about corruption, gross mismanagement, and a presidency full of lies—but things just felt too good.

Maybe the Filipino population should have known better. Maybe they should have questioned Ferdinand's checkered past. He was the son of a politician, but not an honest, upright politician. While Ferdinand was studying law at the University of the Philippines, his father suffered a frustrating loss for a position in the National Assembly. So Ferdinand, his father, and other family members went to the home of the winner, broke in, and shot him dead.

Ferdinand was arrested, tried, convicted, and sentenced to death. The Marcos family appealed the ruling, taking the case all the way to the Supreme Court of the Philippines, where Ferdinand represented himself while studying for the bar in prison. Just after his 23rd birthday, the conviction was overturned and Ferdinand went free.

There was also the money. The Marcos family wasn't poor, but where did Ferdinand get all the money to win the presidency in the first place? How did he finance his historic re-election campaign? Where did all the money come from?

Opponents claimed it came from the National Treasury. Others wondered if it could be the legendary lost treasure known as Yamashita's Gold.

The legend of Yamashita's Gold is pretty interesting. During World War II, the Japanese looted their vanquished enemies throughout Southeast Asia, and shipped the ill-gotten gains first to Singapore and then the Philippines. The seas were too dangerous to move everything all the way back to Japan, so they stashed everything in the Philippines and planned to transport the loot back to the Japanese home islands following victory in World War II. The Japanese didn't win World War II and the treasure remained hidden somewhere in the Philippines.

It came to be known as Yamashita's Gold—named after the Japanese general in command in the Philippines at the time. It was a cache of cash, precious metals, fine art, you name it, plundered from banks, depositories, businesses, museums, private homes and religious buildings. The total haul was estimated to be worth tens of billions of dollars. Some thought it was a myth, some were convinced it was real. Many a treasure hunter descended on the Philippines looking for Yamashita's Gold. Until, according to one theory, Ferdinand Marcos found it and Ferdinand Marcos kept it.[129]

The people of the Philippines eventually caught on to Marcos's deception. The economy slowed. Money for new projects dried up. Public unrest increased in size and volume, and pro-communist forces grew in strength, plotting against the Marcos regime. Demonstrations, riots, and more than 15 public bombings occurred in the two years following Marcos's reelection. Perhaps the most infamous of these was the Plaza Miranda bombing, in which hand grenades were tossed on stage at a political rally with 4,000 people were in attendance, killing nine and injuring 95.

By 1972, a full blown coup d'etat was in the works and Marcos declared martial law, installing himself as dictator and elevating his wife to a position of power. He all but banned the free press, dissolved the media, dismantled civil liberties, shut down Congress and arrested his political opponents and any of their vocal supporters. Thus began a terrible era of violence and greed in which the Marcos family did whatever it took to stay in power.

Over the next dozen years, the Marcoses made more than 70,000 politically motivated arrests, tortured more than 35,000 people and were responsible for the murders and disappearances of 3,257 people.

"It's easier perhaps and more comfortable to look back to the solace of a familiar and mediocre past," Marcos said a year into martial law. "But the times are too grave and the stakes too high for us to permit the customary concessions to traditional democratic processes."

The Marcoses plundered the National Treasury with increasing greed, eventually stealing between $5 to 10 billion dollars, or around $20 billion

---

129   The losers wept. One person eventually took Ferdinand Marcos to court, alleging that Marcos stole the treasure from him, and settled for $13 million. So maybe it wasn't a myth.

today. They used the money to fund their reign of terror, while also paying for a lavish lifestyle that included international travel, high-end Manhattan real estate, and, famously, thousands of pairs of shoes for Imelda.

As international sentiment turned against him, Marcos tried to distract the world from his brutal regime and the country's brewing revolutionary movement by staging a series of massive events to the country.

The Philippines welcomed the Miss Universe Pageant in 1974, featuring special guests Brooke Shields and George Hamilton. The next year, they hosted the Thrilla in Manilla—the much-hyped third and final boxing match between Muhammad Ali and Joe Frazier. Marcos was said to have personally paid Ali $4.5 million pesos to secure the fight.[130]

The smokescreen worked well enough to keep U.S. aid rolling in— growing from tens of millions to billions of dollars and helping keep the Marcoses in power. The Marcos regime appointed family members and trusted advisors to government positions, continued to brutally silence the opposition and quadrupled the Filipino military to 270,000 troops. Death became a part of everyday life in the Philippines.

Under intense pressure, even from supporters, Marcos ended martial law in 1981 and immediately opened elections, running unopposed to win a third term. Anti-Marcos violence from communist groups continued throughout the 1980s with thousands of military, police, and civilian deaths in the constant clashes. The torture and murder continued.

Hope for change landed on the tarmac at Manila International Airport in the summer of 1983. The leader of the Philippine opposition, Benigno Aquino, Jr., had returned to the Philippines after three years in the United States where he was being treated for a heart condition.

Tanned, rested, and ready, Aquino landed in Manila. Less than a

---

130   Ali brought a young woman named Veronica with him to Manila. Veronica was not his wife. Ali's actual wife, Belinda, stayed home in Chicago. Ali and Veronica attended a gala at the Presidential palace, where Marcos complimented Ali on his wife's beauty. Ali failed to correct him. Perhaps due to the large media contingent at the event, word of the gaffe reached Belinda in Chicago, who saw her husband clearly stepping out with his mistress halfway across the world. Belinda flew to Manila immediately, confronted Ali in his hotel, and had a row with her husband that included a lot of yelling and furniture being destroyed. She

minute after stepping off the plane, he was gunned down on the tarmac, killed by members of the Philippine military there to arrest him.

Aquino's murder turned an isolated opposition movement into a national crusade. The U.S. distanced itself from Marcos, now withholding funds sorely needed to prop up the regime. In failing health and losing allies, Marcos was alone and vulnerable. He called a snap election in 1986 and won, though his opponents cried foul over rigged ballot boxes and widespread violence at the polls.

On February 26, 1986, less than three weeks after the election, opposition forces overran parts of capital and seized the offices of the state-run television network. Panicked, Marcos barricaded himself in the presidential palace.

Marcos called the White House for help but was curtly told to "cut and cut cleanly." The Marcoses packed as much stuff as they could and piled into four helicopters that flew them to Clark Air Force base in the Philippines, where they boarded a U.S. Air Force Hercules C-130. They flew first to Guam and eventually to Hickam Air Force Base in Hawaii.

When citizens breached the walls of the palace and stormed the grounds, they discovered evidence of the ridiculously lavish life Imelda and Ferdinand lived, including, notoriously, closets packed with more than 2,700 pairs of Imelda's shoes.

Ferdinand's health deteriorated rapidly. In 1989, three years after he had fled the Philippines, Marcos offered the Philippine government 90% of his personal wealth in exchange for permission to be buried in his homeland next to his mother. The Filipino government declined. Ferdinand Marcos died in Honolulu on September 28, 1989.

Ann Arbor still had its memories of the Marcos visit. Those were the optimistic years before things really went bad and Filipinos started disappearing. A special and hopeful day when the beautiful man and his lovely

---

filed for divorce the next year.

wife landed at Willow Run, graced campus with their presence and ate at the Michigan Union like so many other dignitaries before and after. People change. Though maybe not so dramatically, or violently.

An editorial in the *Ann Arbor News*, dated September 21, 1966, read:

> *"The numerous heads of state that visit these shores every year usually include among them a statesman or two. The conviction with which Marcos articulates the goals for his country and region, and his personal qualifications for leadership, stamp him as an ambassador extraordinaire. Americans can say of his visit here, the pleasure was ours."*

Ferdinand Marcos. Philippine President (and eventual dictator) Ferdinand Marcos stands with law school professor and U-M Executive VP Marvin Niehuss (over his left shoulder) and Michigan Governor George Romney (right) outside the President's House on the campus of the University of Michigan. (Photo by Brian Peters, original courtesy of the *Ann Arbor News*).

THE INVENTION OF THE CUBICLE

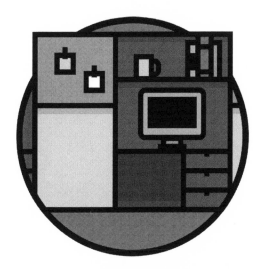

If you've never worked in an office, this about sums it up:

"Thirty years have I served the Philistines, and my neck is not subdued to the yoke. You don't know how wearisome it is to breathe the air of four pent walls without relief day after day."

That was written in the 18th century by a clerk named Charles Lamb—nearly 200 years before the invention of the most dreaded piece of office furniture ever invented: the cubicle.

A three-walled cliche. Three blank sides on which to pin so many "Hang in There" kittycat posters. The cubicle, officially branded the Action Office 2, was invented right here in Ann Arbor. The yoke around the neck of white collar workers everywhere conceived and birthed right on State Street.

Offices aren't new things. Back when Charles Lamb worked for the

East India Company in the 1700s, their headquarters was a buzzing hive of bureaucracy and paperwork. Offices back then were huge rooms packed with rows of long desks at which workers were seated, all facing the same way. These rooms were presided over by supervisors who maximized productivity and minimized luxuries like breaks, snacks and jibber jabber.

Companies and office designers softened throughout the years, trying to make things a little more bearable for the common office worker. Enter water coolers, coffee and cake on birthdays.

The change agent was Robert Probst, an office innovator and brilliant inventor who worked for the Herman Miller furniture company—known for producing the Marshmallow Love Seat, the Noguchi Table, and the Eames Lounge Chair.[131]

Founded and headquartered in Zeeland, Michigan, Herman Miller Inc. didn't want to just make furniture—they wanted to revolutionize the industry. To accomplish this, they created a subsidiary called the Herman Miller Research Corporation and put an office in Ann Arbor at 2285 South State Street.[132] In this unassuming one-story building, they let their change agent and brilliant inventor work, naming him president of the new venture. And right in that building, Probst invented the cubicle.

Probst was a versatile inventor. He'd already created a new kind of heart pump, a quality control system for concrete and a vertical timber harvester, which was apparently a big deal for timber folks. Herman Miller tasked him with a singular mission: "To find problems outside of the furniture industry and to conceive solutions for them."

The Herman Miller company believed in human-centered problem solving. One of its core missions was: "The most important thing in the room is not the furniture—it's the people."

---

131   People who know furniture know how iconic these things are. The Marshmallow Love Seat is the most iconic modernist sofa ever. Only 186 were made and they retail for $15,000 today. The Noguchi Table and Eames Lounge Chair aren't at quite the same level, but even IKEA-level interior designers like me would recognize them immediately.

132   Right across the street from the University of Michigan Tennis Center.

Probst was hired specifically to think about everything but furniture. So he did.

In 1960, Probst saw the U.S. office as a wasteland. "It saps vitality, blocks talent, frustrates accomplishment," he said. "It's the daily scene of unfulfilled intentions and failed effort."

Offices in those days were mostly open spaces with rows of desks out in the open, often surrounded by closed-door offices for executives. Typewriters and phone conversations created a steady din from 9 to 5.

Probst wasn't a fan of the open office style. He felt office workers needed independence, so he designed a three-walled office system that could be customized to any floor plan. It offered privacy and a more efficient workspace, while limiting the surfaces for clutter and storage. To tackle the latter issue, Probst sketched out separate solutions for storage spaces and office features that encouraged workers to leave their desks and move around the office, not just sit and type and talk on the phone.

In 1964, Probst's idea was refined and ready. Herman Miller introduced the Action Office. Think versatile, functional cubicle walls, but prettier and not designed to pen people in. But the components were bulky, complicated and expensive. The Action Office never caught on.

Probst went back to his State Street drawing board. Four years later, in 1968, they launched the Action Office 2. This version was more interchangeable and customizable, providing personal privacy and, in practice, still allowing the worker to interact with their colleagues.

Perhaps Probst made his Action Office 2 system too customizable, its components too interchangeable. Because it was never intended to form a cube. But cubes fit neatly together and don't take up a lot of floor space, so corporate office planners took the Action Office 2 system and used it to cram the maximum number of bodies into their previously open floor plans. They ignored elements of Probst's design that were intended to balance privacy and openness and instead boxed workers in like Tetris pieces.

The cubicle arrived on the market at a perfect time for U.S. businesses. To stimulate business spending, the U.S. Treasury reworked rules for depreciating assets, making it easier to write off the cost of office equipment for tax purposes. Depreciating office furniture could be written off every seven years, while permanent structures like walls couldn't offer companies a tax break for 39 and a half years.

Cubicles qualified as office furniture, not walls, and the phones at Herman Miller rang off the hook. Truckloads of the Action Office 2 took over floor plans in new and old offices, maximizing the number of workers on each floor and giving companies those sweet, sweet tax breaks.

Herman Miller sales rose from $15 million the year they launched the Action Office 2 to $25 million two years later. Competitors copied the design, leading to price wars and cheap knock-offs, segmenting office after office after office with these cubicles. The only loser in the deal was the office worker.

The cubicle became the dominant office layout plan into the 1990s, at the peak of corporate buyouts and mergers. Offices expanded and contracted quickly, necessitating floorplans that could grow and shrink along with staff numbers and payroll. Cubicles were the perfect solution. By 1997, it was estimated 60% of America's white collar work force worked in cubicles.

Probst, who left the company in 1980, was mortified by the bastardization of his invention. As the Action Office system made Herman Miller millions, he watched as depressing knock-off versions spread like a virus to offices across the country. Probst intended to give workers a more flexible and fluid environment, not place them in pens.

In 1997, Probst was interviewed by the *New York Times* about a growing revolution by some of the U.S.'s biggest companies back towards the old open office plan. Probst responded that "the cubiclizing of people in modern corporations is monolithic insanity."

Probst died three years later. The cubicle did not.

Many companies do care about their employees in the workplace. They're constantly rethinking the office, trying to balance efficiency with employee productivity and morale. But the cubicle keeps surviving, and at this rate, may never die.

Herman Miller still markets the Action Office, now in brighter colors, with lower walls, see-through panels—but it's still a cubicle. Nearly 50 years after the Action Office 2 debuted, it's still out there, sectioning call centers, sales offices, anywhere there are fluorescent lights and the option to cram two tons of office workers into a one-ton bag.

Thanks, Herman Miller. Thanks, Robert Probst. Thanks, Ann Arbor.

GERALDINE SEEBACK AND THE MUSIC MOBILE

Geraldine Schlemmer was born in Ann Arbor on July 15, 1908, and lived at 537 3rd Street, just a little north of Madison Street. Geraldine's father owned the Ann Arbor Fluff Rug Company, where he hand-built most of the machines used to make those Fluff Rug Company rugs and supervised a staff of more than 70.

He was a great marketer, sponsoring floats in parades across the Midwest—riding high, waving to the crowds. The Ann Arbor Fluff Rug Company ran ads in newspapers across the country, featuring the company logo—an image of little baby Geraldine, lying nude on a roll of carpet. Fifty sales agents worked coast to coast to sell those rugs, and all this effort combined to make the Ann Arbor Fluff Rug Company the largest rug manufacturing factory in the United States for a time.

Geraldine, like her father, was a musical prodigy. Though he was never formally trained, Mr. Schlemmer could play several instruments by ear if you gave him a few minutes to mess around.[133]

When Geraldine was five, she sang in public for the first time, standing on a stack of three Bibles so people could see her at the front of the church. She pursued her musical education into adolescence, taking piano and voice lessons at the Kempf house with Reuben Kempf and his wife Pauline. The Kempfs had been locally famous for 25 years, providing music lessons to adults and children in their home at 312 South Division. During the day, they left the front door unlocked and their waiting area open so kids could walk in before lessons and wait on their big red sofa inside.

Geraldine attended Bach Elementary, just a few blocks from where she grew up, then Pioneer High School. She continued her musical education with the Kempfs and performed around town—singing in church each Sunday and making regular singing and dancing appearances at the Majestic Theater on Maynard Street. When she graduated from high school, Pauline Kempf helped arrange for her to attend the Cincinnati Conservatory of Music—one of the top music schools in America. Geraldine worked her way through college, teaching music, working in radio and writing for the Cincinnati Enquirer.

After graduation, she stayed in Cincinnati until she received an offer to study music in New York City—packing her bags for a new adventure. But Geraldine's father fell ill and she was forced to change her plans, passing on the Big Apple and moving back to Ann Arbor.

It was 1936 and Geraldine, now 28, was back in the house she grew up in, caring for her father until he passed away in 1945 at the age of 81. She got back into teaching music and pursued a job at the *Ann Arbor News*, showing up at their offices every day for a week until they took her on.

That's where Geraldine met her husband, James Seeback, a linotype operator at the *Ann Arbor News*. The two courted briefly and married on New Year's Day, 1938, at the Michigan League. The bride wore a chiffon velvet frock in a soft blue-green shade with matching slippers and tiara cap with a shoulder-length veil of the same shade. The groom wore whatever.

---

133   Mr. Schlemmer must have been pretty good, because he was the leader of the Odd Fellows Lodge drill and marching teams.

The couple had a son, Dale, and Geraldine quit the News to be a stay-at-home mom. While pregnant with their second child, life got tougher for Geraldine Seeback. People didn't really talk about the fact that James Seeback left her—now a mother of two. Newspaper articles tactfully say Geraldine found herself alone after the birth of her second son. A memoir written by a woman who worked closely with Geraldine later in life says James died—which wasn't true. So Geraldine was either telling people her husband had died, or they just assumed.[134]

Geraldine was now without a partner and in dire need of an income. That's how she got back into teaching music. With her mother pitching in with the kids, Geraldine joined the music department at St. Thomas High School, where she taught music all day, then returned home and gave private music lessons until 10:30 at night. When her last student left, she got to work on the laundry she took in for extra cash. She then got in two or three hours of sleep and got up to do it all over again.

Somewhere in the midst of making ends meet, Geraldine played piano in the fledgling Ann Arbor Symphony Orchestra, right around the time they performed their first concert at the Michigan Theater. She was elected the first female symphony president in 1947 and continued playing until 1950, when she stepped away to focus on making the orchestra bigger and better from behind the scenes.

By the 1950s, Geraldine was teaching music out of a studio on East Liberty Street in the Pretzel Bell building. In 1961, she upgraded to nicer digs at 320 East Washington Street—the current site of the Comerica Bank drive-thru—which served as her home and studio. There, she taught piano and voice lessons year round, and offered special intensive summer music school sessions.

If it had to do with music, performance, or pushing for women's

---

134   She was probably embarrassed to talk about her shitheel ex-husband. James Seeback did something bad enough in Ann Arbor to be put on probation, then went out to Montana to stay with his brother, and was arrested there in 1950 for violating parole. He served whatever time he had to, then returned to Montana where he married Helen Olcott in 1951. They moved to Minneapolis where James' father lived and resided there in 1958 when James' father died. The next blip on the radar is a 1979 obituary in Richland, South Carolina, announcing the death of 81-year-old James Seeback. No wife mentioned.

involvement in either, it's likely Geraldine was involved. She was:

- The founder of the Ann Arbor and Michigan Women's Orchestra Association

- A charter member of the Women's City Club, Ann Arbor Civic Ballet, and Beta Sigma Phi Business Organization

- A member of a number of state and national professional musical organizations

- A member of the Washtenaw and Dexter Historical Societies

- Listed in the Who's Who of American Women, the National Register of Prominent Americans, and in the British Blue Book of Professional Women

And in 1963, she was named Ann Arbor Woman of the Year. That same year, Geraldine added another chapter in her life when she conceived of the wondrous and amazing Music Mobile.

The Music Mobile was...actual serious copyrighted phrase coming...a "Music Lesson on Wheels." As Geraldine saw it, there were two challenges with teaching music. The first was access. Not every kid who wanted or would find value in music lessons could consistently make it to her downtown studio. The second challenge was the home lesson. Teachers like Geraldine and her peers visited homes throughout Ann Arbor, but the modern home was full of distractions—telephones, televisions, barking dogs, siblings, doorbells. The home was often an environment not conducive to focused musical learning.

So Geraldine created a rolling music studio that could bring the lessons to the kids. Her Music Mobile looked like a slightly more inviting version of Walter White's RV. It had the body of a 1963 Ford Condor motor home welded to a Ford truck chassis. An article in the Fall 1963 edition of the *Ford Times* put it this way:

> "*The Music Mobile is tastefully and comfortably furnished. It has a spinet piano just back of the driver's compartment, washroom facilities and a kitchen amidships, and a waiting room at the rear. It can be used for any kind of music lesson; there is even a plug-in socket for an electric*

organ."

The idea for the Music Mobile came to Geraldine a few years earlier. She started talking to an Ann Arbor Ford dealer and together they connected with some higher-ups at Ford to make her dream a reality. The Ford Motor Company custom-designed the Music Mobile for her at a cost of around $5,000.

She used the Music Mobile for five years—driving to central points in different neighborhoods around Ann Arbor and teaching lessons each Saturday. She made snacks in the Mobile's kitchen and sometimes dinner. A few times, when the weather was too rough to safely drive home, Geraldine slept on the waiting room couch, which converted into a bed.

Geraldine was a vocal proponent of the Music Mobile, and happily shared details with anyone who was interested, but it's unclear if Ford ever built a second. When she retired to Dexter in 1969, she parked the Music Mobile on the property where it remained as retired as she was.

She continued to volunteer for a number of causes, and worked on her own project—a children's book called *Learn Music By Crayoning*.[135] Her sons, Dale and Terry, thrived in their respective fields. Dale followed in his mother's musical footsteps, playing violin in the Toledo Symphony and at the Sands Hotel in Las Vegas, where he backed such performers as Liberace, Sammy Davis, Jr., and Elvis Presley. Terry went into business, and worked with companies like the Ann Arbor Bank and the Frisch Big Boy and eventually joined his brother for a stint at the Sands.

In 1981, Geraldine was named an Ann Arbor Symphony Board Member for Life. The honors kept coming. Ann Arbor Mayor Gerald Jernigan proclaimed July 15, 1988 "Geraldine Seeback Day" and designated her the First Lady of the Symphony.[136]

---

135   Sadly, there's no evidence that she finished it.

136   Here's the only potential controversy in the Geraldine Seeback story. There's no record of this proclamation at City Hall, which occasionally designated single, non-recurring days in honor of important people. The Ann Arbor News reported it though, and I find it way too specific for it to have been a mistake. So, let the record show that July 15, 1988, was indeed Geraldine Seeback Day in Ann Arbor.

Geraldine lived locally until 1994, when she moved to Harrison, Arkansas, to be closer to her family. She passed away peacefully the next year, October, 1995. The fate of the beautiful, wonderful Music Mobile is unknown. When Seeback's story ended, so did the Music Mobile's.

Two hard-working musical marvels, who served Ann Arbor well.

DAM ARBOR

The Huron River watershed in Southeast Michigan travels 130 miles from White Lake Township in Oakland County all the way down to Lake Erie. The headwaters originate in Indian Springs Metropark, twisting and turning southwest then southeast, meandering through Dexter, Ann Arbor, Ypsilanti, Belleville, Flat Rock, and Rockwood and branching into 24 major tributaries along the way.

The name "Huron" was chosen by French settlers who attributed it to the Native Americans who lived near the mouth of the river near Detroit. The natives themselves called the Huron Giwitatigweiasibi, or "burnt-oak region," referring to their method of managing the woods on the banks of the river. They burned large patches of trees next to the river to enrich the soil, clear brush for crops, and attract game.

University of Michigan Professor of Civil Engineering William Hoad published an essay on the Huron River in the 1949 Autumn edition of the

Michigan Alumnus called "The Little River of Michigan." His poetic
description of the river's characteristics follows:

"One does not have to be a regularly ordained geologist to note that the
Huron River is a youthful stream. The Huron's headwaters are gathered
haphazardly from little lakes and swamps and spring-fed brooks scattered over
the broad moraine which was built up between the Saginaw and Erie lobes of
the last great ice invasion. From Dexter to Ypsilanti is perhaps the most
beautiful part of the valley, for here the hills close in and the highway crosses
back and forth from side to side seeking an adequate foothold. The bordering
hills, the wooded slopes, the winding roads, the sunny beaches, the overhanging
trees, all these agreeable surroundings are but the setting for the central jewel of
the valley which is the water itself.

The Huron is not a flashy stream; on the contrary it is fairly steady in
its habits, as rivers go. One reason the flow of the Huron is so steady is the
numerous lakes with which it is connected act to some extent as equalizing
reservoirs, filling up to higher levels in winter and spring and doling out their
excess waters during the summer."

Flat-boat operations transported goods along the Huron River from
Ypsilanti to Lake Erie until railroads expanded into the region and another
industry put the river to use. By the 1880s, 17 dams were operating at various
points on the Huron, powering sawmills, flour mills, and wool mills. The Argo
Mills Dam was the only one within the Ann Arbor city limits, built in 1830 to
power flour and wool mills. The power they generated was satisfactory but
meager compared with the the output of the first hydroelectric plant, which was
built in California in 1887. Companies suddenly saw the Great Lakes as a new
source of energy and the Detroit Edison Company (then called the Eastern
Michigan Edison Company) was among the first to harness the Huron River as
a local source of hydropower.

A consultant for the Detroit Edison Company named Gardner Stewart
Williams[137] surveyed the river and drafted a plan for harnessing electricity from

---

137   Gardner Stewart Williams was a Michigan boy, born in Saginaw City in 1866 - a
town his grandfather, Gardner D. Williams, founded. He grew to be known as a worldwide
authority in building dams and was influential enough that the U-M Bentley Historical Library

the Huron. By 1910, Detroit Edison acquired the rights necessary to begin construction. The plan was to build or refurbish nine dams. Six were completed, with the project cut short when the Great Depression hit. Four of these dams were located in Ann Arbor—Barton built in 1912, Argo refurbished in 1913, Geddes built in 1919 and Superior constructed in 1920.

Each dam was built around 30 feet high, but varied in length, storage, and power output, depending on the section of the Huron on which it was located. Barton was the biggest, stretching 1,767 feet and boasting a typical storage of 5,050 acre-feet, while the much smaller Superior was just 496 feet long with a storage volume of 700 acre-feet.

Time for some human drama.

Barton Dam wasn't a year old before tragedy struck. Sunday, March 19, 1913 was a sunny but chilly day in Ann Arbor. Two young men and two young women decided to enjoy it by renting a canoe and paddling around the Barton Reservoir, just upstream of the dam. Three were U-M students and a fourth had recently graduated and returned to Ann Arbor with her fiancé and was on the water this fine day catching up with friends.

Spring floods made the river high and fast, but the foursome didn't have much problem navigating the newly-created reservoir. It was starting to get dark when they decided to head for home. The safest and smartest route around the dam and back down the river to the livery was to paddle opposite the power house and portage down an embankment to the river below, then shove off in the calm waters. For whatever reason, they instead decided to bump to the edge of the dam and carry the canoe down a stairway built into the side of the powerhouse next to a discharge spillway, where spinning turbines expelled water downstream like a giant rapids.

They put the canoe in the water, piled in, and shoved off—and that's when they realized their terrible mistake. Rather than shoot off down the river on a wave of water, they were sucked back towards the powerhouse and into the spillway by the violently churning water.

secured his papers and has them available in their archives. If you're into dams.

They paddled like mad but the vortex drew them closer until it capsized the canoe, sucking all four into the dam's works. They were lucky they didn't drown right then. The force sucked them out of the churn and into the spillway inside the dam itself, which was partially above water. They were able to cling to a thin, four-foot-long ledge in freezing cold water up to their necks. It was 6:30 pm and they were already exhausted.

They clung together in the near pitch black screaming for help, but the sound of the rushing water and the turbines inside drowned them out or played tricks with the acoustics. On-duty plant operator Walter Yost heard voices during one of his regular inspections of the dam, but assumed they came from rowdy kids somewhere along the banks of the river.

After a while, one of the boys in the water took matters into his own hands and decided to swim for it. Three times he dove into the black and tried to swim out of the chamber and three times he was pushed back by the raging water. With a water escape ruled out, they felt along the edges of the chamber for some kind of opening and located a trap door in the ceiling above. They pushed and pushed but it wouldn't budge. Desperate, the boy tried to swim out one more time. He never came back.

The three remaining boaters hoped for the best, but an hour later neither the boy nor the cavalry arrived.

"This is a poor way to entertain a guest," one of the women joked to the visiting graduate, trying to keep their spirits up.

Their bodies got colder. It was nearly impossible to see. Occasionally they spoke through blue lips and chattering teeth to confirm that they were all still alive. Three voices became two. It was now 9:30 pm and they'd been in the freezing cold water for three hours.

At 10 pm, Walter Yost heard voices again and this time suspected they were coming from below. He slid a heavy toolbox off a trapdoor that looked down into the egress chamber, and shone the light from his lantern into the dark. Clinging to the ledge, exhausted, were the two remaining students. Yost took a heavy rope and fashioned a noose, then lowered it to the pair and told the girl to slip it around her waist. Yost yelled for his co-workers to help and together they pulled the rope, raising the girl out of the water. For some reason, the boy beside her grabbed hold of her and clung for his life rather than wait his turn. His hands were useless frozen claws and he quickly lost his grip. If he'd just waited, he would have made it. Instead, he fell back in and disappeared into the cold, dark water.

They wrapped the girl in blankets and called for help to look for the others, but it was too dark and cold and the search was called off until morning. At dawn, they scoured the banks of the Huron but found no sign of the others. A diver arrived from Detroit two days later, equipped with diving gear, air hoses, lead shoes and iron weights. He descended into the river and had to crawl on hands and knees against the churning water below the dam's egress, fighting the force of the turbines' backwash to search for the bodies of the boys. A hundred spectators lined the riverbanks to watch, cheering when the diver came up, but groaning when he came up empty.

Volunteers dragged the river, searching every square inch, but they couldn't find the bodies.[138] Finally, nearly a month after the accident, a boy found the body of one of the kids on shore, partially covered in sand. Dozens of volunteers, reinvigorated, scoured the same site for the others and found the second boy's body nearby at the bottom of the river, mostly covered in sand.

The girl—the visitor from out of town—was still missing until U-M president Harry Burns Hutchins[139] implored the student body to try one final time to find the body of their missing classmate. Two hundred volunteers searched the river all day, then broke out lanterns and continued the search as darkness fell. Two boys in a canoe happened to notice a string in the water and when they pulled it, the dead girl floated to the surface. It was the string of her corset.

---

138   They did find the coats of both boys, though those findings never led to the bodies themselves.

139   The fourth president of U-M and the first alum to become president. Also one of the top 5 most impressive mustaches of any U-M employee, up there with Dr. John F. Holt, U-M noseguard Tim Davis, and longtime Michigan athletics PR man Bruce Madej.

Nearly 70 years after the accident, the *Ann Arbor News* contacted the lone survivor, then 88-years-old and living in Elyria, Ohio. She had gone on to work as a librarian at the Ford Motor Company, then taught languages at Dearborn High School until her retirement in 1959. She preferred not to relive that evening with the reporter, though she said the memories were still vivid. She did share one detail: that day on the Huron River was the first time she'd ever been in a canoe.

Despite the tragedy, Ann Arbor's dams continued producing power for Detroit Edison through the 1950s until coal and natural gas proved more efficient than harnessing hydropower on Michigan's small, relatively flat rivers. In 1963, Detroit Edison sold the four dams back to the city of Ann Arbor, which purchased them for a song—$400,000—$120,000 of which was covered by the federal open spaces program. The deal ensured Ann Arbor had control of the city's main water supply, helped preserve the river and opened more avenues for recreational development.

The return to city control came just in time for the flood of 1968.

In late June 1968, it rained for seven straight days—a total of 8.1 inches—but the worst of it came Monday through Tuesday night when 5.8 inches of rain[140] fell on the city, flooding basically every neighborhood.

The Huron, its tributaries and lakes throughout Ann Arbor overflowed their banks, washing out roads, bridges, and a stretch of the Penn-Central railroad tracks, while also flooding homes, businesses, farms, parks, you name it.

Police scrambled to help panicked residents endangered by flood waters, while fire trucks rushed through fender-high floodwaters to fight sudden blazes caused by electrical shorts. Thousands were without power and 5,000 without phone service in Ann Arbor and Ypsilanti. The Sheriff's Department dispatched police and prisoners from the county jail to sandbag critical areas to prevent further flooding.

---

140   For some context, Hurricane Harvey dumped up to 51 inches of rain on portions of Texas from August 26-30, 2017 including a one-day total of 16 inches of rain recorded at Houston's Bush Intercontinental Airport.

Three of Ann Arbor's four dams held fast, but suffered enough damage to require expensive reconstruction and repairs.[141]

The Geddes dam took the brunt of it. Raging waters knocked the dam out of commission when floodgates jammed only half-open during the heaviest rains, forcing water to rise higher and higher behind the dam. The water level eventually broke over the dam and its banks, cutting a whole new riverbed along the embankment and wiping out 100 feet of Dixboro Road and part of the railroad tracks. It might have been worse, if not for the heroic actions of city employee Jimmy Kennedy, who forced the floodgates fully open while dangling from the side of the dam, suspended by his legs by a few brave colleagues.

Crews fought the downpour, using heavy equipment to cut additional holes in the dam to allow the water to flow through, then dumped truckload after truckload of rocks and dirt to re-route the rushing floodwaters back into the river.

In photos of the event, you'll see cars parked on the street in water past their wheel wells, people standing outside apartment buildings trying to prevent personal effects from washing into the river and a section of the train tracks completely obliterated.[142]

Ann Arbor wasn't the only city affected. Citizens from Lansing to Redford dealt with floodwaters as well. In the first night, there were two fatalities. Eighteen-year-old J.K. Grandy was swept into an open drainage ditch near an apartment complex in Troy and drowned, while 11-year-old Randy Williams was swept through a water pipe in Niles while playing in the flood. The Loch Alpine sewage plant near Saline also sustained heavy damage and lost four 30-gallon drums of chlorine, which went floating down the Huron somewhere.[143]

The Washtenaw Health Department was quick to advise the people to

---

141   Ann Arbor fixed them all in 1971 and 1972, using $3.5 million in bonds approved by city voters in 1970.

142   To appreciate what this looked like, go to oldnews.aadl.org and search for 1968 Flood

143   There's only one mention of these barrels, and no word if they were ever recovered, intact or otherwise.

clean up following the disaster by offering tips on disinfecting tainted water and treating basements full of water from the city's backed-up sewers. The clean up stunk, but the worst part for Ann Arbor's home and business owners was that insurance policies failed to cover most of the flood damage, leaving residents and businesses to foot the bill. Randy Johnston of the Ann Arbor Association of Independent Insurance Agents gave this dismal quote to the *Ann Arbor News* following the flood:

> *"In all of the property insurance policies, there is no coverage in any form that protects an owner from flooding, sewer backup and surface water damage. And you can't buy it anyway."*

Some damaged cars were covered, and some insured personal property had water damage clauses, but Michiganders were out of luck because Michigan isn't a high-risk area for flooding.

In the days following the rains, Ann Arbor was littered with natural and man-made debris left behind by the receding waters. Tens of flatbed trucks and dozens of volunteers crawled Gallup, Huron, and Riverside Parks, trying their best to clear them of trash, tires and dead fish.

The dams were repaired and, for the most part, have held fast since. A few leaks here, some sporadic water pumping into the river there, dealing with zebra mussels, fishing the odd dead body out of the works. Typical dam stuff.

In 1983, Ann Arbor voters approved another bond, this one for $3.2 million, to refurbish Barton and Superior dams to allow for hydropower generation once again. The dams buzzed back to life in 1986, generating power which Ann Arbor sold back to Detroit Edison for between $50-$60 an hour. Back in 1986, Barton Dam alone could generate enough power to fulfill about three percent of Ann Arbor's energy needs, while the smaller Superior could power about two percent.

The city expected that it would pay off the bond debt by the mid-1990s, at which point the funds generated from the dams would turn into city revenue. The city still has a long-term agreement in place where DTE purchases electricity generated by the Huron River.

Today, the dams are pretty solid—but what if another flood of 1968 was to happen.

In 2008, the *Ann Arbor News* decided to ask some experts what they thought.

Matt Naud, then-Ann Arbor environmental coordinator and ~~definitely~~ likely owner of a doomsday shelter said, "There is no doubt it will happen. The only question is when."

City records in 2008 showed 21,083 people living within 100 feet of a floodplain—the areas where water settles. Houses and businesses within this floodplain were at risk of flooding, or worse, collapsing, causing as much as $110 million in damages.

Should a 100-year event or 500-year event occur where Ann Arbor receives a record amount of rain in a single day or gets dumped on over a terrible wet week, as in 1968, "It would cut the city in half," said Naud.

The odds of such an event were put at about 0.2%.[144] That seems pretty slim. But 0.2% is 0.2%. Take heed, basement owners.

---

144   Feel lucky, Ann Arborites, it could be worse. Experts says there's a 19-percent chance of an earthquake on the San Andreas Fault with a magnitude of 6.8 or higher by 2047.

THE CLAIRVOYANT PHYSICIAN

It was a time of spirits and specters and the folks who could contact, communicate and channel them in the ghost world. Like the Fox sisters of Hydesville, New York, who, in 1848, spoke with spirits through a series of knocks. They developed a code with these ghosts. Knocks to represent yes and no—on the wooden floors, on the walls and ceiling—eventually a code of knocks to represent the entire alphabet, used to seek big answers like the riddles of the universe, or small ones like confirming what color dress one of the girls was wearing. The sisters would sit at a table, ask the spirits questions and the knocks from afterlife would answer.

The Fox Sisters debuted their soon-to-be world-famous spiritualism show in Rochester, New York, in front of a paying audience in November 1849. The exhibition would forever be known as the Rochester Rappings. The girls sat on stage in plain view of the audience and called the spirits. Who knocked from below the stage. Blew in the ears of startled audience members. Passed through the bodies of some of those in attendance, filling them with a frightful chill. People wanted to believe. And it was hard not to. That night in Rochester was the first ever demonstration of spiritualism in front of a live, paying audience. But it was far from the last.

A few years later in little Pittsfield Township, a young boy named Daniel B. Kellogg stood in a schoolhouse on a freezing cold night waiting for a traveling mesmerist to arrive. The man was traveling through Michigan and with stories like the Rochester Rappings in the air, it was an irresistible draw for the townsfolk. The performer put down stakes for several nights, showing off his wondrous spiritual skills for a reasonable admission price.

The man lit a candle and, as he spoke, waved his hand back and forth in front of the flame. Young Kellogg was entranced. His vision dimmed. His head got foggy. Kellogg assumed everyone else was experiencing the same thing. A numbness and prickling sensation took over his body. But he was the only one.

The mesmerist singled Kellogg out. Playing to the crowd, he magically controlled parts of Kellogg's body. He made Kellogg stand erect, made him walk against his will, and fed him tobacco and told him it was candy. Kellogg was fully aware of what was going on, but was powerless to stop it. Kellogg saw the tobacco package, smelled the tobacco, chewed the tobacco—he knew full well what he had in his lip was tobacco. But, boy, did it taste like candy.

Kellogg willingly assisted in every performance during the mesmerist's run, learning what he could about his strange power, and his ability to channel it, until the man packed up and moved on. Kellogg turned out to be the perfect vessel to bridge our world and the spirit realm. He devoted his life to harnessing his gift.

Kellogg held his own magic circles and channeled the same knocks like the ones they were talking about in Rochester. He channeled spirits, who took over his body to write messages from the afterlife using ink and paper. Onlookers sat upright in their seats as Kellogg closed his eyes and made parlor furniture dance around him. People flocked from all over Pittsfield Township to witness these amazing occurrences, and word spread throughout the county.

Never a remarkable boy, Kellogg quickly gained popularity as a major spiritualist. According to Kellogg, it was simple: he cleared his mind and focused only on friendship and love, letting positive emotions wash over him, and surrounding objects would glow and the spirits would whisper to him.

He claimed to be able to inspect, with perfect ease, the internal makeup of everyone in the room. Their organs glowing—hearts, brains, spleens, kidneys, livers. Each giving off a different light depending on the organ's state of health. Kellogg never studied medicine, but he had an undeniable gift for diagnosing disease and prescribing appropriate remedies. Bloodletting and purging (giving patients certain oils to make them throw up) were still common treatments at the time, along with opiate injections and mineral water cures. Kellogg's brand of psychic diagnosis and healing offered hope and, because he was actually pretty good at it, yielded positive results.

All this isn't as crazy as it sounds. Medicine in the 1850s was still pretty inexact. This was before hand washing, before the widespread use of plaster casts for broken bones. Surgery of any kind was extremely risky and often a last resort.

Permit a quick digression that's too long for a footnote, but adds a little flavor to this soup of ours.

It's 1799 and the first-ever president of the United States—George Washington—lies in his bedchamber, cold, short of breath, and clutching his chest. The day before, he sat at the dinner table soaked to the bone in wet clothes after spending most of the day riding around on horseback in the snow and sleet in chilly December. He coughed, his nose ran, he had a sore throat, and he stayed in bed the next day to allow his 67-year-old body to try and beat this thing. The doctors arrived soon after and "helped."

The first physician removed 12 to 14 ounces of the president's blood— nearly a pint of the red stuff. Good old bloodletting. The doc gave Washington a tonic of molasses, butter, and vinegar, which didn't seem to help. So they poured another solution down his throat which caused terrible blisters—the idea being that blisters would pull the evil from the president's body so he could just cough and spit it out.

More doctors arrived and took another 18 ounces of blood—more than a pint this time. The human body contains about 10 pints of blood. Washington was down to eight. His situation, shockingly, didn't improve, so doctors took another 32 ounces of blood—now 40% of the president's blood—and followed with a round of purging to make Washington vomit. Later that night, they applied compounds to his feet, arms, and legs to raise more blisters. All these medical miracle attempts failed. A few hours later, the president muttered his final words and died.[145]

This was the state of medical care that George Frickin' Washington received. He wasn't some commoner or some 32-year-old farmer from Ann Arbor. Granted, this case happened 50 years before Daniel B. Kellogg initiated his unique brand of medicine, but these treatments were still in common practice. Could Kellogg's methods really have been much worse than what George Washington's own doctors were practicing at the time?

Digression over.

People came from all over Pittsfield Township to visit Kellogg and present him with their physical and mental ailments. In their presence, Kellogg would slip into a trance, see their bodies and organs glow in his mind and diagnose them like a ghost MRI machine, then prescribe cures based on what he psychically detected. They called him the "clairvoyant physician"—accessing the spirit world to offer help.

As his practice grew, Kellogg set up shop in the Anson Brown Building in Lower Town at 1001 Broadway Street, which is the oldest remaining commercial building in Ann Arbor.[146] He advertised in periodicals across the country, offering to see patients directly or diagnose them by mail. For these remote diagnoses, Kellogg was assisted by two spirit guides named Walapaca and Owosso—the ghosts of Native American medicine men who would speak to him in foreign tongues Kellogg somehow understood.

One of Kellogg's ads in the Ann Arbor City Directory read:

---

145   Washington's final words were: "I am just going. Have me decently buried, and do not let my body be put into the vault in less than two days after I am dead. Do you understand me? Tis well."

146   It's where the St. Vincent De Paul Thrift Store is today.

"Dr. D. B. Kellogg.

Examines and Treats Diseases on Principles.

Special Attention Given to Chronic Complaints.

Full name, age and place of residence required to insure a correct
examination.

Examinations, personally or by letter. 50 cents each.

Office hours, 9 a.m. to 12 and from 1 to 4 p.m."

For these mail order patients, Kellogg received the patient's
information, along with their fee, and dispatched Walapaca or Owosso to
remotely perform the examination and report back. Then Kellogg prescribed
one of his special family remedies.

One correspondence with a patient reads:

"I find you improved and gradually getting better and I am confident I
can cure you and today send you a good compound and one which will help
you—still you will need more when this is employed. Let me again hear from
you when necessary."

Kellogg also saw patients in the flesh in Ann Arbor. These visitors put
up with less-than-ideal conditions in Kellogg's Lower Town office. They were
often assailed by the harsh sounds of a ghost crying child in distress, which
emanated from the lower floors of the building both day and night. Sometimes
furniture moved mysteriously. Strange knockings were heard throughout the
building. A small price to pay for quality medical care, I guess.

Kellogg's fame spread. Ann Arbor's clairvoyant physician with no
formal medical training was curing the sick and afflicted. His practice thrived
as patients filled his office, filled his mailbox, and filled his pockets.

It wasn't all friendship and love, though. Kellogg couldn't always turn
off his spiritual gift. Wherever he traveled, the place became a hazard zone.
Loud knocks awoke him at night—strange tappings on his pillow startled him
awake. One time, he was forced to abandon his office for an entire day because
a flying hair brush wouldn't stop attacking him.

In a growing town with a popular university, he was beset by skeptics and crazy people. Academics constantly challenged his powers, while others overvalued his skills and begged him with money and favors to do things like raise their loved ones from the dead.

Demand for his cures was so high that, with his brother Leverett B. Kellogg[147], he created a line of family medicines under the Kellogg name. Kellogg's Liver Invigorator, Kellogg's Lung Remedy, Kellogg's Magic Red Drops, and Kellogg's Family Cathartic Pills. They used mineral water from a well in the front yard of Daniel's home, located near his office, at 723 Moore Street.[148] The well water was high in iron and sulphur, making it the perfect water cure for patients suffering from bad guts.[149]

Unfortunately, Daniel didn't enjoy this success very long. He died in his home in 1876 at the age of 41, presumably of an inflammation of the bowels. His brother Leverett continued to sell their family cures, while Daniel's son, Albert C. Kellogg, continued to practice his father's profession.

Those magic red drops were sold throughout the 1800s, and Albert practiced his family's brand of medicine—even after the Fox sisters from New York admitted that their famous Rochester Rappings were nothing but a hoax. Apples tied to strings tied to their feet provided the knock knock knocking on the wooden floor. The coordinated, concealed cracking of foot and ankle bones convinced people who wanted to believe to actually believe. It was all a complete hoax. The thing is, nobody cared about their confession.

Spiritualism thrived, as did the Kelloggs, until Leverett died. Then Albert too joined the spirit world, passing to the other side in 1893, taking with him the clairvoyant Kellogg legacy.

---

147   Leverett B. Kellogg farmed with his family in Pittsfield Township until the age of 21, then moved to California and spent time on the West Coast and in Missouri before returning to Ann Arbor to work with his brother.

148   Daniel B. Kellogg's old residence remains in the same place today, though it's a series of apartments now. It holds a special place in my heart for two reasons: 1) I watched a Super Bowl in one of those apartments a long time ago, so I feel like I knew Kellogg before I KNEW Kellogg. 2) My good friend Brian Peters, who is also the recording technician and sound engineer for the Ann Arbor Stories podcast, shattered his kneecap in front of the Kellogg home slipping on a wet, mulberry-coated sidewalk on his walk to work one morning.

149   My completely real and technical medical term, not Kellogg's.

DB Kellog Building. Ann Arbor's clairvoyant physician, Daniel B. Kellogg, practiced out of the Kellogg building in the 1800s, curing the sick and infirm and person and through spiritual means. This photo was taken in 1938 after the top two floors of the building were removed and the structure remodeled. (Photo by Brian Peters, original courtesy of the Bentley Historical Library.)

WE HAD A ZOO!

If you were a student at the University of Michigan, a faculty member, a janitor, a regular old townie, someone visiting from out of state, or, perish the thought, a kid—a delicious little snack of a kid—if you were any of those things from 1929 to 1962 and you found yourself on U-M's campus near where Geddes Road and Washtenaw Avenue meet today, there's a chance you were in imminent danger and didn't even know it.

From that spot, you may have been watched with predatory eyes by bears. Bobcats. Badgers. Red foxes. Raccoons. Porcupines—porcupines eat people, I swear. Otters—like, really mean otters. Not to mention the most savage animal of them all—the wolverine. This assortment of beasts roamed the wilds of Geddes and Washtenaw—in what is now, in the summer of 2017, the rear of the U-M Museum of Natural History and its parking lot.

For more than 30 years, this motley menagerie watched with slavering mouths and sharp teeth—mouths and teeth that would sometimes take food right out of your hands, that is, if they were hungry and you held tasty treats up to the fence surrounding their cages.

Right, cages. I didn't mention the cages. There were cages. And fences. And zookeepers. Wait, I didn't mention. Dear reader…we had a zoo!

From 1929 to 1962, U-M had an honest-to-goodness zoo. The gift of a clutch of animals native to the state of Michigan and a financial appropriation from the U-M Regents paid for and stocked an octagonal paddock 40 feet in diameter—about the length of a school bus. This paddock was split into six equal slices with a small building laid in the middle to store food and supplies. The pens were completely enclosed by regular chain link fence, and a gravel track ran outside the whole business, about five feet wide, separating the cages from a second chain link fence where the public was kept at bay. Most people stood at the outer chain link fence, but there are pictures of visitors touching the animals through holes in the inner cage.

It was the 1930s. This wasn't Fort Knox.

They called it the Museum Zoological Park—dubbed the Animal House by locals. It was staffed by graduate students and a few full-time zookeepers. The donor's idea was that sick kids staying at the hospital across the street could come to the zoo, see the animals, and forget about their daily treatments. The zoo would also be open to students, Ann Arborites and interested visitors—all free of charge.

The zoo was an instant hit. It opened with those first few animals—raccoons, foxes, badgers, porcupines, and skunks, but its popularity led to the construction of a companion reptile pit featuring a shallow pool with running water to accommodate nine species of turtle and seven species of snake, all native to Michigan.

Over the seasons, animals moved to other facilities or were replaced by new specimens or different creatures entirely. They added coyotes, opossums, a bobcat, and the zoo's main attractions—two bears and a wolverine.

The first bears to join the Animal House were a pair of four-week-old black bear cubs found by the Department of Conservation. They were sent to the zoo in 1933 weighing less than two pounds each. Their eyes hadn't even opened yet.[150] The cubs were kept warm inside the zoo's tiny central building, protected from Ann Arbor's February chill—nursed on six-ounce bottles and taking four-hour naps throughout the day—until they got big and strong enough to go outside.

Their names were Brother and Sister—the featured attraction of the zoo. They put their paws up to the chain link fence surrounding the tiny enclosure when people walked by, swaying their big heads and licking their big bear lips. Imagine being just a few feet from a pair of giant bears any time you wanted.

Brother and Sister lived into their 20s before health issues became a problem. By 1955, Sister had severe arthritis and worsening lung problems and had to be euthanized. The death was a shock to Brother—partly because of how the zoo carried out their plan. They euthanized Sister in the cage with Brother, then dragged her out of the enclosure while keeping him at bay. They loaded her into a truck and drove off. For days, Brother raised his nose and sniffed the air any time a vehicle drove by, trying to find his sibling. Brother was heartbroken for weeks.

To cheer him up, the zoo obtained a two-and-a-half year-old bear named Toodles, which reinvigorated Brother, who started setting ground rules immediately. Brother ate first. Got his choice of where he slept in the cage. Normal bear dominance stuff. Brother was the more laid-back bear, according to the zookeepers. He never gave anyone trouble. Toodles, on the other hand, was a different story.

There's a throwaway line in a newspaper report where they write about Toodles gashing or biting a kid visiting the zoo, though it's hand-waved in the article. Yes, Toodles drew blood from a young patron but "some older kids had been teasing the bears all afternoon when they dared the youngster to get close to the cage."

In 1957, Brother and Toodles were shipped to another zoo where they joined a geriatric study of bears. In exchange, the zoo got two new bear cubs,

---

150   Bear cubs don't open their eyes until around six weeks.

courtesy once again of the Department of Conservation. These cubs had been stolen from the woods by poachers looking to sell them. The poachers were arrested and the cubs confiscated by the authorities.

The black bear cubs were shipped to Ann Arbor where the zoo held a contest to name the new arrivals. Thirteen-year-old William A. Close Jr. of 1414 E. Park Place[151] won, coming up with better names than more than 130 other entrants. For his incredibly original names, he won a book. Yes. A book. About mammals in the Great Lakes.

The names he suggested—you're never going to guess these. Maize for the female cub and Blue for the male. William A. Close, Jr. and the rest of Ann Arbor in 1957—you were better than that.

Meanwhile, the zoo continued to restock with cool attractions year after year. In 1958, they added a pair of otters (purchased from the Detroit Zoo for $350 apiece) and built a little water slide and pool. The bobcat came in 1952.

As for the zoo's wolverine—that's an interesting tale that starts back in 1923 with Michigan football coach Fielding Yost.

Yost had a simple request: find me a wolverine. Yost watched the University of Wisconsin bring their caged badger onto the field during a game and the sight lit a slow-burning fire within him to acquire his own live mascot. So he wrote letters to 68 trappers throughout the state, offering a handsome bounty if they'd bring a wolverine to Ann Arbor. All 68 bounties went unclaimed.

Michigan Senator William Alden Smith summoned Yost to Lansing to check out a stuffed wolverine he had in his office. When Yost arrived he scoffed at the senator's taxidermy, which turned out to be a coyote.

Yost increased the bounty for the trappers, and this time included hunters as well: Deliver a wolverine to Ann Arbor—dead or alive. Still, no wolverines were found, shot or captured.

---

151   Because of course the newspaper published the addresses of 13-year-olds in the 1950s.

Pitying Michigan's frustrated coach, the Hudson Bay Fur Company sent him a stuffed wolverine in 1924 to dull his mascot lust, but Yost still pined for the real thing.

Fast forward to 1927, when Yost's dreams finally came true. The Detroit Zoo obtained 10 wolverines from the state of Alaska in exchange for who knows how much treasure. Two of the creatures, nicknamed Bennie and Biff, were loaded into a cage and carried onto the field by four attendants at the Michigan Stadium dedication game against Ohio State on October 22, 1927.

More than 85,000 people roared as Bennie and Biff were paraded along the sidelines. Not surprisingly, Bennie and Biff freaked out. The wolverines scrambled around their cage nervously as the cheering and noise increased, until they began taking swipes at their handlers and the people hanging out on the sidelines. It wasn't the best idea.

Yost wasn't even the football coach in 1927—by then he was serving as athletic director. This may have contributed to his new perspective on bringing vicious beasts onto the field in front of tens of thousands of screaming people, marching bands and pretty much all of the scariest stuff animals could encounter.

"It was obvious that Michigan mascots had designs on the Michigan Men toting them, and those designs were by no means friendly," Yost admitted.

It's unclear exactly how long the experiment lasted. Most accounts say the wolverines were trotted out for big games for a few years before the practice was retired. Some accounts say the wolverines were housed in the zoo between games, but no records of that were found. Regardless, the experiment was pretty short-lived.

The first actual evidence of a wolverine at the Animal House is in 1936—when either the Chevrolet Motor Company, a prestigious alum or a prestigious alum working at the Chevrolet Motor Company donated a wolverine to the zoo.

As was their wont, the zoo held a naming contest for the new arrival and the winning suggestion was Intrepidus. Treppy, for short. There's a rumor that Treppy was brought onto the field at Michigan Stadium for a football game but freaked out and never returned. That sounds about right. He was apparently a big baby and would take food right out of the hands of his keepers.

Treppy was the oldest captive wolverine when he died in his enclosure in May 1950. He'd spent 14 years at the zoo and lived for who knows how long in the Alaskan wilderness prior to that. He was never replaced with another wolverine because, seriously, did you read that whole bit about Yost's obsession? Wolverines are really hard to find in Michigan.[152]

As for the zoo itself, just nine years after it opened, with the town enamored with its new addition, the city developed ambitious and semi-insane plan to create a 40-acre zoological garden near the U-M hospital and the Huron River. It would be a wildlife utopia where animals native to the state would roam free, kept semi-contained by moats, water features, rocky precipices— natural structures that in theory would have kept the wolves from devouring the beavers, buffered the bobcats and the coyotes, and avoided an animal Battle Royale witnessed by some patient way up in the hospital watching from their room.

Contingent on a grant from World Animal Protection, planners engaged architects to sculpt what the habitat might look like, complete with a model of a giant bear mound. Otters, beavers and muskrats would be turned loose on sections of the Huron to build dams and habitats for themselves. There's no way it wouldn't have resulted in some Jurassic Park raptor-level shenanigans. But we never got a chance to find out. The grant never came through and cooler heads didn't have to prevail.

The zoo was ultimately doomed too. Think back to the zoo's dimensions—a 40-foot-wide enclosure divided into six sections. Again, about the length of a school bus. Now imagine that school bus doing 360-degree donuts in a parking lot. Pretty sweet, huh? Now picture the skid marks caused by that donut, they represent the entire footprint of the zoo.[153] Divide that into

---

152   How rare are wolverines in Michigan? There has never, ever been a verified wolverine trapping in the state. And the first verified wolverine *sighting* in the Mitten wasn't until 2004.

153   I know, I know, the wheels of the bus aren't at the very back of the vehicle, meaning

six wedges, put a building in the middle, then add two bears into one of those spaces, two foxes in another, a wolverine in the third. All side by side by side. No spacing.

By the 1960s, calls to renovate or relocate the zoo were frequent. When the nearby Natural History Museum had a $1.2 million expansion and renovation approved in 1962, it was time for the zoo to go.

The city lobbied the Board of Regents to relocate the zoo somewhere else on campus, but the Regents declined to entertain the matter. Ann Arbor City Council tried next, debating a measure on the November ballot to raise $300,000 from a five-year city millage for the cost to build and maintain the zoo, but decided there wasn't enough public interest in the issue, and the measure never made it onto the ballot. The zoo was formally set to close.

Hundreds of letters poured in from 38 states asking to adopt Ann Arbor's animals. Including one from little Betsey Daugherty of Huntington, West Virginia, who wrote:

"How are you? I am good. I saw in mama's paper about you are giving way animals. Would you please send me a skunk? Mama says okay. Thank you."

Based on the requests they received, the zoo estimated it could have provided homes for 165 skunks, 177 turtles, 91 racoons, 43 foxes and 18 bears. But the zoo was only looking to relocate animals to commercial or university facilities, not to private owners.[154]

Maize and Blue were given to a much larger zoo in Athens, Michigan, where the bears had more room to roam. It took the zookeepers a few tries to coax the bears out of their cages and into crates for the trip. Once they arrived in their new home in Athens, they were renamed Dokomac and Athena. A year after the move, Athena, formerly Maize, had cubs.

The zoo in Athens had, you guessed it, a contest to name the new little

---

a proper 360-degree bus donut would create a circle considerably less than 40-feet in diameter. But when the hell else am I going to get to write about a school bus doing a 360-donut in a parking lot in an extremely serious history book?

154   Many of the animals were given away, but unfortunately some were destroyed.

bears. Unfortunately, we don't know the winning name, nor the name of the winner, nor their home address.

University Zoo Shortly Before Closing. In July of 1962, an Ann Arbor family visits the U-M zoo just before it was closed for good. (Photo by Brian Peters, original by Eck Stanger of the *Ann Arbor News*.)

Breaking Ground on the Museum. In April of 1963, a bulldozer rips up the parking area behind the University's Museum Building to make way for construction of a $1.2 million addition to the building. The small structure in the background was the former U-M zoo. (Photo by Brian Peters, original by Doug Fulton of the *Ann Arbor News*.)

A VERY DIXBORO GHOST STORY

This is the story of Martha Crawford. She lived somewhere in Canada with her young son Joseph and a husband who doesn't get a name because he dies before this story really gets going. Right now, actually.

The widow Crawford decides to visit her sister, Ann Mulholland, who lives in Michigan. Ann is a pleasant person living in a pleasant place and the trip is a nice opportunity for Martha and young Joseph to leave some of their sadness behind.

It's 1835. They travel to the village of Dixboro.

A Quick History Lesson

Back in 1824, a 28-year-old retired sea captain named John Dix from Boston, Massachusetts, purchased 469 acres of land in Ypsilanti Township for $1.25 an acre—the same amount Ann Arbor founders John Allen and Elisha Rumsey paid for their 640 acres that same year. Both locations had their advantages. Allen and Rumsey's land had the Huron River, Dix's was nearer to Detroit.

On part of his land, Dix founded the town of Dixboro.[155]

At 28, Captain Dix had already led an amazing life. Off to sea at age 16, he made his mark in the War of 1812, made his fortune after the war and survived a terrible shipwreck somewhere in between.

Dix built his house in 1824, moved in that same year. Sketched a plan for the town and formally platted it in 1826, creating 64 lots on 25 acres, including a public square for a church and school. The first schoolhouse was built sometime between 1828 and the early 1830s.

Dix didn't stick around long. There are conflicting explanations as to why he sold his land to James P. Clements in 1833 and moved his family to Texas. Some say his aggressive nature clashed with the laidback townspeople. Maybe he just got bored. Whatever the reason, the town felt his absence. Dixboro survived, but it couldn't keep up with its neighbors Ann Arbor and Ypsilanti. But that's future Dixboro.

In 1835, Dixboro has two taverns, two general stores, mills—everything a growing town needs.[156]

So when recently-widowed Martha Crawford and her son paid a visit that year, it was still a pretty promising Michigan town.

And it was about to get a ghost story.

Mrs. Crawford Visits Dixboro And A Terrible Secret Is Revealed

Arriving from Canada, Martha stepped out of the carriage and hugged her sister Ann. She shook hands with her brother-in-law, James Mulholland and was introduced to James' brother John. John was single. Young. Handsome, in a Dixboro: population-50-kind-of-way. Martha and John shook hands. Soon they'd do a lot more—jumping straight to the courting. Plans for a small wedding were hastily drawn up. It all seemed like a wonderful turn of fate.

---

155   Originally spelled "Dixborough," in case you run into it in old photos or maps.

156   Dixboro has a history as old as Ann Arbor, but due to events that you'll read about in a second, this is about as good as it gets.

Except for one small thing.

Martha's sister harbored a secret. Why she didn't tell Martha sooner is a mystery. Maybe tip her off before Martha and John's first date?[157] Just a teensy weensy heads-up?

Martha was already debating "tiered cake or cupcake tower" when Ann finally whispered this terrible secret into Martha's ear. Martha broke off the engagement immediately, ran to her room and packed her bags for Canada.

There was a knock at the door. It was Ann's husband, James, come-a-calling. But not in a pleasant "Can I help you with your bags or hail you a horse and buggy" way. No. He was menacing. He was threatening. If Martha fled for Canada, he promised her that she and her son would never make it to the border alive.

Martha was terrified. Her sister was helpless—living her own secret nightmare. Martha unpacked. The wedding was back on. Soon, Martha Crawford became Martha Mulholland.

The Unhappy Life of Martha Mulholland

Shortly after her sister's nuptials, Ann fell ill and wasted away. She died not long after Martha's wedding bouquet wilted. Martha's own husband, John, died less than five years into the marriage—lowered into the ground in 1840.[158]

Twice-widowed Martha and her brother-in-law James were left to divvy up the Mulholland family estate. It was a contentious fight. Martha didn't much like James, and she knew the terrible secret the brothers harbored. And he knew she knew.

Then Martha took ill as well—wasting away as her sister had. Taking advantage of her diminished state, James went to court to declare Martha incompetent and insane, attempting to wrest control of his dead brother's estate

---

157   Why don't history books capture more of the mundane details of life? I would pay good money for a brief account of Martha and John's first date. Was it chaperoned? Did he pick her up on foot or by carriage? Maybe they rode those bikes with the giant front wheel? Took a stroll around the ashery, smelling the fresh potash. Come on, historians of 1835—nobody cares about platting and river flow. I need date deets.

158   There's no explicit link made between Ann and John's deaths. History makes a point of recording that Ann wasted away, while John just dies.

from her. It was a messy battle and Martha was essentially alone in this little town in Michigan.

In 1845, Martha traveled to Ann Arbor seeking help, finally revealing her secret. She confided it to a University of Michigan physician named Dr. Sam Denton, on the condition that he bleed her to death after her confession.

Denton had no intention of assisting this woman's suicide. He faked a broken lancet and turned her away. Hysterical, Martha returned to Dixboro and died shortly thereafter.

Dear reader, you may suspect foul play, but the residents of Dixboro did not. They assumed Martha passed from the same illness that took her sister 10 years earlier. It was 1845. People died from stubbing their toes.

A Very Dixboro Ghost Story

That fall, Isaac Van Woert and his family settled in Dixboro, renting Martha's home from her son Joseph, who was probably smart enough to steer clear of his uncle James Mulholland. After spending only a few nights in Dixboro, Van Woert had a strange and terrible encounter. With a ghost.

While walking through the yard at dusk, Van Woert spied a light inside the house.
"I put my hand on the window sill and looked in. I saw a woman with a candlestick in her hand. She held it in her left hand.....she wore a loose gown, had a white cloth around her head, her right hand clasped in her clothes near the waist. She was bent forward, her eyes large and much sunken, very pale indeed....she moved slowly across the floor until she entered the bedroom and the door closed. I then went up and opened the bedroom door and all was dark. I stepped forward and lighted a candle but saw no one, nor heard any noise, except just before I opened the bedroom door I thought I heard one of the bureau drawers open and shut."

He told a few townspeople what he saw and they told him the story of poor Martha Mulholland. Van Woert saw the spirit again, right before Halloween. He was awakened by a noise at 1 am, opened the bedroom door, and saw a light in the middle of the house, but no candle. Standing five feet away was the same woman in white.

"Don't touch me," the spirit said, and Van Woert stepped back. "He has got it. He robbed me little by little until they kilt me. They kilt me! Now he has got it all."

Van Woert asked, "Who? Who killed you? Who has it all?"

The spirit replied, "James. James has got it at last."

Then everything went dark.

Throughout the fall, the ghost of Martha Mulholland appeared to Van Woert nine times. Each time it gave more and more detail about its fate. The ghost implicated her husband, members of his family and a local doctor in her murder. The ghost also mercifully, finally, told the secret it had shared only once before.

Finally, The Secret!

Martha's ghost implicated the same cabal in several other murders, telling Van Woert that the bodies of these poor souls were dumped in nearby Frain Lake and a town well.

Overcome by the experience and confident in his sanity, Van Woert traveled to Ann Arbor and signed a sworn statement in front of the Justice of the Peace, describing each encounter in great detail. Dixboro was split down the middle on whether or not to believe the newcomer's tale, but authorities exhumed Martha's body anyway. The coroner investigated and ruled that Martha had indeed been poisoned. Authorities searched the lake and the well for the other alleged victims, but failed to turn up further traces of murderous misdeeds.

The police found no evidence linking James Mulholland, his family or the crooked town doctor in any murders, but that didn't stop the whole lot of them from skipping town. Every last one of the suspected killers fled Dixboro and never came back.

The Van Woerts eventually moved out. The haunted house changed hands a few times. Sometime in the 1860s or 1870s, the house burned down under suspicious circumstances. There's been no report of the ghost of the widow Mulholland since.

Bonus Ghost Story!

Though Martha's spirit hasn't been seen in more than a century, Dixboro may still have a ghost. The first victim of the poison posse may haunt Dixboro to this day.

Sometime in the early 1830s, a traveling tin peddler spent the night at a tavern on Cherry Road, right across the street from the Dixboro General Store. He tied up his horse and cart outside, got something to eat, and went to bed. In the morning, the salesman was nowhere to be found—his horse and cart exactly where he'd left them the day before. No one ever saw or heard from him again.

Rumor has it one of the Mulholland brothers murdered the peddler and dumped his body down a well, though no corpse was found and the well was filled in not long after the alleged crime. Why they did it, nobody knows. How they did it, ditto. But a ghost story emerged from the deed.

Stand on the grass across from the Dixboro General Store on Cherry and Plymouth. Maybe grab a handful of old-timey candies, like Mary Janes, before you do.[159] Wait until it gets dark. Look for the moon. On quiet nights, close your eyes, crane your neck. Listen closely.

If you're lucky and you're into these kind of things, you can still hear the tinkle of the dead tin peddler's bell as it sways on his long-abandoned cart.[160]

---

159   Dixboro General Store: Open Monday through Saturday, 10 am to 6 pm and Sundays 11 am to 5 pm.

160   BOO!

SKYSCRAPERS

"Skyscraper"—it's such an elegant word. The oldest confirmed use of the term appeared in print way back in 1883 in the Chicago Daily, tucked into an article about the city's mania for tall buildings. Chicago's first skyscraper, the Home Insurance Building, rose 10 stories above the rest of the city, succeeding in kicking off the skyscraper race.[161]

Two decades later, skyscraper fever had reached Ann Arbor and infected State Treasurer, banker, and semi-shady entrepreneur Frank Glazier. Glazier was already a mover and shaker in Chelsea, building on his father's already-successful business ventures, but his legacy in Ann Arbor was nil. So in 1906, he bought three buildings on the corner of Huron Street and Main

---

161   Today, a skyscraper needs to reach 492 feet to be classified as such (around 45 stories). The Home Insurance Building was just 138 feet. There are also designations for supertall buildings (984 feet or 90-ish stories) and megatall buildings (2,500 feet or 230-ish stories). There's only one megatall building in the world in 2017—the Burj Khalifa in the United Arab Emirates.

Street, right in the heart of Ann Arbor's downtown, and erected the city's first skyscraper. It was called, inventively, the Glazier Building. The mere purchase of the three buildings cost more than any previous construction project in Ann Arbor's young history. That's before Glazier knocked them to the ground and, over the course of the next two years, built his grand seven-story structure on the remains.

The building cost Glazier $210,000, or around $6.2 million dollars today. Back in 1906, he could afford it. But between the start of the project and its grand opening, the Panic of 1907 took hold. This financial disaster caused the collapse of all of Ann Arbor's banks and crippled Glazier's empire. The demise of his fortune revealed some shady dealings. Glazier had been depositing state funds into his own bank, and had put up his Chelsea stove manufacturing company stock as collateral in eight separate loans totaling $1 million. To be technical, it was all super illegal.

While Glazier was off serving time in Jackson State Prison, his building was sold at auction for just $77,000. It was an inauspicious start to Ann Arbor's history of tall buildings.

It was another 20 years before a taller building was erected, one block away from the Glazier Building, at the corner of Main Street and Washington Street. The First National Building went up in 1929—10 stories high and completed in under a year using almost exclusively local contractors. It was a gorgeous building inside and out, with bronze doors, black terrazzo floors, Italian travertine walls, and a richly decorated paneled ceiling. Sixteen 1,000-watt floodlights illuminated the tower, making it a popular city landmark.

A 10-story skyscraper is nothing to sneeze at but it wasn't until 1969 that Ann Arbor got a skyscraper truly worthy of the term.

The Tower Plaza stands 26 stories tall—292 feet from the sidewalk to the tip of the tallest antenna on the roof. It's not exceptionally pretty. Just concrete and glass—but boy, does it scrape the sky.

Rumors of a giant construction project at the corner of William Street and Maynard Street buzzed around town in 1965. A $19 million dollar skyscraper that some thought definitely wouldn't help keep Ann Arbor weird. A photo of the architect's model appeared in the *Ann Arbor News* that summer with details provided by well-known developer Jack Stegeman. Stegeman had already built the 10-story $1.3 million Maynard House in 1962, just across the street from the proposed Tower Plaza project.[162]

The proposed Tower Plaza would be Ann Arbor's ultimate skyscraper— it included 300 studio and one-bedroom apartments and street-level commercial space for a restaurant and retail. Stegeman was well-liked, but the city was hesitant to build something so massive.

City Council debated the project. Should Stegeman be allowed to build so high? And on that spot?

On one side were the pro-development council members who wanted denser downtown housing options and tax revenue. On the other side were council members who worried about the impact on downtown parking, the skyline, and whether or not the giant building would dwarf the iconic 11-story Burton Memorial Tower. City Council debated and debated and debated.

On the night on August 30, 1965, some weird stuff went down in City Hall. City Council met to debate the 26-story development, but a few key voices were on vacation. Missing in action were City Manager Guy Larcom, City Attorney Jacob Fahrner, and Planning Director Raymond Martin. Who knows if the outcome would have been different if they'd been present, but the vote was taken, and the Tower Plaza project was approved, 7-4, with Mayor Wendell Hulcher leading the winning side.

It wasn't a done deal. The project experienced delays and appeasements, like when the city demanded the developers furnish additional parking spaces within close proximity of the building before an occupancy permit could be issued. But by 1966, the foundation was in place and the tower slowly went up, higher and higher and higher. Most of the exterior work on the building was complete by the fall of 1968—behind schedule but still 26 stories above Ann Arbor. By the summer of 1969, the building was ready and leases were signed to accept tenants for its 300 apartments.

---

162   Stegeman had a thing for tall buildings. He'd later complete the 15-story, $5 million Campus Inn on Huron Street, as well as other building projects throughout the city.

The building scraped the sky high above Maynard and William. It had two sides flanked by windows and two sides of sheer concrete. The developers thought they might marble the sides to make them more attractive, but the cost was prohibitive. They held a contest in 1974 to propose a more attractive solution, offering the winner a $500 prize. There was a winning design, but nothing was ever implemented.

On a clear day, high above the city in one of the Tower Plaza's upper apartments, the Detroit skyline was visible, and fantastic views of Ann Arbor could be had, from the bell tower to the Big House. One of the coolest things about the building had nothing to do with the interior. It was the roof. The 26-story Tower Plaza was the tallest building between Detroit and Chicago, which made it an ideal location for all kinds of antennae. In 1996, the roof sported between 25 and 30 antennas—TV, ham radio, and cell phone, relaying signals throughout the state and beyond thanks to their lofty perch above Ann Arbor.

In 1986, the building was purchased and the apartments converted to condos. The Tower Plaza was a hot place to live, with occupants from University of Michigan students to 86-year-old retirees living side by side, separated by eight-inch-thick concrete walls.

Several condos in the building go on the market each year. They run from $130,000 to $400,000, not including association fees. Studios range from 380 to 430 square feet, while one-bedrooms offer between 430 and 700 square feet. There are a few custom-built two-bedrooms, but good luck getting those, moneybags.

There's another skyscraper story in Ann Arbor, but it takes place outside the confines of downtown. Local businessman, CEO of Domino's Pizza, and multi-multi-millionaire Tom Monahan wanted to build a monumental building to serve as company headquarters at the Domino's Farms campus.

In the 1980s, he asked the architects that inherited Frank Lloyd Wright's firm to carry out a design the master himself had sketched out but never built.[163] The 52-story structure was called The Golden Beacon, and was conceived of by Wright in 1956, with the intent of building it as an office and apartment tower in Chicago. Ultimately, Monahan and the architects agreed they couldn't do the design justice, so Monahan hired the firm that built the existing Domino's Farms compound to make his dream come true. They designed a 30-story tower that rose up at a constant 15-degree angle.[164] The building would be made of concrete and steel, encased in glass, bronze, and copper. The price tag was in the neighborhood of $180 million dollars—which comes to about double that amount in today's dollars. The media dubbed the project "The Leaning Tower of Pizza."

The firm created a 50-foot scale model—but that was the extent of the construction on the project. Monahan moved on to other things and the Tower Plaza remained the tallest building in Ann Arbor.

However, the Leaning Tower of Pizza does exist in Ann Arbor. It's just not the skyscraper it was intended to be.

Head up to the Domino's Farms and cruise around the track surrounding the campus. There, not far from the bison, you'll see a weird, slanted structure in the distance. Drive a little closer and you'll see Ann Arbor's weirdest (sort of) skyscraper. It's the 50-foot scale model of the Leaning Tower of Pizza, still standing there today.

---

163   Monahan was obsessed with Wright. By the late 1980s, he'd spent more than $14 million to acquire more than 300 objects designed by Wright—the largest collection anywhere.

164   Monahan apparently loved tall things. He proposed a 25-story crucifix be built just outside Ann Arbor to celebrate his strong faith in the biggest way possible. The monument would have been just 51 feet shorter than the Statue of Liberty's torch.

Tower Plaza. The Tower Plaza is the tallest building project ever approved in the city of Ann Arbor. This photo taken in February of 1967 shows the beginnings of the project that wouldn't be complete until the summer of 1969. (Photo by Brian Peters, original by Brian Fulton of the *Ann Arbor News*.)

100% TRUE: THE STORY
OF WILLIAM DOUGLAS STREET

This is a story about a man. He may seem too good and too weird to be true. But what you're about to read is 100% real.

William Douglas Street was born January 7, 1951, in Detroit. He was the oldest of five children born to a family of modest means. He attended Detroit Central High School, got good grades, and excelled at sports. Street was smarter and more charismatic than many kids his age. It wasn't clear if it was an academic or an athletic scholarship in his future, but he was going places.

A nasty knee injury dashed hopes for athletic stardom and that may have derailed his interest in academics as well. It's not clear why Street didn't attend college after graduating in 1969, but he decided to stay home and work alongside his father, installing burglar alarms.

This wasn't the life Street was meant to lead, so he joined the Navy in

1969 and served on the carrier USS Midway off the coast of Vietnam for the next two years. During the summer of 1970, Street took leave to go have a try at making it in the world of professional sports. It turned out that he was good enough for the Boston Red Sox to sign him to their rookie league team. He pitched for the Sox that summer, but didn't advance in the organization. His curve broke too late and he didn't have much of a fastball. Still, Street was popular with his teammates, who called him "Billy D" around the clubhouse. He planned to use the nickname as the title of his future autobiography.

After being discharged from the Navy in 1971, Street went back to baseball. He flew to Lakeland, Florida, for a tryout with his hometown Detroit Tigers at spring training. He didn't make the team, and was sick of toiling in the minors, so he switched sports.

In 1972, as a member of the University of Michigan football team, he was invited to San Francisco to play in the East/West Shrine Game, where his team won 9-3. Later that month, Street landed a job with *Time* magazine despite no formal writing experience.

He wasn't in the gig long before Street was pulled to a new vocation. He was accepted to and zipped through medical school, hired at Henry Ford Hospital in 1973, then landed a residency position at Illinois Masonic Hospital in Chicago. He specialized in women's and children's health, but the job wasn't a good fit, so he returned to Michigan nine months later.

Never one to be idle, Street next made the decision to switch from medicine to law. He earned his law degree from U-M, then began his Master's work in Ann Arbor in 1981. At the same time, he interned with the Human Rights Department in the city of Detroit, working on high-profile cases in the city.

Street thrived at law, but it was the 1980s and the stock market was booming. He applied for stock broker training at Merrill Lynch in Ann Arbor but was turned down. He teamed up with another failed enrollee and together they started their own firm. Despite a limited bankroll, Street earned thousands in the first few months. Despite his success in finance, Street returned to his studies at the U-M law school in 1983. He was a regular fixture at law school social events around town, and sometimes wore his full naval uniform to class.

If it isn't obvious by now, Street wasn't content to stay in one place for too long. In the fall of 1983, he transferred from U-M's law program to Yale University's medical school in New Haven, Connecticut. Like most things in Street's life, his time in Connecticut didn't last long. He left after a year, returning to Michigan in the spring of 1984.

Not much is known about Street's adventures in the mid to late 80s, but his life did catch the eye of Hollywood. An independent film was made about his life called *Chameleon Street*, and had a limited release in 1989. It didn't garner a lot of critical acclaim, but auteur Steven Soderbergh noticed the genius in the story and re-released it at the Sundance Film Festival in 1990 where it won the Grand Jury Prize.

Unfortunately, Street suffered from chronic health problems throughout the early 1990s, so for a period, his tales go from torrent to trickle. When Street surfaced again, in 2013, he was working at the U-M Health System as a cardiologist. By then, Street's health problems were behind him—he ran marathons (which earned him a national magazine profile), earned degrees from Duke and West Point, and began moonlighting as a defense contractor for the U.S. government. Street proudly sported his West Point class ring while speaking at alumni events around Michigan.

He'd also become very, very wealthy. Street wore a $7,000 Rolex on his wrist, spent hundreds on dry cleaning, and drove a brand new Ford Fusion. He looked good in his 60s—maybe a little tired.

William Douglas Street never wrote that autobiography he planned to title Billy D.

Most of what we know about him comes from newspaper articles and the Michigan Department of Corrections website. It's there that we get the most accurate picture of William Douglas Street, AKA Doug Street, AKA Brian Davis, AKA William Street, Jr., AKA Victoria Reason.

So here's the real story of William Douglas Street. He was born January 27, 1951, in Detroit. His athletic ability and charisma levels are unknown—though from all the shenanigans he would go on to pull over the next 40 years, it can be assumed he possessed ample amounts of both. Street never graduated from Detroit Central High School, never worked with his dad (who was a bus driver), and he never joined the Navy. The Navy wouldn't take him, and according to Street's mother, it was one of the biggest disappointments in his life.

Street did dabble in professional baseball, though the Boston Red Sox organization would have you know that he was terrible. Street tried out for the Sox in 1969 and 1970 and never saw the field. "After a 10-minute workout, it was obvious he had no baseball talent," a spokesperson for the Sox said. He wasn't around long enough for anyone to nickname him "Billy D" or even to most of them to remember his name.

The 1971 Tigers tryout did happen, but not quite as advertised.

Street was married to a woman who enjoyed the finer things in life, and Street couldn't afford those finer things. So he set up a plan to earn $50,000 extorting Detroit Tigers superstar slugger Willie Horton—telling him he had incriminating photos of Horton with another woman.

Street called Detroit Tigers General Manager Jim Campbell and pretended to be Jerry LeVias—a college football superstar-turned-wide receiver for the Houston Oilers. Street, acting as LeVias, told the Tigers GM he wanted to quit football and try his hand at baseball. Would the Tigers give him a tryout?

The Tigers organization jumped at the chance. It'd be public relations gold, if nothing else. The Tigers sent Street a $165 plane ticket to their spring training facility in Florida and prepared to roll out the red carpet. A day before the tryout, Street paid a visit to a Detroit bar owned by former Tiger's great Gates Brown and, pretending to be LeVias, gave a sob story about losing his luggage. Brown gave him $300, which Street pocketed before heading to Lakeland.

When Street arrived, the Tigers gave him his own locker and a uniform, took publicity photos, and issued a glowing press release. In all the hubbub, Street didn't have a chance to sidle up to Horton and initiate his extortion plan before hitting the field. The ruse was quickly discovered when either Street showed how bad he was at baseball, or someone called the Houston Oilers organization for a comment.

"We were taken by a pro," former Tigers outfielder and farm club official Hoot Evers said after the tryout. Street was kicked out of the stadium and paid for his own way home.

It would be a shame to let a perfectly good extortion plot go to waste. A few weeks later, Street changed his plan a bit and hand delivered a death threat to Willie Horton's front door in the Sherwood Forest neighborhood in suburban Detroit. Mrs. Horton answered the knock, Street handed her an envelope and skedaddled. Inside was a note threatening to kill the two Horton children unless $20,000 cash was delivered to a secure location.

Street may have gotten away with the plot, if Mrs. Horton hadn't recognized him immediately. She had sat only a few seats away from him in first class when both flew to Lakeland for the start of Tigers spring training. She knew right away he was the charlatan who had tried to make the team. Mrs. Horton called the police.

Street was arrested, tried, and convicted of extortion and sent to Jackson State prison in 1973. While out on bail during his trial, Street traveled to San Francisco, posing as a University of Michigan football player, and joined in the festivities at the college football East/West Shrine Game. His ruse didn't last long. He was discovered and removed, and again paid his own way home.

Street's prison sentence began in September, 1973. It took him 29 days to escape. As a non-violent offender, authorities didn't try too hard to track him down.

Maybe they should have.

That same year, Street popped up at Henry Ford Hospital, posing as a medical school graduate from either Wayne State University or the U-M. They sussed out the fake in their midst pretty quickly—Street was arrested and charged with false pretenses and escaping from prison. He was back in the clink in 1974, but as a nonviolent offender, the system didn't want to waste a jail cell on Street.

Paroled in 1975, Street headed to Chicago where once again he posed as a medical school graduate, landing a residency at Illinois Masonic Hospital in Chicago. Street practiced medicine for nine months before his lies were uncovered. During his time there, he treated sick kids, delivered babies, and possibly performed 36 hysterectomies.[165]

Authorities kicked down the door of his fancy apartment overlooking Lake Michigan and found more than enough evidence to arrest him. How did they uncover this ruse? Staff became suspicious after Street took frequent bathroom breaks during surgery. A member of the OR team followed him into the bathroom one day and discovered him consulting stacks of heavily-indexed medical books.

Street was never prosecuted—just sent back to Michigan and returned to prison for breaking parole. He spent a short time there before being paroled again.

In 1981, Street decided to switch from lying about being a doctor to lying about being a lawyer. Posing as a U-M law school graduate, he landed an internship at the Human Rights Department in the City of Detroit. He used the credentials of a real lawyer named Douglas Street, and fooled everyone, except for his own ex-wife, who he happened to run into at a black tie event he was attending with colleagues from the Human Rights Department. She told everyone about his lies and the internship ended early.

Street bounced from crap job to crap job. He washed dishes, delivered handbills, worked as a janitor. He sold plasma. It was the 1980s and the stock

---

165   Street doesn't admit to performing the surgeries, but a newspaper account of this nine-month lie gives this very specific number. Too specific to be false, right?

market was booming. Street applied for broker training with Merrill Lynch in Ann Arbor but was turned down. So he and another failed enrollee formed their own stock trading outfit, but it never formally launched. Street managed to make thousands off the venture, though not from trading. Instead, he swindled his partner out of $2,000 cash and, impersonating his partner, took out a bank loan and signed up for a credit card with a high spending limit at a swanky clothing store.

Street next obtained the diploma and official documents of a real U.S. Naval Academy graduate, and used the credentials to enroll at U-M law school. He really did attend classes dressed in full naval uniform. He had a roommate, whom he bilked out of $600, then forged a check under the alias he was using for an emergency loan from the university. Another student unlucky enough to get close to Street was also bamboozled out of $1,600, though that person never pressed charges.

Street was a social butterfly in Ann Arbor, he attended law school functions regularly, though maybe he should have kept a lower profile. He was spotted at a U-M banquet by a Detroit lawyer familiar with Street's lies. The lawyer alerted the university to the impostor in their midst, and it didn't take them long to send the cops after Street.

Unfortunately, the authorities were a little too late. Street had already skipped town for New Haven, Connecticut, and Yale medical school, where he enrolled under another student's name, attending classes, and laying low this time. The school eventually uncovered the impersonation and police arrested Street in his home. When they searched the apartment, they found diplomas from the Naval Academy and Oxford University in other people's names. Warrants in Ann Arbor came up when they ran Street's real identity, and he was extradited to Michigan, where he was charged with a list of crimes and sentenced to his first stretch of real time.

Street's crimes caught the attention of the indie film community. The fictionalized *Chameleon Street*, released in 1989, is based on Street's true story and though it wasn't a critical success, it slowly picked up a cult following. In

1990, it was screened at the Sundance Film Festival where it won the Grand Jury Prize.

Street was paroled sometime in the early 1990s and went right back to his grifter lifestyle, racking up 10 charges of health care fraud and a number of other offenses that put him back behind bars until 2003. After his release, Street spent the next decade working crap jobs and stealing under the radar, always on the lookout for his next opportunity.

"I can't be happy mopping someone's floor or doing someone's dishes," Street said. "I have too much ability for that, I need someone who will trust me and give me a career opportunity."

He had seven known aliases—one a woman he impersonated named Victoria Reason. He wasn't above putting on a wig, earrings, and donning a dress if it he could earn a few bucks.

In 2013, the law caught up to Street once again. He'd purchased a $7,000 Rolex in an Ann Arbor jewelry store and paid with a bad check. He wrote another bad check for hundreds of dollars' worth of dry cleaning in Detroit.

The cops tracked him down to his ex-wife's house, where he was arrested in the driveway, sitting in his Ford Fusion. On his finger was a class ring from West Point bearing the name of the man he was impersonating—a defense contractor from Virginia with dual degrees from West Point and Duke University. Street had read a profile of the man in a national magazine—he was a marathoner and all-around All-American guy.

Street confessed that his goal with this impersonation was to get a good job and to meet women. Street hadn't just written bad checks and plagiarized the man's life history for his resume—he had also impersonated him at Michigan West Point alumni events. He'd even given speeches at some of those gatherings, which were actually said to be pretty eloquent.

At the age of 64, Street was convicted of his crimes in 2015. He was paroled February 22, 2017, and sent to a halfway house in Detroit.

While on parole, Street can't leave the state. He can't associate with anyone with a felony record and undergoes regular alcohol and drug testing. He can't own a gun, have bank accounts or credit cards, and must pay for the costs of his treatment, restitution, and crime victim's costs. He still looks pretty good, considering he's had 17 convictions and 47 years of documented crime. Maybe a little tired.

Street served time for everything from fraud to forgery, violating parole, failing to pay court costs and failure to follow through on court-ordered psychiatric help. He spent time behind bars in Jackson, Kenross Facility in Sault Ste. Marie, Phoenix Facility in Plymouth, and Muskegon Correctional Facility, not to mention prison work camps in Northern Michigan and halfway houses in Detroit.

For now, William Douglas Street, AKA Brian Davis, AKA Doug Street, AKA Victoria Reason is walking the straight and narrow. But who knows what his other identities are up to.

THE PIG BOWL

1969 was a rough year in and around Ann Arbor. Before autumn even fell, five young women had been found murdered in Ann Arbor and Ypsilanti—beaten, strangled, stabbed, raped, shot—plus three other killings. Police caught John Norman Collins that summer—known in the papers as the Michigan Murderer, the Co-Ed Killer, and the Ypsilanti Ripper. The devil was off the streets, but people still double-bolted their doors and tried to stay inside after dark.

To ease the tension, the Ann Arbor City Police and the Washtenaw County Sheriff's Department got together and organized a full-contact football game. This was a perfect way to take people's minds off the horrors of 1969, put on a silly spectacle, and raise money for Christmas presents for needy kids.

They dubbed it the Pig Bowl—county cops vs. city cops. The Sheriff's Department called their team the Pigs, while the townie cops nicknamed themselves the Goats, after a pet goat named Fuzz that served as their mascot for the big game.

It was a full contact affair, eleven men per side, regulation rules. The University of Michigan adopted the Goats, outfitting them in official U-M gear—from the crown of their winged helmets to the tips of their cleats. The then-Division II Eastern Michigan University Hurons outfitted the Sheriff's Department in green and white.

But uniforms and pads were only half the battle. These men weren't college football players. Sure, some were former high school and college athletes—some even standouts—but only some. The majority of the players spent their days riding in squad cars and filling out paperwork, not toting the pigskin and tackling aggressive, moving targets.

Each team held a half dozen informal practices that fall. Ann Arbor Police Chief Walter Krasny and his Goats practiced on a field in town, while Sheriff Douglas A. Harvey's Pigs did the same at EMU. These practices led to injuries of their own. Officers suffered sprains, charley horses, cuts and bruises up and down the line.

On a cold and rainy Sunday afternoon, December 7, 1969, 50 men suited up and met on the field of battle. Fans paid $1.50 each to get into EMU's Briggs Field to watch these cop combatants knock heads for the Pig Bowl trophy. The trophy itself was an old battered dairy farm cream can from 1913, about the size of a man's torso. It had been repurposed as a pig slop bucket until some farmer cleaned it up, stenciled "Pig Bowl Trophy" on the side, and donated it to the cause.

Heavy rain throughout the previous day and night had made the field a muddy mess. More than 1,000 brave souls weathered the wet and cold to root for one side of cops or the other. Both teams brought along mascots: the Pigs brought a pig named DJ, and the Goats were accompanied by their buddy Fuzz.

The Pigs and the Goats trotted out into the quagmire and gave the people what they wanted. Within minutes, every man was covered in mud, their jerseys nearly indistinguishable.

The Goats struck early and often, putting up 19 points in the first half through a series of long runs and deft passes. Once the field conditions deteriorated, neither team could manage to cross the goal line. The fans watched a deadlocked second half—a back and forth of bruised, beaten, and increasingly exhausted men trying to claim victory and escape the afternoon in one piece.

There were casualties. A member of the Sheriff's Department was taken to St. Joseph's Hospital with a serious knee injury and another exited the game with a severe ankle bruise. Most others escaped with only bumps and bruises.

"It hurts when I blink," one city patrolman was quoted as saying after the final whistle had sounded.

They raised more than $5,000, which purchased toys that were distributed to kids throughout the county. The Pig Bowl was a huge hit, and the victorious Goats proudly displayed the trophy at police headquarters.

The next year's Pig Bowl was bigger and better. Tickets were sold across town and the game was moved to Pioneer High School's Hollway Field to accommodate the increase in spectators. There was infinitely more trash talk and a series of high profile pranks between the departments leading up to the kickoff.[166]

More than 7,000 fans packed the stands for Pig Bowl II, which raised $15,000 this time around. The sides were matched similarly to the first contest, except that the Sheriff's Department added a young crop of EMU campus officers to their roster.

The Pigs scored early, taking a 7-0 lead, but the Goats responded with a touchdown of their own. But the extra point failed, and the Pigs' 7-6 lead would hold until the end of the game, as cops from both sides limped off the field.

In Pig Bowl III, the Goats blanked the Pigs, then won again the next year in Pig Bowl IV on a last minute two-point conversion. By then, ticket sales were down and the novelty of the whole thing had started to wear off. There

---

166   Washtenaw County Sheriff's deputies faked a ruse to gain entrance to the Ann Arbor Police Station, swiping the Pig Bowl Trophy before the game. The fact that a bunch of cops were able to sneak into the police station unnoticed, steal such a large item and then sneak back out didn't seem to bother anyone when the story was printed in the *Ann Arbor News*.

was no Pig Bowl V. The series ended in 1973 with the Ann Arbor Police
retaining the coveted slop bucket.[167]

The Pig Bowl briefly took the city's mind off that horrible year in 1969
and gave the cops a chance to do something a little silly to serve the community.
It generated friendly competition, generated some laughs, and raised a lot of
money. The Pig Bowl served its purpose and it's worth celebrating those brave
Pigs and valiant Goats and all the bumps, bruises and sprains they suffered.

---

167   We're not sure where the Pig Bowl Trophy resides today. Maybe in the basement of
an Ann Arbor police officer. Maybe in the police station itself. Or maybe a couple jokers from
the Sheriff's Department sneaked in and made off with it again, and the city cops are too
embarrassed to admit it. Who knows?

HOW THE HIPPIES ALMOST KILLED FOOTBALL

In the summer of 1970, the hippie movement and youth counterculture scene wasn't what it was during the 1967 Summer of Love, or even what it was during the summer of Woodstock in 1969.

Nixon was in the White House and the Vietnam draft was in full swing. An 18-year-old had been stabbed to death 20 feet from the Rolling Stones during a concert at the Altamont Speedway Free Festival, and the public was just learning all the grisly details of the Manson family murders.

In 1970, a lot of people weren't thinking "peace and love" when they heard the word "hippie." Instead, they were thinking sex, drugs, draft dodging, and murder.

On August 7, 1970, Michigan experienced its own version of Woodstock. The three-day festival was packed with more than 200,000 hippies, burnouts, wastoids, and pinkos who swarmed tiny Leoni Township for the Goose Lake International Music Festival.

Promoter Richard Songer bought 350 acres of farmland in Goose Lake Park—a quiet corner of Jackson County—to create a permanent outdoor music arena, with tall fences, restrooms, showers, kitchens—infrastructure sorely lacking at Woodstock.

When Songer proposed the Goose Lake International Music Festival as the first event held at this new facility, townsfolk freaked. More than 400,000 people had descended on Woodstock the summer before—everyone had seen the pictures and the clips on the news. There had been rain, mud, hippies, nudity, drugs, hippies, free love, hippies, long hair, hippies, and hippies.

The Goose Lake International Music Festival was proposed in March and the Goose Lake Property Owners Association immediately dragged Songer into court to try to block it. They argued about zoning laws and tried to appeal to the court in the interest of the preservation of law and order, detailing how the festival would surely pollute the area with "an invasion of hippies or gypsies or whatever."

Songer moved ahead with his plans, hoping for a positive outcome. He cleared land for parking and camping and built a state of the art amphitheater called The Goose Nest. He surrounded the property with a 12-foot tall fence, topped with three rows of barbed wire to keep non-paying customers out. Songer booked acts for the festival—Joe Walsh, Jethro Tull, and Chicago, along with home-grown acts like MC5, The Stooges, and Mitch Ryder.

Songer won the first round in court, but the Jackson County prosecutor made a last-ditch effort to stop the festival, filing for an immediate injunction on the grounds that the gathering would be too big, too crazy, and too lewd for local law enforcement to handle. The plea was denied.

Festival-goers arrived the day before the event, pitched tents on the campground, made use of the kitchen facilities, and purchased stuff from the vendors. Kids traveled in from both coasts. Songer hired 400 security guards, including a number of White Panther Party members[168], to work the gates and

---

168   The White Panthers were a far-left, anti-racist movement most active in and around Detroit and Ann Arbor.

patrol the fenceline, preventing some of the chaos seen at Woodstock. Songer's plan to keep non-paying festival goers from crashing the event didn't work very well. Guards were bribed to let people slip through holes in the fence, and when gate receipts were counted, Songer estimated only 45,000 of the 200,000-plus people in attendance actually paid to get in.

Songer didn't seem to mind. The weather was lovely, the bands were great, and the atmosphere was full of peace, love, and happiness. There was also casual nudity, outdoor sex, and lots of open drug use. Police kept a tight grip on their billy clubs just outside the fence, aware that their presence on the property could spark a riot. Residents in the surrounding area were also on edge. Some families sent their women and children to stay with relatives out of town, while the remaining menfolk kept watch from their porches with loaded shotguns to protect against the inevitable invasion of a hippie mob.

In the end, not a single act of violence was reported during the festival. Authorities did stop and search many of the festival-goers as they left, making 160 drug-related arrests.[169]

Meanwhile, 32 miles away—a straight shot east on I-94—Ann Arbor was having its own rock 'n' roll-related issues. The counterculture movement didn't sit well in a lot of Michigan communities—not just those in the middle of nowhere. Here's a quick anecdote to set the mood:

In 1967, local psychedelic band The Seventh Seal played a show on Belle Isle in Detroit, which culminated in what the press referred to as "a love-in."[170] The music whipped the crowd into such a frenzy that they rioted—at least according to reports made by authorities. Concert-goers said the trouble began when Detroit police started forcibly clearing Belle Isle and the hippies fought back.

The headline "Local Group Denies Playing Riot-Causing Music"

---

169   The County Sheriff's office noted that they issued more drug charges in that one day than the two previous years combined.

170   Official definition: A gathering at which people are encouraged to express feelings of friendship and physical attraction.

actually appeared in 30-point type in the *Ann Arbor News*. The Seventh Seal denied their music caused people to lose their minds and beat each other up.

Watched with a wary eye, the band played their mind-altering music throughout Ann Arbor, often as part of a series of afternoon Sunday rock concerts held in parks throughout the city—West Park, Gallup, and Huron Flatlands.[171] They drew crowds of all sorts—wearing bright orange saris, dungarees, togas, bare feet, sleeveless black leather jackets, bells on their ankles, and rings in their noses. Hippies of all stripes.

These Sunday rock concerts were a regular thing by 1970. The city was still worried about these gatherings causing love-ins, riots, and noise, but most of the concerts went off without a hitch, other than some minor drug use and the lingering scent of patchouli.

Ann Arbor City Council was well acquainted with the plots and plans at Goose Lake, and kept an eye on court proceedings to block Michigan's Woodstock. Five days before the start of the Goose Lake Festival, Ann Arbor's situation inflamed.

At a Sunday afternoon rock concert in Gallup Park on August 2, 20-year-old David Lee Hunter shot 21-year-old Ypsilanti motorcycle club member Richard Morris after the two got into an altercation. Hunter was arrested, Morris was severely wounded, and the anti-rock 'n' rollers in Ann Arbor shook their heads and mouthed "I told you so."

The Ann Arbor Blues Festival was planned for the following Friday, which City Council made no attempt to curb. But they did keep one eye on Goose Lake and the other on the next Sunday rock concert scheduled for August 16 at Huron Flatlands—one week after Michigan's Woodstock would wrap up.

City Council, particularly 5th ward councilman Lloyd Fairbanks, feared that holdovers from the Goose Lake Festival would linger in the area and attend the Ann Arbor rock concert a week later. Fairbanks urged City Council to cancel the August 16 concert unless assurances were made that the Goose

---

171   Huron Flatlands was a large park area adjacent to Huron High School where many festivals and musical events were held.

Lake hippies, burnouts, and wastoids had indeed dispersed. The concert was eventually allowed to continue, but City Council tightened its leash on rock 'n' roll in their town.

Fallout from Goose Lake didn't just affect Ann Arbor. It came back to bite Songer as well. He'd planned a smaller three-day rock festival at his Goose Lake venue for Labor Day weekend—starting Sunday, September 6. The Thursday before the concert, Jackson County Circuit Judge John C. Dalton ruled in favor of a petition asking that the park be closed indefinitely to all rock concerts that posed "a public and common nuisance."

Songer took the blow in stride, instead staging a political rally at Goose Lake to celebrate a resolution passed in the Michigan House and Senate allowing 18-year-olds to vote. Ten thousand kids, mostly from out of state, streamed into Goose Lake, only to be turned away at the gates due to the cancellation of the festival. Many relocated to Portage State Lake Park, about seven miles away, and made the best of the Labor Day weekend, but very few attended the Sunday rally—estimates put the crowd at less than 1,000.

Police made one drug-related arrest.

Legal precedent is a funny thing, and when wielded by a former Michigan Daily sports editor-turned-janitor-turned-union-steward-turned-counterculture-sympathizer—it can threaten an American institution. Even an American institution like college football.

The aforementioned multi-hyphenate Joel Block filed suit in Washtenaw County Circuit Court, seeking to stop the sold-out October 17, 1970, Michigan-Michigan State game at the Big House. In addition to the suit, Block requested that Michigan Stadium be permanently closed as a site for future football games.[172]

Block cited precedent set in the cancellation of the second Goose Lake rock festival and the indefinite closure of the venue. Block employed the same language used against Goose Lake, adding:

---

172   This wasn't Block's first act of public protest. As a senior, he was sentenced to seven days in jail and fined $240 for participating in a student sit-in at the U-M.

"I am not against football, but I am for equal law enforcement. If the law applies to rock festivals, it should also apply to football games."

Block obtained affidavits from 10 people who attended an October Michigan home game against Texas A&M, in which eyewitnesses reported:

- Marijuana joints being smoked and passed openly

- Illegal consumption of alcoholic beverages

- Alcoholic beverages being given to minors

- Thievery in full view of police

- Flags and banners symbolizing revolution against the American government

- An attack on a popcorn vendor

- Public swearing and profanity

- Inadequate and overcrowded restroom facilities

- Traffic jams of a dangerous nature[173]

A hearing was set for the Friday before Saturday's kickoff, where it was expected that U-M representatives would present evidence as to why the game should be played.

Ann Arbor Police Chief Walter Krasny didn't dispute Block's gameday claims. Krasny said his men averaged three arrests per game for drunk and disorderly conduct, but that, "drunkenness in the stadium usually fluctuates with the weather."

Krasny did say things had improved from the olden days. He credited the near-extinction of excursion trains for the decline in the number of rowdy drunks in the stadium. Previously, trains packed with football fans from distant cities would pull into Ann Arbor and disgorge hundreds of liquored-up visitors right at the tracks near the stadium. Fights inside and outside the stadium were

---

173   The *Michigan Daily* offered specifics: Two truckloads of empty alcohol bottles carted out of the stadium after the game, grade-school kids swigging from half-empty wine bottles, and marijuana and drug use throughout the stands.

commonplace. Krasny admitted that game drunks, as he called them, were often ignored in favor of those who needed medical attention or mediation—people suffering from heat stroke, illnesses,[174] or altercations.

Block's suit was ridiculous, right? Wasn't it?

Legal precedent is a funny thing.

Judge Ross W. Campbell heard the case. U-M lawyers called the suit patently frivolous and said that nothing would be a greater absurdity than to grant this injunction. Block's lawyer stuck to his guns—the rock concert at Goose Lake was canceled and the venue shut down for similar reasons. He demanded to know the difference.

The verdict was delivered less than 24 hours before the scheduled kickoff. The judge ruled against Block's suit, and allowed the game to go on as scheduled. No irreparable harm would be done to the public when the two teams met on the field.[175]

The game went off without a hitch. Under perfect weather conditions, Michigan cruised to a 34-20 win over the Spartans, while police made just one arrest for drunk and disorderly conduct. Traffic moved smoothly, people were nice to each other, and none of the expected protests or demonstrations materialized.[176]

The Wolverines went on to win the first nine games of that season before losing to Ohio State in Columbus. The Spartans only won four games that year and wouldn't beat the Wolverines again until 1978.

The sportos won. The hippies lost. And really, what's more American than that?

---

174   Krasny added a crazy little footnote, admitting that his squad handled heart attack victims at nearly every Michigan-Michigan State game in the Big House.

175   You didn't really think they'd cancel the game, did you?

176   One hiccup—the county health department halted the sale of all hot dogs at halftime because the frankfurters were being sold cold.

TRAIN CRASHES

Ann Arbor has a rich history of trains and railroads. So, so much rich train history. In the late 1830s, the Michigan Central Railroad expanded west from Detroit, reaching Ann Arbor in 1839. And … that's enough train history. Let's get to the TRAIN CRASHES!

Sorry, a little more set up.

The new railway line was first used to transport cargo—livestock, coal, wool, general stuff. Passengers eventually rode to and from Detroit, and later to and from other destinations in Michigan, Ohio, and Illinois. These trains were loud, dirty, dangerous beasts, rolling along tracks cut through fields and towns throughout Michigan. This took some getting used to. Livestock wandered onto the tracks, pedestrians wandered onto the tracks, horse-drawn carriages and automobiles stopped where they shouldn't have. Moo, smash, crash.

In addition to those regular, run of the mill train wrecks were some larger accidents.

During the Huron Valley Bridge collapse of 1904, a bunch of freight cars fell off the elevated tracks of the Huron Valley Bridge to the frozen ground below.

In 1940 there was a big, messy freight wreck at the Michigan Central Railroad Station.

Dexter saw a smash-up involving a 70-car freight train versus a 250-passenger express train in 1952. The wreck injured seven and caused $1 million in damage.

But those were all minor compared to the train crashes in this chapter. These were the real blockbusters—one that broke the bank, and another that literally shaped history.

Train Crash Number One

It was a hot midsummer night in 1927 and the engine on a fully-loaded freight train just couldn't finish the job. The train had moved west through downtown Ann Arbor and was slowly chugging uphill near the Washtenaw County Fairgrounds, where Veterans Park is today. The engine strained and wheezed but just couldn't pull the heavy freight cars to the top of the hill. It slowed and eventually came to a dead stop.

It was getting late and rather than burn out the engine attempting the Jackson Road incline, the crew came up with a solution. The railmen divided the cars and pulled each smaller, more manageable section up the incline separately. It was hot, it was getting late, and the crew started to hurry to get the job done. It was a recipe for an accident.

The crew failed to adequately rejoin two sections of the train, and four fully-loaded freight cars began slowly, slowly sliding back down the hill. They moved so slowly at first, heading east towards downtown. But the big metal wheels turned a little faster after every revolution. What began as a walking pace quickened to a dead sprint as the train continued to build momentum just one mile from downtown. Freight cars weigh tons, and the men and their puny man flesh had no way to stop them. The conductor, Fern Garn, clung to the side of the train, desperately trying to think of a solution.

The train gained speed as it moved down the hill. It was probably going 40 miles per hour by the time it hit the first curve in the track, where Jackson Road turns into Huron Street at Dexter Avenue. The wheels screeched, but the four cars stayed on the tracks, and sped even faster as Ann Arbor's downtown grew nearer.

This is where the train cars really got going. The train rolled under the Ann Arbor Railroad viaduct, crossed Ashley Street, and headed for the sharp bend at Main Street. Even though the train was now traveling uphill, it had gained enough speed for conductor Fern Garn to know this bend would be a problem. He jumped for his life and survived, but was knocked unconscious and missed the big finale.

One person who didn't miss a thing was the night janitor at the *Ann Arbor Times News*. He was cleaning offices on the upper floors when he heard a steady rumble. He often heard trains roll through downtown, and knew at once that this was something different.

He looked west at the four runaway freight cars racing toward the corner of Huron and Main. They were on a trajectory that would take them either farther up Huron—where there were no tracks—or straight into the Farmers & Mechanics Bank.[177]

Those four fully-loaded freight cars tried to take the turn, but ended up jumping the tracks and plowing straight into the lobby of the Farmers & Mechanics Bank, traveling at an estimated 50 miles per hour. The impact pulverized the side of the building and threw up clouds of dust so thick that witnesses could barely see each other as they staggered onto the street to survey the damage.

Late night diners at two restaurants beside the bank—Prochnow's Dairy Lunch and the Sugar Bowl—heard the rumble, felt the impact, and thought the crash was an earthquake. The restaurant walls bulged and bricks

---

177   PNC Bank at the corner of Huron and Main today.

flew into the street. People were knocked off stools.

Remarkably, no one was hurt. One of the bank's board of directors was later quoted as saying: "This is the largest deposit in the history of the Farmers & Mechanics bank. I hope we shall never have another like it."

The damage to the building has long been repaired. Not so with the wreckage left by our next train crash, which happened two years later in Ypsilanti.

Train Crash Number Two

A freight train passing through Depot Town on the morning of January 21, 1929 left an impression on Ypsilanti that remains to this day. Michigan Central baggage handler Fred Beck was doing his thing on board the train when he heard a peculiar sound. Beck noticed that a single wheel on the 85-car freight train was off the track, hanging dangerously to the side.

This was bad news. Especially for an 85-car freight train, and especially for an 85-car freight train passing through town. Trains that heavy aren't easy to stop. The crew tried valiantly, but couldn't slow it in time to prevent car number 12 from bouncing off the track, uncoupling from the rest of the train, and skidding across Cross Street, where it smashed into the side of the building next to the tracks—a building that houses Sidetrack Bar & Grill today.

Back then, it was known as the Caldwell Building. The ground floor was a restaurant rented and run by Bert and Cestia Ollett, while the Caldwells lived on the upper floor. At the time of the crash Mrs. Caldwell was out back, but the Olletts were inside the restaurant preparing for the morning rush.

The freight car wasn't traveling 50 miles an hour like the Ann Arbor bank crash, but a runaway freight car can cause a ton of damage regardless of speed. The car hit the side of the building nearest the tracks, caving in the east wall and blowing many of the Caldwells' household effects into the street. The roof on that side of the building sagged, then collapsed. The restaurant too was disemboweled—the shock of the collision sent tables, chairs, and assorted supplies scattering onto the tracks and into the street.

The Olletts miraculously survived. Bert escaped with minor cuts and bruises, while Cestia suffered a broken arm and fractured skull. The crash had torn open the building, leaving the Caldwell's second floor home broken open and giving a perfect view of their interior to all of Cross Street. It also destroyed a portion of the restaurant and sent the Olletts' cash register tumbling into the rubble.

The crash site was roped off by the authorities, who tried to make sense of the damage and take care of the injured. The cash register was eventually recovered, but it was empty. Mrs. Ollett's purse was found, but her money and checks had been removed.

Mrs. Caldwell had a canary named Bobby, whose cage was flung from the second story into the street when the wall caved in. Rescue workers found the empty, battered cage and feared the worst. But several hours later, Bobby was found in a pile of rubble, shell-shocked and dusty but otherwise okay.

The building was not okay. The crash shaved off the corner and created an odd 45-degree angle of damage. Rather than rebuild that section to make the building whole and square again, they walled everything off, creating the distinctive building footprint visible today. Sidetrack Bar & Grill uses the old caved-in section as an outdoor patio, where people eat, drink, and cheer at the trains that roll by, hoping they all stay on the tracks.

THE BLIND PIG

On February 23, 2017, Swisher Commercial listed the Blind Pig and 8-Ball Saloon for sale—6,970 square feet, two stories, two half-baths, no bedrooms, no list price. Best offer only. Liquor license included.

The brick building that houses the Blind Pig and 8-Ball is 150 years old, built as an addition to the larger complex it's attached to, which started as a brewery way back in the 1850s. In Ann Arbor's first city directory in 1860, the main building is listed as G.F. Hauser's City Brewery. In 1868, it's listed as John Reyer's City Brewery, and in 1872, Ekhardt Bros. Brewery. The breweries went out of business after the Panic of 1873[178], and the main building became Ann

---

178   The Panic of 1873 was a multi-layered financial crisis that caused a depression in Europe and North America lasting from 1873 to 1879. Coupled with post-Civil War inflation, a railroad speculation bubble, and both the Great Chicago and Great Boston Fires that destroyed large portions of both cities, you'd think MORE people would want to drink beer, but the Panic all but killed Ann Arbor's breweries.

Arbor Central Mills in 1882. The brick addition where the Pig and the 8-Ball reside was built in 1865 and serve as offices, storage space, and a walk-in safe.

The Blind Pig officially opened in 1972 and has had three phases of ownership. Tom Isaia and Jerry Del Giudice opened the Pig in 1972, then sold to David Whitmore in 1979, who sold to the Goffett family in 1983.

Isaia was a senior at the University of Michigan when he and business partner Del Giudice bought the Mill's add-on building and converted it into a European-style coffee bar/blues club. The partners built a little stage and a bar in the basement, and on the main floor, they added tables, chairs, and a top of the line espresso machine. They called it The Blind Pig Cafe—which refers to one of two things:

A "blind pig" was a term used by speakeasy owners back during Prohibition to describe cops who were on the take and would look the other way for a regular second income. It also refers to low-class establishments that operated during Prohibition that enticed customers to come inside to witness a weird attraction (like a literal blind pig) and serve a complimentary alcoholic beverage, staying within the law.

The Blind Pig Cafe was one of the pioneers in Ann Arbor's now-entrenched coffee culture, serving cappuccinos, fancy coffees, and pastries in the cafe by day and hosting blues acts in the intimate, 60-seat space by night.

The Blind Pig Cafe quickly established itself as the best place in Ann Arbor for blues, attracting talent and crowds beyond its meager capacity. The blues scene at the Pig got so hot that in 1977, Del Giudice and another friend started their own record label called Blind Pig Records, signing and releasing their favorite acts.

With the business turning a regular profit and cementing itself as a cornerstone for live music in the city, Isaia and Del Giudice sold. That was always the plan. They were 20 and 21 when they first bought the place and didn't want to hang on to it into old age. They built it, sold for a profit and went on to do other things while they were still young. People were pissed, but the partners had other ambitions to chase. Del Giudice drove to the west coast to run Blind Pig Records full time—eventually signing and releasing multiple Grammy-nominated artists—while Isaia pursued his love of coffee full time.

Not much is written of the second owner, David Whitmore. The official history on the Blind Pig website ignores him completely. But in 1983, the story picks up again, when Roy and Betty Goffett became the third owners of the Pig. Roy grew up in Liverpool, England, and watched the Beatles rise to fame. He made a fortune in the steel business and married a woman named Betty whose family wasn't hurting for money either. Roy always dreamed of owning a music club, so Betty bought him one.

Their ambitions were bigger than the cafe and its small blues space. They expanded the business, taking over the old woodworking studio at the front of the building called "The Treehouse," gutting it, and building a larger stage and a bar in the space. They scrapped the stage in the basement but kept the bar, and rebranded the lower level of the business as the 8-Ball Saloon.

If expansion and moving the famed Blind Pig to a brand new space wasn't enough, the Goffetts did something next that all but guaranteed they'd alienate the last remaining holdouts from the old blues club days.

"Blind Pig Expands, Adds Dance Floor, Disc Jockey." That was the *Ann Arbor News* headline on April 7, 1984. The old Pig faithful were floored. To keep up with the times and make their venue actually turn a profit, the Goffetts made the Blind Pig a live music AND electronic music venue. They'd book live bands most of the week and have DJs spin on non-live nights—a departure from the live-or-nothing olden days.[179] They must have also read some weird books on branding, giving the Blind Pig a Capone-era Chicago speakeasy makeover, which included decorating the new space with tons of mirrors, cheesy black and white gangster movie posters, and a garish coat of paint—all of which prompted one reviewer to write that it looked like a Las Vegas nightmare.

---

179   One practical amenity that gets brought up over and over again in relation to Blind Pig upgrades is air conditioning. There is an actual honest-to-goodness quote in an article from 1983 that says, "Air conditioning would be a great idea."

To bring quality acts to the remodeled Pig, the Goffetts hired the same booker who was getting acts to play Rick's American Cafe. The Pig felt like it was getting Rick's leftovers, so this idea was quickly proven to be flawed. Instead, early in 1985, they stepped up and hired well-known local booking company Prism Productions to bring in acts that would help get the Pig back on its feet. At the same time, they also reimagined the 8-Ball Saloon as more of a games room—pool, darts, shuffleboard, that kind of thing. Live acts, DJs, and dancing on the main floor, and drinking and games in the basement. The modern ecosystem of the businesses was set.

The Capone-branded makeover didn't go over very well and eventually they removed the ugliness. Thanks to the skills of Lee Berry at Prism, the Blind Pig started booking national acts that were touring through the Midwest. This was the heyday of the Pig, bringing in Pearl Jam, Soundgarden, The Smashing Pumpkins, The White Stripes, Dave Matthews, John Mayer, Wiz Khalifa, Sonic Youth, Soul Asylum, and, most famously, Nirvana.

If you've heard of the Blind Pig, you've probably heard that Kurt Cobain called it his favorite venue of all time. Twice, apparently.

Nirvana visited the Blind Pig during their 1990 Bleach tour, which, up to that point, was not going well. The show at the Pig was different. They played to a sold-out and enthusiastic crowd, partied late into the night and slept on the floor of the Prism Productions office because they didn't want to pay for a motel. That show, all 50 minutes of which you can watch on YouTube, turned their spirits around and the band never forgot Ann Arbor's little Pig.

In 1990, the Blind Pig also briefly flirted with adding topless go-go dancers to the mix, but opted not to fight city hall and Ann Arbor's conservative businessmen, who had just snuffed out the city's infamous red light district.[180]

The Blind Pig continued booking major national and international acts as a well-respected mid-size venue in town that was easy to deal with. Ann Arbor residents were willing to pay for live music and with a well-off student

---

180   Read that story in this very book!

population, the venue could charge decent ticket prices, giving bands a financial reason to play the Pig.

But what truly kept the Pig and the 8-Ball in the black all these years wasn't the music. It was the booze. Lots and lots of booze. Through fat times and lean, the fine people of Ann Arbor swilled beer and knocked back well liquor during live shows, but, more importantly, in that dingy 8-Ball basement.

On the day it was listed for sale, the 8-Ball was the only remaining dive bar left in Ann Arbor.[181]

Somebody will buy the Blind Pig and the 8-Ball. And someone will change it. Tear down a stage here, put a bar there, maybe hang up a bunch of black and white gangster movie posters. If not the next buyer, maybe the buyer after that. Or the buyer after that. For a lot of people, that sucks. Like it must have sucked when the original owners sold in 1979, ending the good thing they had going. Like it must have sucked when the Goffetts added a dance floor and DJs. Like it must have sucked when Aaron Carter played two shows at the Blind Pig in 2016.

It's okay, readers. If you live long enough, you're around when things you care about die. So grab a handful of free popcorn, pay in cash, and raise a glass to the old Blind Pig and 8-Ball Saloon.

---

181   At the time of printing, there's a rumor that the Blind Pig has been sold. But nothing confirmed. Regardless, it won't be the last time the Pig will be bought or sold.

Blind Pig. The brick building that houses the Blind Pig is more than 150 years old. The Pig itself opened in 1972 as a European-style coffee bar slash blues club. (Photo by Richard Retyi, courtesy of the Ann Arbor District Library.)

ACKNOWLEDGMENTS

This book wouldn't have been possible without a small army of editors, archivists, and ego strokers. Chief among them is Sara Wedell, who is the main reason I started this book and the only reason I finished it. An amazing editor, organizer, and friend—every writer should dream of having her work on their project.

These stories would have been so much harder to research if not for the Ann Arbor District Library archives staff. The work they do is essential. Huge thanks to Amy Cantu, Debbie Gallagher, Andrew MacLaren, Lucy Roehrig, and Darla Welshons.

Thanks to Eli Neiburger and Mariah Cherem for being instrumental in the origins of the Ann Arbor Stories podcast, which spun into this book you were kind enough to pick up. Their support from day one has been steady and invaluable. Also thanks to Matt Dubay on the podcast side of things for making sure all the ones and zeros line up for each episode.

Thanks to Jen Harley for the covers and chapter illustrations in this book. Nobody would read a Rich Retyi history book if it didn't look like this one does, and I knew right away that Jen would lure you suckers in with her great work, at which point you'd feel bad not reading at least a chapter or two. Check out more of her work at JenHarley.com and help me pressure her into making her lighthouse posters, please.

Thanks to the Ann Arbor District Library and Fifth Avenue Press team, especially Erin Helmrich, Sairah Husain, Nicco Pandolfi, and graphic designer Amanda Szot. Also thanks to photographer and friend Melanie Maxwell for the best Ann Arbor author photo of all time (no offense, John

Bacon) and for being a huge supporter of Ann Arbor Stories from the beginning.

Brian Peters got the dedication, but his support can't be overstated. He's the reason this book has so many cool then-and-now photos, and his garbage radar helped shape many of these stories, which would be a lot worse if not for his level head and rugged good looks.

Finally, since I may never get the opportunity to thank people in quite this fashion again, to the following people, thanks for making life better: Rachel, Sasha, Charlie, Mam, Maggie, Fred, Jason, Jon, Nick, Pete, Courtney, Dr. Tinycat WebMD, Bola, Doo Doo, Henry, Andrew, and M. If I left a few of you off, assume it's because I didn't want to make it weird.